Revolution, Industry and Empire

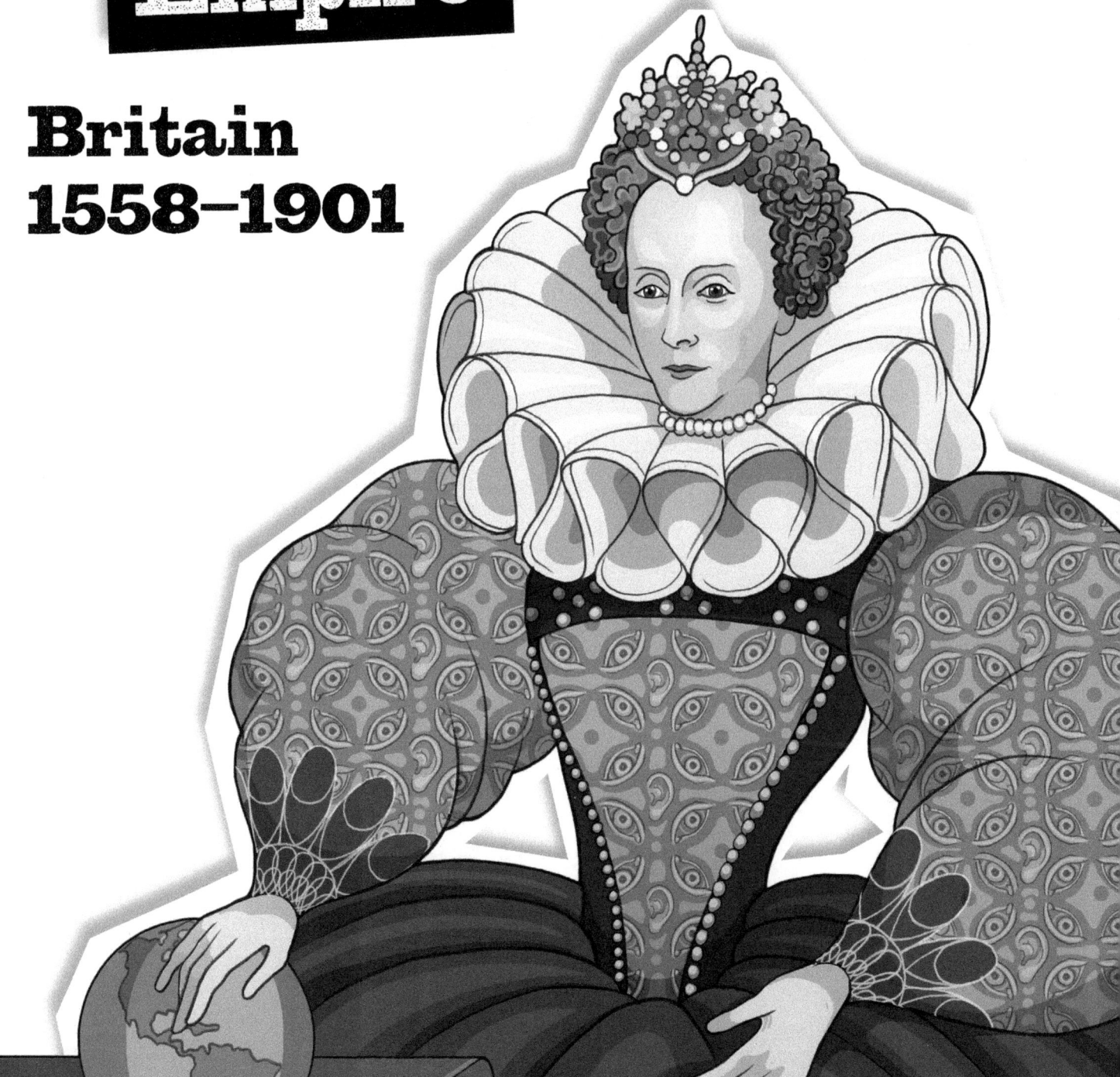

Britain 1558–1901

FOURTH EDITION

Curriculum and Assessment Planning Guide

Aaron Wilkes   Lindsay Bruce

OXFORD

OXFORD
UNIVERSITY PRESS

Great Clarendon Street, Oxford, OX2 6DP, United Kingdom

Oxford University Press is a department of the University of Oxford.

It furthers the University's objective of excellence in research, scholarship, and education by publishing worldwide. Oxford is a registered trade mark of Oxford University Press in the UK and in certain other countries

© Oxford University Press 2020

The moral rights of the authors have been asserted

First published in 2020

All rights reserved. No part of this publication may be reproduced, stored in a retrieval system, or transmitted, in any form or by any means, without the prior permission in writing of Oxford University Press, or as expressly permitted by law, by licence or under terms agreed with the appropriate reprographics rights organization. Enquiries concerning reproduction outside the scope of the above should be sent to the Rights Department, Oxford University Press, at the address above.

You must not circulate this work in any other form and you must impose this same condition on any acquirer

British Library Cataloguing in Publication Data
Data available

978-019-849468-3

10 9 8 7 6 5 4 3 2 1

Paper used in the production of this book is a natural, recyclable product made from wood grown in sustainable forests.

The manufacturing process conforms to the environmental regulations of the country of origin.

Printed and bound by CPI Group (UK) Ltd, Croydon, CR0 4YY

Acknowledgements

The publisher would like to thank the following for permissions to use copyright material:

Cover illustration by Matthew Hollings

Artworks: Moreno Chiacchiera

Photos: p45: ClassicStock/Alamy Stock Photo; **p52:** Heritage Image Partnership Ltd/Alamy Stock Photo; **p60:** North Wind Picture Archives/Alamy Stock Photo; **p78:** Chronicle/Alamy Stock Photo; **p106:** © The British Library Board/BRIDGEMAN ART LIBRARY; **p113:** Artokoloro Quint Lox Limited/Alamy Stock Photo; **p127:** The Royal Mint

We are grateful for permission to reprint extracts from the following copyright texts.

Clement Attlee: speech from Hansard is © Parliamentary copyright and is used under the Open Parliament Licence v3.0

Niall Ferguson: 'Why we ruled the world', 1 May 2003, www.niallferguson.com/journalism, reprinted by permission of the author.

Shashi Tharoor: '"But what about the railways...?" The Myth of Britain's Gifts to India', *theguardian.com*, 8 Mar 2017, copyright © Guardian News and Media Ltd 2017, reprinted by permission of GNM Ltd.

Although we have made every effort to trace and contact all copyright holders before publication this has not been possible in all cases. If notified, the publisher will rectify any errors or omissions at the earliest opportunity.

Links to third party websites are provided by Oxford in good faith and for information only. Oxford disclaims any responsibility for the materials contained in any third party website referenced in this work.

From the authors Lindsay Bruce and Aaron Wilkes: Special thanks to the fabulous Kate Buckley at OUP, who has steered the creation of this handbook from beginning to end. Thanks also to the team at OUP – Janice Mansel-Chan, Alison Schrecker, Emma Jones, Melanie Waldron, Sarah Flynn, Georgia Styring and Jade Coyle.

Contents

Introduction	5
Using this guide	8
Scheme of work	10

Curriculum planning — 19

- Ofsted inspection framework and curriculum planning questions for your department — 19
- Building a historical vocabulary and closing the word gap — 23
- Sample curriculum plans — 26
  - AQA — 27
  - Edexcel — 29
  - OCR — 31
  - Eduqas — 32

Assessment and progression to GCSE — 33

- AQA — 33
- Edexcel — 35
- OCR A and OCR B — 36
- Eduqas and WJEC — 38
- Progression to GCSE: closing the word gap — 40

Chapter 1: Queen Elizabeth — 43

Links to the KS3 History National Curriculum	43
Skills and processes covered in this chapter	43
Lesson sequence	44
Links to the GCSE Curriculum	45
Exam-style questions covered in this chapter	45
A brief history and timeline	46
Further reading for teachers and for students	47
Beyond the classroom	47
Answers guidance for each lesson	48
Answers guidance for Have you been learning?	51
Chapter 1 Assessment summary	52
• Entering student outcomes into the Kerboodle Markbook	53
• Links to GCSE	54
• Links to KS3 History resources	54
• Mark scheme	55
• Sample student answers	56

Chapter 2: Life in Tudor Times — 58

Links to the KS3 History National Curriculum	58
Skills and processes covered in this chapter	58
Lesson sequence	59
Links to the GCSE Curriculum	60
Exam-style questions covered in this chapter	60
A brief history and timeline	61
Further reading for teachers and for students	62
Beyond the classroom	62
Answers guidance for each lesson	63
Answers guidance for Have you been learning?	65
Chapter 2 Assessment summary	66
• Entering student outcomes into the Kerboodle Markbook	66
• Links to GCSE	67
• Links to KS3 History resources	67
• Mark scheme	68
• Sample student answers	69

Chapter 3: Exit the Tudors, enter the Stuarts — 71

Links to the KS3 History National Curriculum	71
Skills and processes covered in this chapter	71
Lesson sequence	72
Links to the GCSE Curriculum	72
Exam-style questions covered in this chapter	72
A brief history and timeline	73
Further reading for teachers and for students	74
Beyond the classroom	74
Answers guidance for each lesson	75
Answers guidance for Have you been learning?	77
Chapter 3 Assessment summary	78
• Entering student outcomes into the Kerboodle Markbook	79
• Links to GCSE	80
• Links to KS3 History resources	80
• Mark scheme	81
• Sample student answers	82

Chapter 4: From Civil War to Commonwealth — 84

Links to the KS3 History National Curriculum	84
Skills and processes covered in this chapter	84
Lesson sequence	85
Links to the GCSE Curriculum	86
Exam-style questions covered in this chapter	86
A brief history and timeline	87
Further reading for teachers and for students	88
Beyond the classroom	88
Answers guidance for each lesson	89
Answers guidance for Have you been learning?	92
Chapter 4 Assessment summary	93
• Entering student outcomes into the Kerboodle Markbook	93
• Links to GCSE	94
• Links to KS3 History resources	94
• Mark scheme	95
• Sample student answers	96

Chapter 5: The Restoration: the Merry Monarch — 98

Links to the KS3 History National Curriculum	98
Skills and processes covered in this chapter	98
Lesson sequence	99
Links to the GCSE Curriculum	99
Exam-style questions covered in this chapter	99
A brief history and timeline	100
Further reading for teachers and for students	101
Beyond the classroom	101
Answers guidance for each lesson	102
Answers guidance for Have you been learning?	104
Chapter 5 Assessment summary	105
• Entering student outcomes into the Kerboodle Markbook	107
• Links to GCSE	108
• Links to KS3 History resources	108
• Mark scheme	109
• Sample student answers	110

Chapter 6: Exit the Stuarts, enter the Georgians — 112

Links to the KS3 History National Curriculum	112
Skills and processes covered in this chapter	112
Lesson sequence	113
Links to the GCSE Curriculum	114
Exam-style questions covered in this chapter	114
A brief history and timeline	115
Further reading for teachers and for students	116
Beyond the classroom	116
Answers guidance for each lesson	117

Contents

Answers guidance for Have you been learning?	119
Chapter 6 Assessment summary	120
• Entering student outcomes into the Kerboodle Markbook	120
• Links to GCSE	121
• Links to KS3 History resources	121
• Mark scheme	122
• Sample student answers	123

Chapter 7: The Industrial Revolution: from farming to factories — 125

Links to the KS3 History National Curriculum	125
Skills and processes covered in this chapter	125
Lesson sequence	126
Links to the GCSE Curriculum	127
Exam-style questions covered in this chapter	127
A brief history and timeline	128
Further reading for teachers and for students	129
Beyond the classroom	129
Answers guidance for each lesson	130
Answers guidance for Have you been learning?	133
Chapter 7 Assessment summary	134
• Entering student outcomes into the Kerboodle Markbook	134
• Links to GCSE	135
• Links to KS3 History resources	135
• Mark scheme	136
• Sample student answers	137

Chapter 8: Terrible towns — 139

Links to the KS3 History National Curriculum	139
Skills and processes covered in this chapter	139
Lesson sequence	140
Links to the GCSE Curriculum	141
Exam-style questions covered in this chapter	141
A brief history and timeline	142
Further reading for teachers and for students	143
Beyond the classroom	143
Answers guidance for each lesson	144
Answers guidance for Have you been learning?	148
Chapter 8 Assessment summary	149
• Entering student outcomes into the Kerboodle Markbook	149
• Links to GCSE	150
• Links to KS3 History resources	150
• Mark scheme	151
• Sample student answers	152

Chapter 9: The slave trade — 154

Links to the KS3 History National Curriculum	154
Skills and processes covered in this chapter	154
Lesson sequence	155
Links to the GCSE Curriculum	155
Exam-style questions covered in this chapter	155
A brief history and timeline	156
Further reading for teachers and for students	157
Beyond the classroom	157
Answers guidance for each lesson	158
Answers guidance for Have you been learning?	160
Chapter 9 Assessment summary	161
• Entering student outcomes into the Kerboodle Markbook	161
• Links to GCSE	162
• Links to KS3 History resources	162
• Mark scheme	163
• Sample student answers	164

Chapter 10: Britain versus France — 166

Links to the KS3 History National Curriculum	166
Skills and processes covered in this chapter	166
Lesson sequence	167
Links to the GCSE Curriculum	167
Exam-style questions covered in this chapter	167
A brief history and timeline	168
Further reading for teachers and for students	169
Beyond the classroom	169
Answers guidance for each lesson	170
Answers guidance for Have you been learning?	172
Chapter 10 Assessment summary	173
• Entering student outcomes into the Kerboodle Markbook	173
• Links to GCSE	174
• Links to KS3 History resources	174
• Mark scheme	175
• Sample student answers	176

Chapter 11: India: a British Empire case study — 178

Links to the KS3 History National Curriculum	178
Skills and processes covered in this chapter	178
Lesson sequence	179
Links to the GCSE Curriculum	179
Exam-style questions covered in this chapter	179
A brief history and timeline	180
Further reading for teachers and for students	181
Beyond the classroom	181
Answers guidance for each lesson	182
Answers guidance for Have you been learning?	184
Chapter 11 Assessment summary	185
• Entering student outcomes into the Kerboodle Markbook	186
• Links to GCSE	187
• Links to KS3 History resources	187
• Mark scheme	188
• Sample student answers	189

Chapter 12: From Tudor to Victorian Britain: what changed? — 191

Links to the KS3 History National Curriculum	191
Skills and processes covered in this chapter	191
Lesson sequence	193
Links to the GCSE Curriculum	194
Exam-style questions covered in this chapter	194
A brief history and timeline	195
Further reading for teachers and for students	196
Beyond the classroom	197
Answers guidance for each lesson	198
Answers guidance for Have you been learning?	203
Chapter 12 Assessment summary	204
• Entering student outcomes into the Kerboodle Markbook	204
• Links to GCSE	205
• Links to KS3 History resources	205
• Mark scheme	206
• Sample student answers	207

Introduction

A unique approach

Oxford's *KS3 History* series by Aaron Wilkes has become one of the best-selling secondary school History series in recent years. This is its Fourth Edition, published in line with the latest National Curriculum framework. This new KS3 series also allows you to cater for the demands of the new GCSE History qualifications by ensuring that the relevant History content and skills needed to access the various question styles at a higher level are covered.

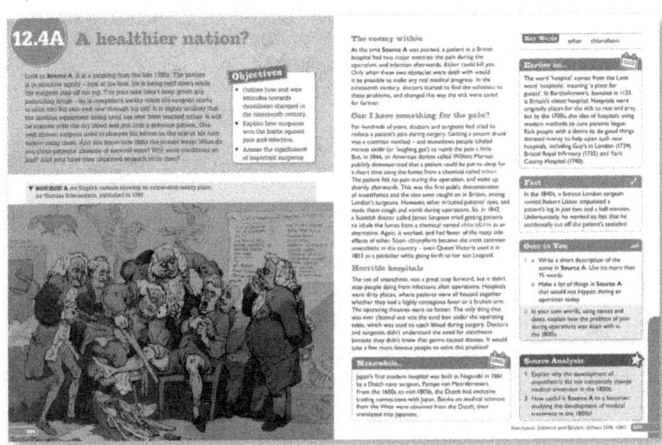

The series is based on the idea that any resources used with students should be as accessible and relevant as possible because children learn best when they are interested and engaged in activities that they think are both challenging and worthwhile. If a group of students are hooked early on in a lesson by an unusual picture, a curious title or a thought-provoking objective, a highly proactive learning environment can be created. Each topic in the *Student Book* aims to get the students involved, and keep them involved – through imaginatively presented double-page lessons with a clear route through them, headed by progressive learning objectives and finished off with an Over to You work section that aims to make the written part of any lesson as inspiring and as challenging as possible.

The *Student Book* contains differentiated activities and assessment opportunities, and essential historical vocabulary in the Glossary and in the Key Words feature. The *Kerboodle Lessons, Resources and Assessment* provides animations and film clips, summative and formative assessments, customisable differentiated worksheets, interactive activities, and more (see page 9). The accompanying *Curriculum and Assessment Planning Guide* (available in both print and digital format) provides further teacher support, including the key historical concepts and skills covered in each chapter, a brief introduction to each topic (ideal for those History departments where a non-specialist might teach), as well as further reading recommendations for both teachers *and* students, ideas for beyond the classroom, and answers guidance for each question.

A rich curriculum

KS3 History is not just a series of textbooks. The materials that accompany them make up a complete scheme of work for a comprehensive Key Stage 3 History course. However, the scheme is not meant to be prescriptive. Experienced teachers may want to plunder the materials for suitable resources and ideas, while supply teachers, non-specialists or those just starting out in the profession will soon understand why the series has been shown in recent research to inspire and motivate young historians[1].

This is a flexible two- or three-year course that matches the requirements of the KS3 History National Curriculum and lays the foundations for the rigours of further study in History. The series is based on the following curriculum principles:

- coherently planned and sequenced towards developing historical knowledge and understanding
- presenting subject matter clearly and making History engaging
- building a wide vocabulary to ensure students acquire the necessary language to access their learning and reduce the word gap[2]
- developing extended writing skills
- checking students' understanding systematically.

[1] The Oxford Impact Framework is a systematic approach to evaluating the impact of OUP products and services. It was developed through a unique collaboration between the National Foundation for Educational research (NFER) and is supported by the Oxford University Department of Education. A 2017 impact study (**www.oxfordsecondary.co.uk/ks3historyimpact**) found that the KS3 3rd Edition series motivates students, impacts positively on student preparedness for GCSE, helps students develop History exam skills and engages students of all abilities.

[2] The term 'word gap' is typically used to refer to pupils entering primary school with a vocabulary far below age-related expectations. However, we know that this issue affects a wider range of children. This word gap can be present throughout a child's education and beyond. The *Oxford Language Report* (2018) (**oxford.ly/wordgap**) found that half the 1,000 teachers surveyed reported that at least 40% of their pupils lacked the vocabulary to access their learning. Over 60% of secondary school teachers believe the word gap is increasing.

Introduction

Guided by these principles, great emphasis has been placed on designing activities that help students understand key historical concepts and develop the skills needed to become excellent historians. We don't believe in teaching to the test but we understand that progression is a vital component of any good KS3 curriculum. We know that History teachers want their curriculum to be ambitious and designed to give all students the knowledge and cultural capital needed for success. We have tested this material with teachers during development to ensure it allows students to build substantive knowledge and skills to progress at a higher level. Furthermore, we know that many History departments are planning KS3 with GCSE in mind. We've not overtly filled our *Student Book* full of GCSE references that might overwhelm students and put some off, but behind the scenes (in this guide) we've mapped our new resources carefully to basic GCSE requirements.

Developing knowledge and skills for young historians

The *Student Books* in this series are written in chronological order. With each book and accompanying *Kerboodle* package, students are encouraged to develop their historical understanding by using precise dates, correct vocabulary and chronological terms. A student's sense of chronology, sequence and duration is developed through the use of overviews, timelines, key date features such as 'Meanwhile' and 'Earlier/Later on…', and summative assessments. We have also ensured that there are numerous opportunities for students to demonstrate their understanding of second order historical concepts such as continuity and change, cause and consequence, similarity, difference and significance.

The series also provides a stimulating backdrop for promoting students' knowledge, and for encouraging their extended writing skills and their understanding of historical evidence. Some topics, such as *3.3 Were the gunpowder plotters framed?* and *8.7A/B Why did the police fail to catch Jack the Ripper?* are presented as a 'History Mystery' for students to weigh evidence and analyse sources. Students are required to use strategies and enquiry techniques to arrive at reasoned conclusions. The *Student Book* also has specific lessons that are designed to help students develop insights into values, beliefs and culture of the time, as well as encouraging their understanding of key processes. For example, lessons such as *2.2 What were Tudor schools like?* focus on the idea of change and continuity. The key concept of cause and consequence forms the central focus of topics such as *4.1 Why did the English start fighting each other?* and *8.1B What made towns and cities stink?* In Chapter 7 *The Industrial Revolution: from farming to factories,* students are encouraged to explore the causes and the impact of the Industrial Revolution, and they are challenged to assess the significance of an individual, while in the end-of-chapter assessment, students have the chance to give their opinion on one identified cause of the Industrial Revolution.

Progression throughout the curriculum

We have also ensured that the skills and concepts that are central to the development of excellent historians have been appropriately mapped.

- The skills and concepts covered in the *Student Book* have been audited and grids that map them throughout each chapter (question by question) have been included in this guide.
- You will see a star in the purple question boxes in many lessons. This indicates to you that the last question in the purple box is linked to GCSE in some way – it might be a genuine GCSE-style question, or simply part of a question that will help students build up to full questions as they make greater progress.

> **Change**
> 1 Write a paragraph explaining how the following changed during the Interregnum:
>   a churches
>   b entertainment.
> 2 In what ways did the lives of people in England change during the Interregnum?

- You will also see a star in all of the end-of-chapter assessments, which show you that the assessments are based on GCSE exam-style question stems. There are grids showing exam-style questions covered in each chapter which identify questions linked to specific GCSE exam boards.

Literacy in History

A key curriculum principle in this *KS3 History* series is to build a historical vocabulary and close the word gap. With this in mind, each lesson contains a selection of vital Key Words. Students should be encouraged to look up their meanings in a dictionary and/or use the Glossary and Index at the back of the *Student Book*. The tasks will ask students to define and deploy these words with precision. Some of these words will be the vital substantive concepts, also known as 'first order concepts' (such as democracy, empire or revolution), that are essential for students to become familiar with as they progress through the subject. Also, it might be interesting to reference some of these concepts as you revisit them again during the course. For example, the same concept can have very different meanings when used in relation to different episodes, events and eras in

History. For example, the concept of 'revolution' takes on different meanings in relation to the Glorious Revolution and the Industrial Revolution.

Students are also asked to cover basic literacy competencies in the Over to You sections. They are taught to construct a proper paragraph, make a point, 'evidence it', and explain what they mean. There is also a range of activities that employ a variety of creative literacy strategies.

Schools now have a greater focus on learning key historical vocabulary and extended writing – the new 'Literacy Focus' activities at the end of each chapter will help with this. These activities will test students' abilities to spell and punctuate correctly, back up their views properly, and construct detailed paragraphs – essential skills for doing well in History.

kerboodle

Kerboodle Lessons, Resources and Assessment provides over 400 lively digital resources to help you deliver the content and skills needed for your KS3 curriculum and to prepare students for progression (see page 9 for more information). You can adapt many of these resources to suit you and your students' individual needs. You can upload your existing resources so everything can be accessed from one location – to help bring History to life in your classroom.

Assessment and progression

Each *Student Book*, and the accompanying *Kerboodle* package and *Curriculum and Assessment Planning Guide*, includes a ready-made set of formative and summative assessment tasks.

- The Over to You sections at the end of each lesson allow students to demonstrate their knowledge and understanding. These sections have been designed to get progressively more challenging as students work through the tasks, meaning we can successfully give all students the chance to demonstrate and apply their knowledge.
- The 'Have you been learning?' sections of each chapter contain 'Quick Knowledge Quizzes', which test students' knowledge, and 'Literacy Focus' activities, which help to improve students' essay-writing skills and grammar. This formative low stakes testing allows students one of many opportunities to recall and apply the knowledge they have acquired. These short activities allow you to check students' understanding systematically, identify misconceptions accurately, and provide clear, direct feedback.
- History skills assessments at the end of each chapter close with a 'big question' summative task, which has been designed to test students' understanding of historical concepts such as continuity and change, cause and consequence, similarity, difference and significance. Step-by-step guides model an approach to answering a challenging exam-style question. This is followed by a similar question that includes scaffolded support and coaching to help students write an extended answer. This guide contains guidance on how these tasks or assessments link to GCSE specifications, differentiated sample student answers, and a banded/graded mark scheme.
- Comprehensive assessment support on *Kerboodle* includes: step-by-step presentations for front-of-class use, differentiated worksheets, and auto-marked tests and quizzes.
- Baseline tests are included to help teachers try to establish the level of knowledge and learning that students have acquired in primary school.

The whole *KS3 History* package allows you to concentrate on delivering memorable History underpinned by a strong curriculum and a foundation of knowledge and skills that students will benefit from, whether they go on to study GCSE or not.

We sincerely hope that *KS3 History* helps you deliver the outstanding lessons that we all aspire to, and that the History series we've developed helps inspire and engage a new generation of students.

Aaron Wilkes   Lindsay Bruce

Using this guide

Curriculum and Assessment Planning Guide

This guide aims to help teachers design a coherent knowledge-rich curriculum with detailed guidance on assessment, key History knowledge and skills, and support for non-specialists.

Matched to each chapter of the *Student Book*, you'll find:
- Links to the KS3 History National Curriculum and to GCSE History curricula
- History skills and processes covered in the chapter
- Lesson sequence
- Exam-style questions covered in the chapter
- A brief history of the chapter topic, and a timeline
- Further reading for teachers and students, and activities that go beyond the classroom
- Answers guidance for all *Student Book* activities
- Comprehensive support for the end-of-chapter assessment, including a mark scheme and sample student answers.

You'll also find sample curriculum plans and support for different GCSE specifications throughout the guide.

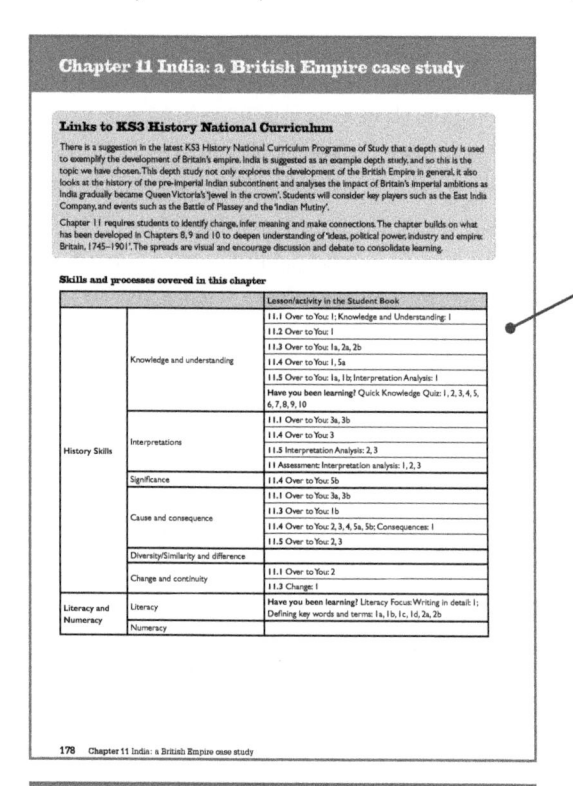

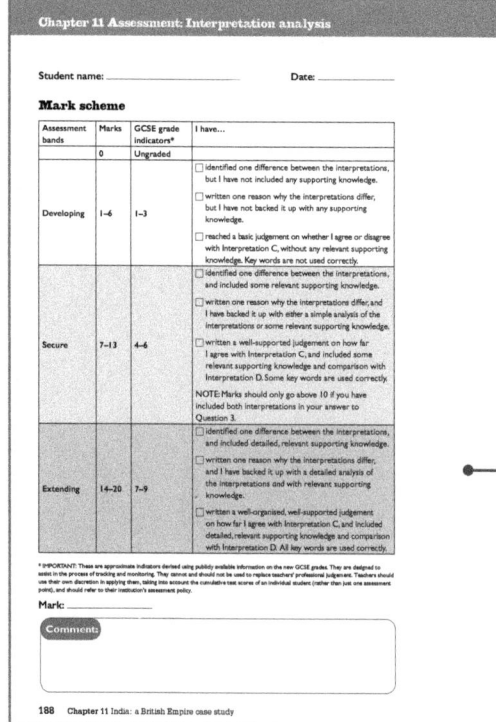

Skills and processes covered in this chapter
Content and assessments are mapped to the KS3 History National Curriculum, to help you plan a coherent curriculum

A brief history
A brief history and Timeline for every chapter, along with further reading suggestions

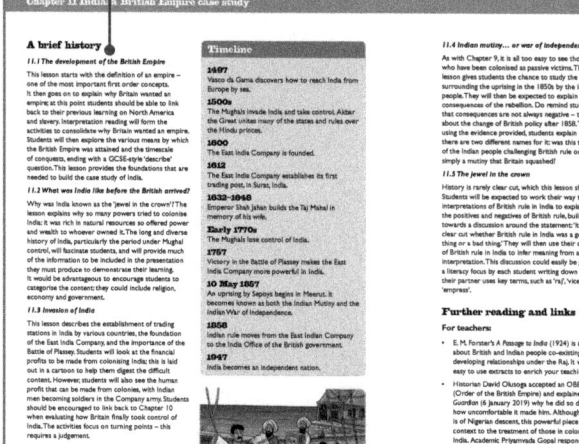

Assessment summary
Assessment planning, mark schemes and differentiated sample answers are available for each end-of-chapter assessment

Using this guide

Kerboodle

kerboodle Lessons, Resources and Assessment (annual subscription)

978 019 8393283

- An online package to support the *Student Book*
- Saves you time and enhances your lessons with over 400 ready-to-use resources, including **resource planners** for each lesson, **knowledge organisers, animations, film clips, history skills interactive activities, auto-marked quizzes** and much more
- Comprehensive support for assessment with **differentiated assessment worksheets**, **presentations, mark schemes and sample answers** to help your students as they progress through the curriculum

- **Digital version** of the *Student Book* can be used front-of-class, packed full of resources launching straight from the page
- Teacher access to the **digital** *Curriculum and Assessment Planning Guide* is included
- Regular updates to content and functionality to ensure you and your students are fully supported with the latest advice

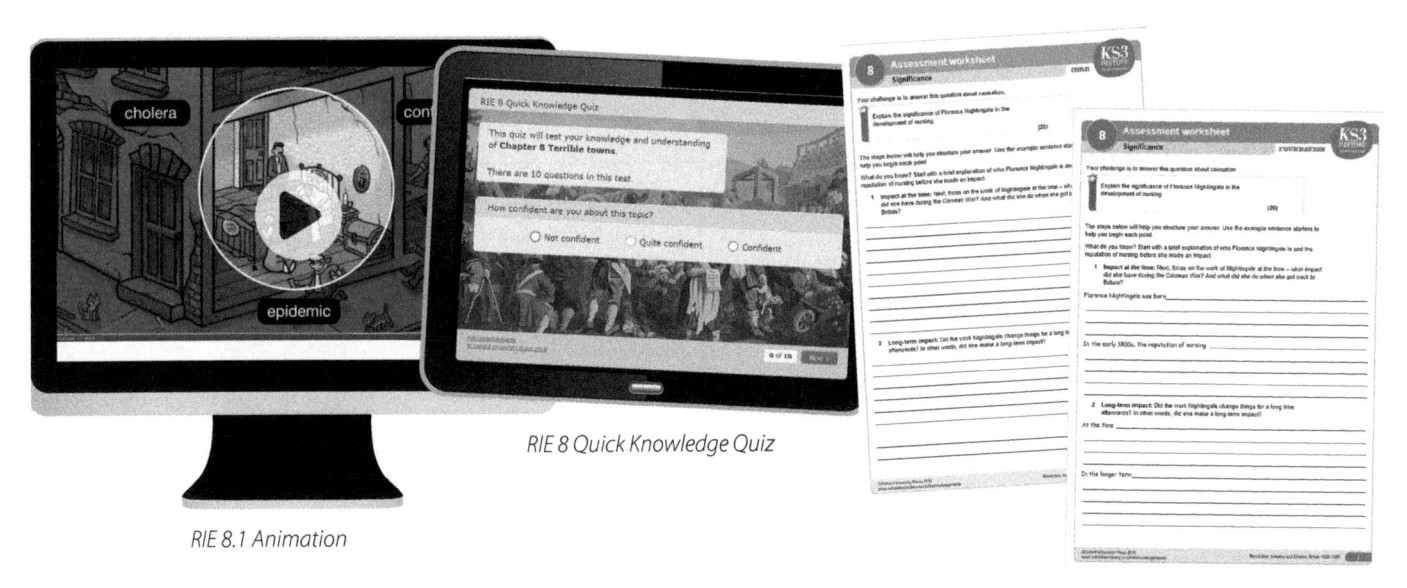

RIE 8.1 Animation

RIE 8 Quick Knowledge Quiz

RIE 8 Assessment worksheet: Significance

kerboodle Book (annual subscription)

978 019 839332 0

- **Student access** to the digital *Student Book*
- Includes **tools for annotation** and can be accessed on a **range of devices**

To find out more: www.oxfordsecondary.co.uk/ks3history

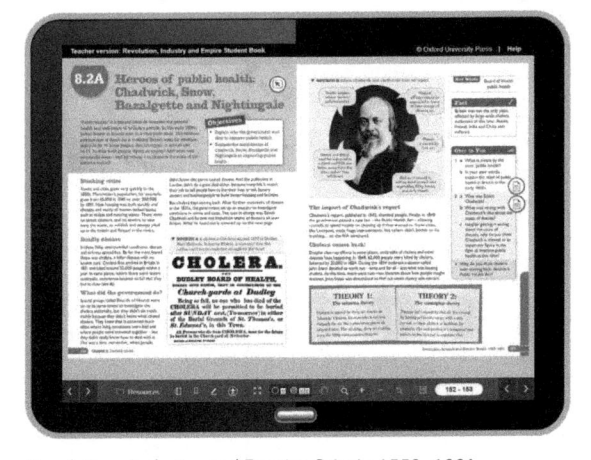

Revolution, Industry and Empire: Britain 1558–1901 Kerboodle Book

Revolution, Industry and Empire: Britain 1558–1901 | 9

Scheme of Work

KS3 History Scheme of Work

This table shows all the lessons available in the *Revolution, Industry and Empire Student Book*, in the *KS3 History* series, so that you can easily navigate through the book and supporting digital material on Kerboodle to select the key themes and topics that you might use to inform your own scheme of work.

Key to resources

SB – Student Book

TG – Curriculum and Assessment Planning Guide (Teacher Guide)

K – Kerboodle

Lesson title	Key Question	Resources	
Introduction			
Timeline from 1558 to 1901	What will we be learning this year in History?	• SB pp. 6–7	• TG p. 48
Chapter 1: Queen Elizabeth		• K RIE 1 Knowledge organiser	
1.1 What was Britain like in 1558?	What was early Tudor society like and how was it ruled?	• SB pp. 8–9 • TG pp. 46, 48 • K RIE 1.1A Worksheet (Core): Change and continuity	• K RIE 1.1 Worksheet (Foundation): Change and continuity • K RIE 1.1 History skills: Knowledge and understanding • K RIE 1.1 End of lesson assessment
1.2 Young Elizabeth: what was she like?	Who was Princess Elizabeth Tudor and what difficulties did she face in her early life?	• SB pp. 10–11 • TG pp. 46, 48 • K RIE 1.2 Worksheet (Core): Knowledge and understanding	• K RIE 1.2 Worksheet (Foundation): Knowledge and understanding • K RIE 1.2 History skills: Source analysis • K RIE 1.2 End of lesson assessment
1.3 Queen Elizabeth's middle way	What changes did Queen Elizabeth make to religion in England?	• SB pp. 12–13 • TG pp. 46, 48–49 • K RIE 1.3 Worksheet (Core): Interpretation	• K RIE 1.3 Worksheet (Foundation): Interpretation • K RIE 1.3 History skills: Diversity • K RIE 1.3 End of lesson assessment
1.4 Why did Queen Elizabeth kill her cousin?	What led to the execution of Mary Queen of Scots?	• SB pp. 14–15 • TG pp. 47, 49 • K RIE 1.4 Worksheet (Core): Source analysis	• K RIE 1.4 Worksheet (Foundation): Source analysis • K RIE 1.4 History skills: Chronology • K RIE 1.4 End of lesson assessment
1.5A Match of the day: England versus Spain	How did King Philip II of Spain plan to invade England and was it successful?	• SB pp. 16–17 • TG pp. 47, 49 • K RIE 1.5A Worksheet (Core): Similarity and difference	• K RIE 1.5A Worksheet (Foundation): Similarity and difference • K RIE 1.5A History skills: Knowledge and understanding • K RIE 1.5A Film clip: Cannons • K RIE 1.5A End of lesson assessment
1.5B Match of the day: England versus Spain	How was the Spanish Armada defeated?	• SB pp. 18–19 • TG pp. 47, 49–50 • K RIE 1.5B Worksheet (Core): Cause and consequence	• K RIE 1.5B Worksheet (Foundation): Cause and consequence • K RIE 1.5B Animation • K RIE 1.5B End of lesson assessment
1.6 Britain begins to build an empire	What is an empire and how was the British Empire built?	• SB pp. 20–21 • TG pp. 47, 50 • K RIE 1.6 Worksheet (Core): Cause and consequence	• K RIE 1.6 Worksheet (Foundation): Cause and consequence • K RIE 1.6 History skills: Cause and consequence • K RIE 1.6 End of lesson assessment
1.7 What did Queen Elizabeth look like?	How do we know what Queen Elizabeth looked like?	• SB pp. 22–23 • TG pp. 47, 50 • K RIE 1.7 Worksheet (Core): Source analysis	• K RIE 1.7 Worksheet (Foundation): Source analysis • K RIE 1.7 History skills: Interpretation analysis • K RIE 1.7 End of lesson assessment
1 Have you been learning?	What can you recall from this chapter? How can a paragraph on the Spanish attempt to invade England in 1588 be improved?	• SB pp. 24–25 • TG p. 51	• K RIE 1 Quick knowledge quiz
1 History skills and Assessment	1 Give two things you can infer from Source C about how Queen Elizabeth wanted to be portrayed. 2 Give two things you can infer from Source D about Queen Elizabeth and her views of her reign as queen.	• SB pp. 26–29 • TG pp. 52–57 • K RIE 1 Assessment: Making inferences (source analysis) worksheet (Core)	• K RIE 1 Assessment: Making inferences (source analysis) worksheet (Foundation) • K RIE 1 Assessment: Making inferences (source analysis) presentation

Scheme of Work

Lesson title	Key Question	Resources	
Chapter 2: Life in Tudor times		• K RIE 2 Knowledge organiser	
2.1A Who's who?	How was Tudor society divided?	• SB pp. 30–31 • TG pp. 61, 63 • K RIE 2.1A Worksheet (Core): Similarity and difference	• K RIE 2.1A Worksheet (Foundation): Similarity and difference • K RIE 2.1A History skills: Diversity • K RIE 2.1A End of lesson assessment
2.1B Who's who?	How were the poor treated in Tudor society?	• SB pp. 32–33 • TG pp. 61, 63 • K RIE 2.1B Worksheet (Core): Knowledge and understanding	• K RIE 2.1B Worksheet (Foundation): Knowledge and understanding • K RIE 2.1B History skills: Knowledge and understanding • K RIE 2.1B End of lesson assessment
2.2 What were Tudor schools like?	How were Tudor children educated?	• SB pp. 34–35 • TG pp. 61, 63 • K RIE 2.2 Worksheet (Core): Knowledge and understanding	• K RIE 2.2 Worksheet (Foundation): Knowledge and understanding • K RIE 2.2 Film clip: Teacher • K RIE 2.2 End of lesson assessment
2.3 How did people have fun in Tudor times?	What kind of hobbies and sports did people do in the Middle Ages?	• SB pp. 36–37 • TG pp. 61, 64 • K RIE 2.3 Worksheet (Core): Knowledge and understanding	• K RIE 2.3 Worksheet (Foundation): Knowledge and understanding • K RIE 2.3 History skills: Source analysis • K RIE 2.3 End of lesson assessment
2.4 And now for your Shakespeare lesson...	What made William Shakespeare famous and why do we still study his work today?	• SB pp. 38–39 • TG pp. 61, 64 • K RIE 2.4 Worksheet (Core): Interpretation	• K RIE 2.4 Worksheet (Foundation): Interpretation • K RIE 2.4 History skills: Source analysis • K RIE 2.4 End of lesson assessment
2.5 Fashion victims	What did women in Tudor times do to make themselves look beautiful?	• SB pp. 40–41 • TG pp. 62, 64 • K RIE 2.5 Worksheet (Core): Change and continuity	• K RIE 2.5 Worksheet (Foundation): Change and continuity • K RIE 2.5 History skills: Interpretation analysis • K RIE 2.5 End of lesson assessment
2.6 Tudor Masterchef	What mealtime routines did Tudor people have – and what were the differences between the rich and the poor?	• SB pp. 42–43 • TG pp. 62, 64 • K RIE 2.6 Worksheet (Core): Similarity and difference	• K RIE 2.6 Worksheet (Foundation): Similarity and difference • K RIE 2.6 History skills: Similarity and difference • K RIE 2.6 End of lesson assessment
2.7A Tudor crime and punishment	What were the most common Tudor crimes?	• SB pp. 44–45 • TG pp. 62, 64 • K RIE 2.7A Worksheet (Core): Knowledge and understanding	• K RIE 2.7A Worksheet (Foundation): Knowledge and understanding • K RIE 2.7A Animation • K RIE 2.7A End of lesson assessment
2.7B Tudor crime and punishment	How were Tudor criminals punished?	• SB pp. 46–47 • TG pp. 62, 65 • K RIE 2.7B Worksheet (Core): Knowledge and understanding	• K RIE 2.7B Worksheet (Foundation): Knowledge and understanding • K RIE 2.7B History skills: Chronology • K RIE 2.7B End of lesson assessment
2 Have you been learning?	What can you recall from this chapter? How can sentences about the poor in Tudor society be improved?	• SB pp. 48–49 • TG p. 65	• K RIE 2 Quick knowledge quiz
2 History skills and Assessment	Explain two ways in which the lives of the upper and lower classes in Tudor times were similar. Explain two ways in which they were different.	• SB pp. 50–53 • TG pp. 66–70 • K RIE 2 Assessment: Similarity and difference (Core)	• K RIE 2 Assessment: Similarity and difference worksheet (Foundation) • K RIE 2 Assessment: Similarity and difference presentation
Chapter 3: Exit the Tudors, enter the Stuarts		• K RIE 3 Knowledge organiser	
3.1 King James I: the scruffy Stuart!	Who was James I and who did he upset?	• SB pp. 54–55 • TG pp. 73, 75 • K RIE 3.1 Worksheet (Core): Interpretation	• K RIE 3.1 Worksheet (Foundation): Interpretation • K RIE 3.1 History skills: Knowledge and understanding • K RIE 3.1 End of lesson assessment
3.2 Remember, remember the fifth of November!	What was the Gunpowder Plot?	• SB pp. 56–57 • TG pp. 73, 75 • K RIE 3.2 Worksheet (Core): Knowledge and understanding	• K RIE 3.2 Worksheet (Foundation): Knowledge and understanding • K RIE 3.2 History skills: Source analysis • K RIE 3.2 End of lesson assessment
3.3 History Mystery: Were the gunpowder plotters framed?	Is there another side to the story of the Gunpowder Plot?	• SB pp. 58–59 • TG pp. 73, 75–76 • K RIE 3.3 Worksheet (Core): Source analysis	• K RIE 3.3 Worksheet (Foundation): Source analysis • K RIE 3.3 History skills: Source analysis • K RIE 3.3 End of lesson assessment

Scheme of Work

Lesson title	Key Question	Resources	
3.4 Which witch is which?	How did King James try to catch witches?	• SB pp. 60–61 • TG pp. 74, 76 • K RIE 3.4 Worksheet (Core): Source analysis	• K RIE 3.4 Worksheet (Foundation): Source analysis • K RIE 3.4 Film clip: Dungeon • K RIE 3.4 End of lesson assessment
3.5A Why do Americans speak English?	Who travelled to America in Tudor and Stuart times?	• SB pp. 62–63 • TG pp. 74, 76 • K RIE 3.5A Worksheet (Core): Chronology	• K RIE 3.5A Worksheet (Foundation): Chronology • K RIE 3.5A Animation K RIE 3.5A End of lesson assessment
3.5B Why do Americans speak English?	What was life like for the early British settlers in America?	• SB pp. 64–65 • TG pp. 74, 76 • K RIE 3.5B Worksheet (Core): Knowledge and understanding	• K RIE 3.5B Worksheet (Foundation): Knowledge and understanding • K RIE 3.5B History skills: Knowledge and understanding • K RIE 3.5B End of lesson assessment
3 Have you been learning?	What can you recall from this chapter? How can the writing of historical narratives be improved?	• SB pp. 66–67 • TG p. 77	• K RIE 3 Quick knowledge quiz
3 History skills and Assessment	1 What can Source A tell us about the views of James VI of Scotland/James I of England? 2 What can Source B tell us about the views of James VI of Scotland/James I of England? Use the two sources and your own knowledge to support your answer.	• SB pp. 68–71 • TG pp. 78–83 • K RIE 3 Quick knowledge quiz • K RIE 3 Assessment: Source analysis worksheet (Core)	• K RIE 3 Assessment: Source analysis worksheet (Foundation) • K RIE 3 Assessment: Source analysis presentation
Chapter 4: From Civil War to Commonwealth		• K RIE 4 Knowledge organiser	
4.1 Why did the English start fighting each other?	Why were people from the same country driven to fight each other?	• SB pp. 72–73 • TG pp. 87, 89 • K RIE 4.1 Worksheet (Core): Knowledge and understanding	• K RIE 4.1 Worksheet (Foundation): Knowledge and understanding • K RIE 4.1 History skills: Cause and consequence • K RIE 4.1 End of lesson assessment
4.2 Match of the day: Roundheads versus Cavaliers	Who dared to fight against the King of England?	• SB pp. 74–75 • TG pp. 87, 8 • K RIE 4.2 Worksheet (Core): Similarity and difference	• K RIE 4.2 Worksheet (Foundation): Similarity and difference • K RIE 4.2 History skills: Similarity and difference • K RIE 4.2 End of lesson assessment
4.3 What was new about the New Model Army?	What was it like to live and fight in the New Model Army?	• SB pp. 76–77 • TG pp. 87, 89–90 • K RIE 4.3 Worksheet (Core): Source analysis	• K RIE 4.3 Worksheet (Foundation): Source analysis • K RIE 4.3 Film clip: Musketeer • K RIE 4.3 End of lesson assessment
4.4 Why was King Charles I sentenced to death?	Who and what was responsible for the execution of the King of England?	• SB pp. 87–79 • TG pp. 87, 90 • K RIE 4.4 Worksheet (Core): Cause and consequence	• K RIE 4.4 Worksheet (Foundation): Cause and consequence • K RIE 4.4 Animation • K RIE 4.4 End of lesson assessment
4.5 Charlie for the chop!	What happened on the day that King Charles I was executed?	• SB pp. 80–81 • TG pp. 88, 90 • K RIE 4.5 Worksheet (Core): Cause and consequence	• K RIE 4.5 Worksheet (Foundation): Cause and consequence • K RIE 4.5 History skills: Source analysis • K RIE 4.5 End of lesson assessment
4.6 Cromwell: the man who banned Christmas	What was life like living in a country without a monarch?	• SB pp. 82–83 • TG pp. 88, 90 • K RIE 4.6 Worksheet (Core): Change and continuity	• K RIE 4.6 Worksheet (Foundation): Change and continuity • K RIE 4.6 History skills: Change and continuity • K RIE 4.6 End of lesson assessment
4.7 Why does Cromwell divide opinion?	Who was Oliver Cromwell and what did he do?	• SB pp. 84–85 • TG pp. 88, 91 • K RIE 4.7 Worksheet (Core): Interpretation analysis	• K RIE 4.7 Worksheet (Foundation): Interpretation analysis • K RIE 4.7 History skills: Knowledge and understanding • K RIE 4.7 End of lesson assessment
4.8 The monarchy returns – but what happened to Cromwell's head?	Why was Oliver Cromwell's body dug up after it was buried?	• SB pp. 86–87 • TG pp. 88, 91 • K RIE 4.8 Worksheet (Core): Significance	• K RIE 4.8 Worksheet (Foundation): Significance • K RIE 4.8 History skills: Chronology • K RIE 4.8 End of lesson assessment
4 Have you been learning?	What can you recall from this chapter? What are the key facts about the English Civil War?	• SB pp. 88–89 • TG p. 92	• K RIE 4 Quick knowledge quiz

Scheme of Work

Lesson title	Key Question	Resources	
4 History skills and Assessment	Write a narrative account of the events during the reign of Charles I (between 1625 and 1642) that led to the start of the English Civil War.	• SB pp. 90–91 • TG pp. 93–97 • K RIE 4 Quick knowledge quiz • K RIE 4 Assessment: Write a narrative account (causation) worksheet (Core)	• K RIE 4 Assessment: Write a narrative account (causation) worksheet (Foundation) • K RIE 4 Assessment: Write a narrative account (causation) presentation
Chapter 5: The Restoration: the Merry Monarch		• K RIE 5 Knowledge organiser	
5.1 Who was the Merry Monarch?	What was life like during the reign of King Charles II?	• SB pp. 92–93 • TG pp. 100, 102 • K RIE 5.1 Worksheet (Core): Source analysis	• K RIE 5.1 Worksheet (Foundation): Source analysis • K RIE 5.1 History skills: Change and continuity • K RIE 5.1 End of lesson assessment
5.2A How deadly was the Great Plague?	What were the symptoms of the Great Plague of 1665?	• SB pp. 94–95 • TG pp. 100, 102 • K RIE 5.2A Worksheet (Core): Cause and consequence	• K RIE 5.2A Worksheet (Foundation): Cause and consequence • K RIE 5.2A Animation • K RIE 5.2A End of lesson assessment
5.2B How deadly was the Great Plague?	What caused the Great Plague and what impact did it have?	• SB pp. 96–97 • TG pp. 100, 102–103 • K RIE 5.2B Worksheet (Core): Source analysis	• K RIE 5.2B Worksheet (Foundation): Source analysis • K RIE 5.2B Film clip: Plague doctor • K RIE 5.2B End of lesson assessment
5.3 Was the Great Fire of London an accident – or arson?	What caused the Great Fire of London, and how fast did it spread?	• SB pp. 98–99 • TG pp. 100, 103 • K RIE 5.3 Worksheet (Core): Source analysis	• K RIE 5.3 Worksheet (Foundation): Source analysis • K RIE 5.3 History skills: Chronology • K RIE 5.3 End of lesson assessment
5.4 London: a city reborn	Who was involved in the plans to rebuild the city of London, and how did they shape a new London?	• SB pp. 100–101 • TG pp. 101, 103 • K RIE 5.4 Worksheet (Core): Cause and consequence	• K RIE 5.4 Worksheet (Foundation): Cause and consequence • K RIE 5.4 History skills: Cause and consequence • K RIE 5.4 End of lesson assessment
5 Have you been learning?	What can you recall from this chapter? How can paragraphs on the Great Fire of London be structured properly?	• SB pp. 102–103 • TG p. 104	• K RIE 5 Quick knowledge quiz
5 History skills and Assessment	1 Describe two features of the streets and buildings in the centre of London in 1666. 2 How useful are Sources A and B for an enquiry into the impact of the Great Fire of London in 1666? Explain your answer, using both sources and your knowledge of the historical context. 3 How could you find out more about the impact of the Great Fire? Name two sources (other than Sources A and B) you could use, and explain your reasons.	• SB pp. 104–107 • TG pp. 105–111 • K RIE 5 Quick knowledge quiz • K RIE 5 Assessment: Source analysis (historic environment) worksheet (Core)	• K RIE 5 Assessment: Source analysis (historic environment) worksheet (Foundation) • K RIE 5 Assessment: Source analysis (historic environment) presentation
Chapter 6: Exit the Stuarts, enter the Georgians		• K RIE 6 Knowledge organiser	
6.1A The Glorious Revolution	What happened to the monarchy after the death of Charles II?	• SB pp. 108–109 • TG pp. 115, 117 • K RIE 6.1A Worksheet (Core): Cause and consequence	• K RIE 6.1A Worksheet (Foundation): Cause and consequence • K RIE 6.1A History skills: Cause and consequence • K IPM 6.1 End of lesson assessment
6.1B The Glorious Revolution	What happened to King James II, and how did the monarchy change as a result?	• SB pp. 110–111 • TG pp. 115, 117 • K RIE 6.1B Worksheet (Core): Significance • K RIE 6.1B Worksheet (Foundation): Significance	• K RIE 6.1B History skills: Significance • K RIE 6.1B End of lesson assessment
6.2 From Stuarts to Georgians	How did the 'Act of Settlement' and the 'Act of Union' change Britain?	• SB pp. 112–113 • TG pp. 115, 117–118 • K RIE 6.2 Worksheet (Core): Chronology	• K RIE 6.2 Worksheet (Foundation): Chronology • K RIE 6.2 History skills: Chronology • K RIE 6.2 End of lesson assessment
6.3 The Battle of Culloden, 1746	Who were the Jacobites and what threat did they pose to King George?	• SB pp. 114–115 • TG pp. 116, 118 • K RIE 6.3 Worksheet (Core): Knowledge and understanding	• K RIE 6.3 Worksheet (Foundation): Knowledge and understanding • K RIE 6.3 Film clip: Conflict • K RIE 6.3 End of lesson assessment

Scheme of Work

Lesson title	Key Question	Resources	
6.4A From Tudor to Georgian times: what changed?	What were some of the key discoveries and inventions of the 16th to early 18th centuries?	• SB pp. 116–117 • TG pp. 116, 118–119 • K RIE 6.4A Worksheet (Core): Change and continuity	• K RIE 6.4A Worksheet (Foundation): Change and continuity • K RIE 6.4A History skills: Change and continuity • K RIE 6.4A End of lesson assessment
6.4B From Tudor to Georgian times: what changed?	What was Georgian society like?	• SB pp. 118–119 • TG pp. 116, 119 • K RIE 6.4B Worksheet (Core): Change and continuity	• K RIE 6.4B Worksheet (Foundation): Change and continuity • K RIE 6.4B Animation • K RIE 6.4B End of lesson assessment
6 Have you been learning?	What can you recall from this chapter? How can key words be applied?	• SB pp. 120–121 • TG p. 119	• K RIE 6 Quick knowledge quiz
6 History skills and Assessment	In what ways did the lives of British people change, and in what ways did they stay the same between the late Tudor period and the beginning of the Georgian period (c.1550s-c.1700s)?	• SB pp. 122–123 • TG pp. 120–124 • K RIE 6 Quick knowledge quiz • K RIE 6 Assessment: Change and continuity worksheet (Core)	• K RIE 6 Assessment: Change and continuity worksheet (Foundation) • K RIE 6 Assessment: Change and continuity presentation
Chapter 7: The Industrial Revolution: from farming to factories		• K RIE 7 Knowledge organiser	
7.1 From homeworkers to factory workers	How did the way in which goods were made change in the 1700s?	• SB pp. 124–125 • TG pp. 128, 130 • K RIE 7.1 Worksheet (Core): Knowledge and understanding	• K RIE 7.1 Worksheet (Foundation): Knowledge and understanding • K RIE 7.1 History skills: Knowledge and understanding • K RIE 7.1 End of lesson assessment
7.2A How did factories create towns?	What were the key changes that took place in the way goods were made?	• SB pp. 126–127 • TG pp. 128, 130 • K RIE 7.2A Worksheet (Core): Cause and consequence	• K RIE 7.2A Worksheet (Foundation): Cause and consequence • K RIE 7.2A History skills: Cause and consequence • K RIE 7.2A End of lesson assessment
7.2B How did factories create towns?	How were new factories powered?	• SB pp. 128–129 • TG pp. 128, 130 • K RIE 7.2B Worksheet (Core): Significance	• K RIE 7.2B Worksheet (Foundation): Significance • K RIE 7.2B History skills: Cause and consequence • K RIE 7.2B End of lesson assessment
7.3 Peggy the pauper	Why did children work in factories and what were conditions like?	• SB pp. 130–131 • TG pp. 128, 130 • K RIE 7.3 Worksheet (Core): Similarity and difference	• K RIE 7.3 Worksheet (Foundation): Similarity and difference • K RIE 7.3 History skills: Knowledge and understanding • K RIE 7.3 End of lesson assessment
7.4 How were factory working conditions improved?	How did the Sadler report help to improve working conditions in factories?	• SB pp. 132–133 • TG pp. 128, 131 • K RIE 7.4 Worksheet (Core): Change and continuity	• K RIE 7.4 Worksheet (Foundation): Change and continuity • K RIE 7.4 History skills: Source analysis • K RIE 7.4 End of lesson assessment
7.5 'Black gold' and the new 'Age of Iron'	What was 'Black gold' and why was it so important? Why was this known as an 'Age of Iron'?	• SB pp. 134–135 • TG pp. 129, 131–132 • K RIE 7.5 Worksheet (Core): Significance	• K RIE 7.5 Worksheet (Foundation): Significance • K RIE 7.5 Film clip: Miner • K RIE 7.5 End of lesson assessment
7.6 From roads to canals to railways	What developments and inventions completely changed Britain's transport system?	• SB pp. 136–137 • TG pp. 129, 132 • K RIE 7.6 Worksheet (Core): Change and continuity	• K RIE 7.6 Worksheet (Foundation): Change and continuity • K RIE 7.6 Animation • K RIE 7.6 End of lesson assessment
7.7A An age of invention	What were some of the greatest achievements of Britain's great inventors, designers and scientists?	• SB pp. 138–139 • TG pp. 129, 132 • K RIE 7.7A Worksheet (Core): Knowledge and understanding	• K RIE 7.7A Worksheet (Foundation): Knowledge and understanding • K RIE 7.7A History skills: Chronology • K RIE 7.7A End of lesson assessment
7.7B An age of invention	Who was the 'greatest inventor and designer of the time' - and why?	• SB pp. 140–141 • TG pp. 129, 132–133 • K RIE 7.7B Worksheet (Core): Significance	• K RIE 7.7B Worksheet (Foundation): Significance • K RIE 7.7B History skills: Knowledge and understanding • K RIE 7.7B End of lesson assessment
7.8 So what was the Industrial Revolution?	What was the Industrial Revolution and what caused it to take place?	• SB pp. 142–143 • TG pp. 129, 133 • K RIE 7.8 Worksheet (Core): Cause and consequence	• K RIE 7.8 Worksheet (Foundation): Cause and consequence • K RIE 7.8 History skills: Change and continuity • K RIE 7.8 End of lesson assessment
7 Have you been learning?	What can you recall from this chapter? How can sources help us describe the changes that took place in Manchester between 1740 and 1850?	• SB pp. 144–145 • TG p. 133	• K RIE 7 Quick knowledge quiz

Scheme of Work

Lesson title	Key Question	Resources	
7 History skills and Assessment	'Britain's entrepreneurs were the main cause of the Industrial Revolution.' How far do you agree with this statement?	• SB pp. 146–147 • TG pp. 134–138 • K RIE 7 Quick knowledge quiz • K RIE 7 Assessment: Causation worksheet (Core)	• K RIE 7 Assessment: Causation worksheet (Foundation) • K RIE 7 Assessment: Causation presentation
Chapter 8: Terrible towns		• K RIE 8 Knowledge organiser	
8.1A What made towns and cities stink?	What was life like for ordinary people in industrial towns and cities in the nineteenth century?	• SB pp. 148–149 • TG pp. 142, 144 • K RIE 8.1A Worksheet (Core): Source analysis	• K RIE 8.1A Worksheet (Foundation): Source analysis • K RIE 8.1A History skills: Source analysis • K RIE 8.1A End of lesson assessment
8.1B What made towns and cities stink?	Why was disease common for the people living in newly expanded nineteenth century towns?	• SB pp. 150–151 • TG pp. 142, 144 • K RIE 8.1B Worksheet (Core): Cause and consequence	• K RIE 8.1B Worksheet (Foundation): Cause and consequence • K RIE 8.1B Animation • K RIE 8.1B End of lesson assessment
8.2A Heroes of public health: Chadwick, Snow, Bazalgette and Nightingale	Why was the 'Public Health Act' introduced?	• SB pp. 152–153 • TG pp. 142, 144–145 • K RIE 8.2A Worksheet (Core): Cause and consequence	• K RIE 8.2A Worksheet (Foundation): Cause and consequence • K RIE 8.2A History skills: Cause and consequence • K RIE 8.2A End of lesson assessment
8.2B Heroes of public health: Chadwick, Snow, Bazalgette and Nightingale	What contribution did Edwin Chadwick, John Snow, Joseph Bazalgette and Florence Nightingale make to public health in the nineteenth century?	• SB pp. 154–155 • TG pp. 142, 145 • K RIE 8.2B Worksheet (Core): Knowledge and understanding	• K RIE 8.2B Worksheet (Foundation): Knowledge and understanding • K RIE 8.2B Film clip: John Snow • K RIE 8.2B End of lesson assessment
8.3 How divided was society?	What class divisions were there in the eighteenth and nineteenth century and what was life like for people in different classes?	• SB pp. 156–157 • TG pp. 142, 145 • K RIE 8.3 Worksheet (Core): Similarity and difference	• K RIE 8.3 Worksheet (Foundation): Similarity and difference • K RIE 8.3 History skills: Knowledge and understanding • K RIE 8.3 End of lesson assessment
8.4 Crime and punishment	Who was responsible for keeping law and order – and how were criminals punished?	• SB pp. 158–159 • TG pp. 143, 145–146 • K RIE 8.4 Worksheet (Core): Source analysis	• K RIE 8.4 Worksheet (Foundation): Source analysis • K RIE 8.4 History skills: Knowledge and understanding • K RIE 8.4 End of lesson assessment
8.5 How did the first police force begin?	Who were the 'Bow Street Runners' and how did they compare to Robert Peel's 'Bobbies'?	• SB pp. 160–161 • TG pp. 143, 146 • K RIE 8.5 Worksheet (Core): Knowledge and understanding	• K RIE 8.5 Worksheet (Foundation): Knowledge and understanding • K RIE 8.5 History skills: Source analysis • K RIE 8.5 End of lesson assessment
8.6 Why was Elizabeth Fry on a £5 note?	What were prisons like in the 1800s – and what did Elizabeth Fry and John Howard do to improve them	• SB pp.162–163 • TG pp. 143, 146–147 • K RIE 8.6 Worksheet (Core): Cause and consequence	• K RIE 8.6 Worksheet (Foundation): Cause and consequence • K RIE 8.6 History skills: Chronology • K RIE 8.6 End of lesson assessment
8.7A History Mystery: Why did the police fail to catch Jack the Ripper?	How did Jack the Ripper strike fear across London in 1888?	• SB pp.164–165 • TG pp. 143, 147 • K RIE 8.7A Worksheet (Core): Source analysis	• K RIE 8.7A Worksheet (Foundation): Source analysis • K RIE 8.7A History skills: Source analysis • K RIE 8.7A End of lesson assessment
8.7B History Mystery: Why did the police fail to catch Jack the Ripper?	Why was it so difficult for police to find out who Jack the Ripper was?	• SB pp.166–167 • TG pp. 143, 147 • K RIE 8.7B Worksheet (Core): Source analysis	• K RIE 8.7B Worksheet (Foundation): Source analysis • K RIE 8.7B History skills: Source analysis • K RIE 8.7B End of lesson assessment
8 Have you been learning?	What can you recall from this chapter? What can an academic text tell us about the development of public health?	• SB pp. 168–169 • TG p. 148	• K RIE 8 Quick knowledge quiz
8 History skills and Assessment	Explain the significance of Florence Nightingale in the development of nursing.	• SB pp. 170–171 • TG pp. 149–153 • K RIE 8 Quick knowledge quiz • K RIE 8 Assessment: Significance worksheet (Core)	• K RIE 8 Assessment: Significance worksheet (Foundation) • K RIE 8 Assessment: Significance presentation

Revolution, Industry and Empire: Britain 1558–1901

Scheme of Work

Lesson title	Key Question	Resources	
Chapter 9: The slave trade		• K RIE 9 Knowledge organiser	
9.1A What was the slave trade?	How was the slave trade organised?	• SB pp. 172–173 • TG pp. 156, 158 • K RIE 9.1A Worksheet (Core): Knowledge and understanding	• K RIE 9.1A Worksheet (Foundation): Knowledge and understanding • K RIE 9.1A Animation • K RIE 9.1A End of lesson assessment
9.1B What was the slave trade?	What was Britain's role in the slave trade?	• SB pp. 174–175 • TG pp. 156, 158 • K RIE 9.1B Worksheet (Core): Interpretation	• K RIE 9.1B Worksheet (Foundation): Interpretation • K RIE 9.1B History skills: Source analysis • K RIE 9.1B End of lesson assessment
9.2A A life of slavery	What was life like for the African men, women and children when they were traded as slaves?	• SB pp. 176–177 • TG pp. 156, 158–159 • K RIE 9.2A Worksheet (Core): Source analysis	• K RIE 9.2A Worksheet (Foundation): Source analysis • K RIE 9.2A History skills: Chronology • K RIE 9.2A End of lesson assessment
9.2B A life of slavery	What happened to the slaves once they became the property of their owners?	• SB pp. 178–179 • TG pp. 156, 159 • K RIE 9.2B Worksheet (Core): Source analysis	• K RIE 9.2B Worksheet (Foundation): Source analysis • K RIE 9.2B History skills: Cause and consequence • K RIE 9.2B End of lesson assessment
9.3A Why was slavery abolished?	What factors contributed to the abolition of slavery?	• SB pp.180–181 • TG pp. 157, 159 • K RIE 9.3A Worksheet (Core): Source analysis	• K RIE 9.3A Worksheet (Foundation): Source analysis • K RIE 9.3A History skills: Knowledge and understanding • K RIE 9.3A End of lesson assessment
9.3B Why was slavery abolished?	When did the slave trade end in Britain and the British Empire?	• SB pp.182–183 • TG pp. 157, 159 • K RIE 9.3B Worksheet (Core): Cause	• K RIE 9.3B Worksheet (Foundation): Cause • K RIE 9.3B Film clip: William Wilberforce • K RIE 9.3B End of lesson assessment
9 Have you been learning?	What can you recall from this chapter? What are the key facts about Britain's involvement in the slave trade?	• SB pp. 184–185 • TG p. 160	• K RIE 9 Quick knowledge quiz
9 History skills and Assessment	Which of the following was the more important reason why the slave trade was abolished in the British Empire in 1807: • the efforts of the slaves themselves, and former slaves • the anti-slavery campaign in Britain? Explain your answer with reference to both reasons.	• SB pp. 186–187 • TG pp. 161–165 • K RIE 9 Quick knowledge quiz • K RIE 9 Assessment: Causation worksheet (Core)	• K RIE 9 Assessment: Causation worksheet (Foundation) • K RIE 9 Assessment: Causation presentation
Chapter 10: Britain versus France		• K RIE 10 Knowledge organiser	
10.1A Britain versus France… in North America	What happened when European settlers arrived in North America?	• SB pp. 188–189 • TG pp. 168, 170 • K RIE 10.1A Worksheet (Core): Interpretation	• K RIE 10.1A Worksheet (Foundation): Interpretation • K RIE 10.1A Animation • K RIE 10.1A End of lesson assessment
10.1B Britain versus France… in North America	What happened during the Seven Years War?	• SB pp. 190–191 • TG pp. 168, 170 • K RIE 10.1B Worksheet (Core): Knowledge and understanding	• K RIE 10.1B Worksheet (Foundation): Knowledge and understanding • K RIE 10.1B History skills: Cause and consequence • K RIE 10.1B End of lesson assessment
10.2 In what way is the execution of a French king linked to Britain?	What is the 'Declaration of Independence' and how is it connected to the French Revolution?	• SB pp. 192–193 • TG pp. 168, 170–171 • K RIE 10.2 Worksheet (Core): Source analysis	• K RIE 10.2 Worksheet (Foundation): Source analysis • K RIE 10.2 History skills: Significance • K RIE 10.2 End of lesson assessment
10.3 Napoleon versus Nelson: Battle of Trafalgar	Who were Napoleon Bonaparte and Vice Admiral Horatio Nelson – and what happened at the Battle of Trafalgar?	• SB pp. 194–195 • TG pp. 169, 171 • K RIE 10.3 Worksheet (Core): Significance	• K RIE 10.3 Worksheet (Foundation): Significance • K RIE 10.3 History skills: Source analysis • K RIE 10.3 End of lesson assessment
10.4 Waterloo: Napoleon's last stand	What happened at the Battle of Waterloo?	• SB pp. 196–197 • TG pp. 169, 171 • K RIE 10.4 Worksheet (Core): Source analysis	• K RIE 10.4 Worksheet (Foundation): Source analysis • K RIE 10.4 Film clip: Waterloo • K RIE 10.4 End of lesson assessment

Scheme of Work

Lesson title	Key Question	Resources	
10 Have you been learning?	What can you recall from this chapter? How can paragraphs about the conflict between Britain and France in the 1700s and 1800s be improved?	• SB pp. 198–199 • TG pp. 172	• K RIE 10 Quick knowledge quiz
10 History skills and Assessment	Explain the following: • the importance of the treaty, signed in Paris (1763), for Britain's position in North America • the importance of the Battle of Trafalgar for relations between Britain and France.	• SB pp. 200–201 • TG pp. 173–177 • K RIE 10 Quick knowledge quiz	• K RIE Assessment: Consequences worksheet (Core) • K RIE Assessment: Consequences worksheet (Foundation) • K RIE Assessment: Consequences presentation
Chapter 11: India: a British Empire case study		• K RIE 11 Knowledge organiser	
11.1 The development of the British Empire	How and why did Britain gain an empire?	• SB pp. 202–203 • TG pp. 180, 182 • K RIE 11.1 Worksheet (Core): Knowledge and understanding	• K RIE 11.1 Worksheet (Foundation): Knowledge and understanding • K RIE 11.1 History skills: Knowledge and understanding • K RIE 11.1 End of lesson assessment
11.2 What was India like before the British arrived?	Why was India such a rich prize for anyone who conquered it?	• SB pp. 204–205 • TG pp. 180, 182 • K RIE 11.2 Worksheet (Core): Knowledge and understanding	• K RIE 11.2 Worksheet (Foundation): Knowledge and understanding • K RIE 11.2 History skills: Chronology • K RIE 11.2 End of lesson assessment
11.3 Invasion of India	How did trading by European countries in India lead to war?	• SB pp. 206–207 • TG pp. 181, 182 • K RIE 11.3 Worksheet (Core): Change	• K RIE 11.3 Worksheet (Foundation): Change • K RIE 11.3 Animation • K RIE 11.3 End of lesson assessment
11.4 Indian mutiny… or war of independence?	How can the events in India of 1857 and 1858 be interpreted differently?	• SB pp. 208–209 • TG pp. 181, 182–183 • K RIE 11.4 Worksheet (Core): Consequences	• K RIE 11.4 Worksheet (Foundation): Consequences • K RIE 11.4 History skills: Cause and consequence • K RIE 11.4 End of lesson assessment
11.5 The jewel in the crown	Why was India considered to be the 'jewel' in Britain's crown?	• SB pp. 210–211 • TG pp. 181, 183 • K RIE 11.5 Worksheet (Core): Interpretation analysis	• K RIE 11.5 Worksheet (Foundation): Interpretation analysis • K RIE 11.5 Film clip: Soldier • K RIE 11.5 End of lesson assessment
11 Have you been learning?	What can you recall from this chapter? How can a paragraph about India in the 1500s be improved?	• SB pp. 212–213 • TG pp. 184	• K RIE 11 Quick knowledge quiz
11 History skills and Assessment	1 Interpretations C and D give different views on the impact of British control of India. What is the main difference between the views? 2 Suggest one reason why Interpretations C and D give different views about the impact of British control of the British Empire. 3 How far do you agree with Interpretation C about the impact of British control of the British Empire? Explain your answer, using both interpretations and your own knowledge of the historical context.	• SB pp. 214–217 • TG pp. 185–190 • K RIE 11 Quick knowledge quiz	• K RIE 11 Assessment: Interpretation analysis worksheet (Core) • K RIE 11 Assessment: Interpretation analysis worksheet (Foundation) • K RIE 11 Assessment: Interpretation analysis presentation
Chapter 12: From Tudor to Victorian Britain: what changed?		• K RIE 12 Knowledge organiser	
12.1A 1848: How close was a British revolution?	How and why did British people fight for improved rights?	• SB pp. 218–219 • TG pp. 195, 198 • K RIE 12.1A Worksheet (Core): Interpretation	• K RIE 12.1A Worksheet (Foundation): Interpretation • K RIE 12.1A Film clip: Massacre Witness • K RIE 12.1A End of lesson assessment
12.1B 1848: How close was a British revolution	Were the protests successful – and what changes resulted from the action taken by British people?	• SB pp. 220–221 • TG pp. 195, 198 • K RIE 12.1B Worksheet (Core): Knowledge and understanding	• K RIE 12.1B Worksheet (Foundation): Knowledge and understanding • K RIE 12.1B History skills: Source analysis • K RIE 12.1B End of lesson assessment
12.2A Was this an age of improvement for women?	What position in society did women have in the eighteenth and nineteenth centuries?	• SB pp. 222–223 • TG pp. 195, 198–199 • K RIE 12.2A Worksheet (Core): Source analysis	• K RIE 12.2A Worksheet (Foundation): Source analysis • K RIE 12.2A History skills: Source analysis • K RIE 12.2A End of lesson assessment

Scheme of Work

Lesson title	Key Question	Resources
12.2B Was this an age of improvement for women?	How important was the Match Girls Strike of 1888?	• SB pp. 224–225 • TG pp. 195, 199 • K RIE 12.2B Worksheet (Core): Knowledge and understanding	• K RIE 12.2B Worksheet (Foundation): Knowledge and understanding • K RIE 12.2B History skills: Interpretation • K RIE 12.2B End of lesson assessment
12.3 What were Victorian schools like?	What was life like in a Victorian schoolroom – and how and why did schools change in the 1800s?	• SB pp. 226–227 • TG pp. 195, 199 • K RIE 12.3 Worksheet (Core): Change and continuity	• K RIE 12.3 Worksheet (Foundation): Change and continuity • K RIE 12.3 History skills: Change and continuity • K RIE 12.3 End of lesson assessment
12.4A A healthier nation?	How and why did attitudes to cleanliness change in the nineteenth century?	• SB pp. 228–229 • TG pp. 196, 200 • K RIE 12.4A Worksheet (Core): Source analysis	• K RIE 12.4A Worksheet (Foundation): Source analysis • K RIE 12.4A History skills: Knowledge and understanding • K RIE 12.4A End of lesson assessment
12.4B A healthier nation?	Who were the key individuals that helped win the battle against pain and infection?	• SB pp. 230–231 • TG pp. 196, 200 • K RIE 12.4B Worksheet (Core): Significance	• K RIE 12.4B Worksheet (Foundation): Significance • K RIE 12.4B History skills: Source analysis • K RIE 12.4B End of lesson assessment
12.5A How did people have fun during Victorian times?	Why did the amount of leisure time people had in the 1800s increase – and where did people go in their free time in the 1800s?	• SB pp. 232–233 • TG pp. 196, 201 • K RIE 12.5A Worksheet (Core): Change and continuity	• K RIE 12.52A Worksheet (Foundation): Change and continuity • K RIE 12.5A History skills: Cause and consequence • K RIE 12.5A End of lesson assessment
12.5B How did people have fun during Victorian times?	What did different sections of society do with their leisure time in the 1800s?	• SB pp. 234–235 • TG pp. 196, 201 • K RIE 12.5B Worksheet (Core): Change and continuity	• K RIE 12.5B Worksheet (Foundation): Change and continuity • K RIE 12.5B History skills: Source analysis • K RIE 12.5B End of lesson assessment
12.6 The high street	What did a typical Victorian high street look like?	• SB pp. 236–237 • TG pp. 196, 201–202 • K RIE 12.6 Worksheet (Core): Source analysis	• K RIE 12.6 Worksheet (Foundation): Source analysis • K RIE 12.6 History skills: Knowledge and understanding • K RIE 12.6 End of lesson assessment
12.7 Why are Charles Darwin and a chimpanzee on a £2 coin?	What is Darwin's theory of evolution and why did it cause so much controversy?	• SB pp. 238–239 • TG pp. 196, 202 • K RIE 12.7 Worksheet (Core): Significance	• K RIE 12.7 Worksheet (Foundation): Significance • K RIE 12.7 History skills: Knowledge and understanding • K RIE 12.7 End of lesson assessment
12.8 The Great Hunger	What were the causes of the Great Hunger – and did the British government do enough to help?	• SB pp. 240–241 • TG pp. 196, 202 • K RIE 12.8 Worksheet (Core): Interpretation	• K RIE 12.8 Worksheet (Foundation): Interpretation • K RIE 12.8 History skills: Cause and consequence • K RIE 12.8 End of lesson assessment
12.9 What was Britain like by 1901?	How did Britain change between 1558 and 1901?	• SB pp. 242–243 • TG pp. 196, 202 • K RIE 12.9 Worksheet (Core): Change and continuity	• K RIE 12.9 Worksheet (Foundation): Change and continuity • K RIE 12.9 Animation • K RIE 12.9 End of lesson assessment
12 Have you been learning?	What can you recall from this chapter? What do sources and interpretations tell us about the Peterloo Massacre?	• SB pp. 244–245 • TG pp. 203	• K RIE 12 Quick knowledge quiz
12 History skills and Assessment	How far do you agree that science and medicine saw the largest change between 1558 and 1901 in Britain?	• SB pp. 246–247 • TG pp. 204–208 • K RIE 12 Quick knowledge quiz	• K RIE 12 Assessment: Change (Core) • K RIE 12 Assessment: Change (Foundation) • K RIE 12 Assessment: Change presentation

Curriculum planning

Curriculum planning: Ofsted inspection framework

A new Ofsted inspection framework has been used with schools from September 2019. The most notable change to this framework is that schools will be judged on the 'quality of education' – a judgement that is based around Ofsted's working definition of the 'curriculum'. Ofsted is clear that the new framework will credit schools that promote a rich and broad curriculum, and have announced that the main points of focus when assessing the quality of education will be related to the **'intent, implementation and impact'** of the curriculum. The aim of this section is to provide teachers, department leaders and faculty leaders with some guidance on how to ensure you are prepared for both the new framework, and, at the same time, delivering a *KS3 History* course that is coherently sequenced, ambitious, relevant and ideally placed to prepare students for study at a higher level. As educators, you will no doubt have given your *KS3 History* curriculum much thought up to this point. It is now even more important that your *KS3 History* curriculum helps to enhance the *whole-school* curriculum.

1 Reviewing your KS3 curriculum

Let's start by digging into what is meant when Ofsted say that the three main points of focus within the quality of education judgement will be 'intent, implementation and impact' – and think about where your History curriculum fits:

> **Intent:**
> - *The curriculum is ambitious and designed to give **all** students the knowledge and cultural capital they need to succeed in life.*
> - *The curriculum is coherently planned and sequenced towards cumulatively sufficient knowledge and skills for future learning and employment."*

As a department, your challenge here then is to ensure that the 'History diet' you offer in school earns its place in the whole school curriculum. It might be useful as a department to think about these questions relating to **curriculum intent:**

- ☐ What is the curriculum we offer? What knowledge, cultural capital and skills will be gained by a student undertaking our course?
- ☐ Why have we made those curriculum choices – and how are these choices 'ambitious'?
- ☐ How is our curriculum/scheme of work sequenced (and why was it sequenced this way)?
- ☐ How is progression built into the course/scheme of work?
- ☐ How does our curriculum/scheme of work help ensure students make progress?
- ☐ How can/will this curriculum/scheme of work be developed over time?

> **Implementation:**
> - *Teachers have good knowledge of the subject and courses they teach.*
> - *Teachers present subject matter clearly, promoting appropriate discussion about the subject matter being taught. They check students' understanding systematically, identify misconceptions accurately and provide clear, direct feedback.*
> - *Over the course of study, teaching is designed to help students to remember in the long term the content they have been taught and to integrate new knowledge and concepts.*
> - *Teachers and leaders use assessment well, for example to help students embed and use knowledge fluently or to check understanding and inform teaching.*
> - *The resources and materials that teachers select reflect the school's ambitious intentions for the course and study and clearly support the curriculum."*

As you are reading some of these points, I am sure that you are thinking how well History as a subject promotes many of the curriculum ideas highlighted. It is a subject that invites discussion and allows us to embed and use knowledge fluently. You could consider these questions relating to **curriculum implementation**:

- ☐ How can the resources in the curriculum/scheme of work help us to present subject matter clearly?
- ☐ How can this curriculum/scheme of work help to reduce teacher workload (including, how does it help us with subject knowledge and knowledge of the course)?
- ☐ How is progression built into the course/scheme of work?
- ☐ How does our curriculum/scheme of work help to ensure students make progress?
- ☐ What assessments do we set and how do they help to form part of the process of evaluating progress and identifying next steps?
- ☐ Are there other ways that we establish what knowledge and skills students have gained?
- ☐ How does our KS3 curriculum contribute to the broader aims of the school in providing students with the cultural capital they need to succeed in life?

> **Impact:**
> - *Students develop detailed knowledge and skills across the curriculum and, as a result, achieve well.*
> - *Students are ready for the next stage of education."*

Curriculum planning

Any forward thinking, relevant, coherently planned History curriculum should be able to hit the two points above. History is a subject that allows students to develop detailed knowledge and skills while helping to build a comprehensive historical vocabulary, enhance their writing skills and generally prepare students for the rigours of further study. Again, it might be worth asking these questions around the **impact** of your own curriculum:

- How do our students develop detailed knowledge and skills, and how do we test this?
- How do we build strong literacy skills in our teaching (vocab, writing, etc.)?
- How do we prepare students for the rigours of further study from an early age?
- How do we measure impact?

2 How the Oxford *KS3 History* course can be part of your school's rich and ambitious curriculum

Our vision is a *KS3 History* series that helps teachers ensure that all students make progress and achieve their potential, and also allows teachers the flexibility to deliver a rich and broad curriculum that could be adapted to allow *all* students to develop as historians.

Supporting curriculum intent with coherently planned textbooks

Using the framework laid out in the KS3 History National Curriculum, the three textbooks in our *KS3 History* series chart the history of the British Isles as a coherent narrative. The topics in the books are sequenced chronologically (from pre-1066 to the present day) and the chapters are themed to help students accumulate sufficient knowledge. This helps you to teach both chronologically and thematically, which will ultimately help students grapple with the demands of History content at KS3 and beyond.

We focus on how people's lives have shaped this nation and how Britain has influenced and been influenced by the wider world. For example, in ***Invasion, Plague and Murder 1066–1558* (Book 1)** we explore the impact of William the Conqueror and his Norman Conquest, culminating in a lesson that assesses how life changed under the Normans. In later books we examine some of the great inventors and leaders that have made an influential and lasting impact on both this country and the world. As well as individuals, we look at key events, developments and ideas. In ***Revolution, Industry and Empire 1558–1901* (Book 2)**, for example, we assess the Industrial Revolution – a significant aspect of world history – and the factors that made it happen, as well as the impact it made on both Britain and the wider world. Book 2 also looks at the expansion of the British Empire, with particular focus on India, while ***Technology, War and Independence: 1901–Present Day* (Book 3)** examines the decline of Britain's empire and the reasons behind this.

We ensure that all students are supported in the design of the curriculum with, for example:

- Over to You activities that are ramped in difficulty, so students can access and apply the key information.
- Engaging features like Fact boxes and Key Words which give all students the 'knowledge and cultural capital'.
- And in this guide, you can find further reading suggestions and activities for students to stretch and support those who will relish taking their learning 'beyond the classroom'.

Supporting curriculum implementation

By offering accessible, engaging content that builds into a solid body of historical knowledge and understanding, and by supporting the acquisition of key history skills, this *KS3 History* series can ensure that students develop a good knowledge and understanding of the subject. This will help them to 'remember in the long term the content they have been taught and to integrate new knowledge and concepts'.

Second-order concepts

Throughout the series we continually reference the second-order concepts that help us organise the process of studying history, such as continuity and change, cause and consequence, similarity, difference and significance. We use them to get students to make connections, draw contrasts, frame historically-valid questions and create their own structured accounts.

It is vital that students understand the methods of historical enquiry, including how evidence is used and how and why contrasting arguments and interpretations of the past have been constructed. In Book 1, for example, we look at the way actions of William the Conqueror have been interpreted, while in Book 2 students assess the reputation and legacy of Oliver Cromwell and get the chance to justify the sort of reputation they think Cromwell deserves.

Checking understanding systematically

Throughout the course we have built in regular opportunities for students to demonstrate the knowledge and understanding they have learned. This is done through a variety of assessments and activities. Every chapter and every lesson in each book follows a consistent approach, with features that have been successfully trialled and tested – Fact boxes, Over to You activities, and History Skills activities. Activities and assessments progress in difficulty as students work through the chapters and through the three textbooks.

Further, by offering a consistent mixture of low- and high-stakes assessment opportunities at the end of each chapter, we allow students to demonstrate progress and help them to retain knowledge in the long term. The mix of **summative** (Quick Knowledge Quizzes; Literacy Focus activities; auto-marked end-of-lesson self-assessments on Kerboodle) and **formative** assessments (end-of-chapter assessment questions with mark schemes and differentiated assessment worksheets on Kerboodle) help you to 'check understanding and inform teaching' so you can ensure that students 'embed and use knowledge fluently'.

Supporting curriculum impact

An impact study[3] on Oxford's *KS3 History* series (Third editions) was undertaken in order to gain an in-depth understanding of how teachers and Heads of History perceived the course had impacted both student motivation and preparedness for the next stage of education. Teachers who took part discussed the positive impact of the series and told us that this series:

- motivates students
- impacts positively on student preparedness for GCSE
- helps students develop History exam skills
- engages students of all abilities.

The chart below summarises some of the key questions you may have around the curriculum principles that inform this textbook series.

[3] see **Oxford University Press** (2017) Impact Study: KS3 History by Aaron Wilkes 3rd Edition

Key question	How OUP can help you:
What is the curriculum offered by this course (including what knowledge, cultural capital and skills will be gained)?	This is a flexible two- or three-year course that matches the requirements of the KS3 History National Curriculum and lays the **foundations** for the study of all GCSE History specifications. Our curriculum principles are to: • provide a coherently planned and sequenced curriculum towards developing historical knowledge and understanding • build a historical vocabulary and close the word gap • develop extended writing skills • present subject matter clearly and make History engaging • check students' understanding systematically • focus on how people's lives have shaped this nation and how Britain has influenced and been influenced by the wider world. This course has been proven (in its last edition) to engage and motivate KS3 students, and to support progression by preparing students for the rigours of further study in History.
Why were those curriculum choices made (including any research findings) and how are these choices 'ambitious'?	We understand that the teaching and learning landscape at KS3 and KS4 has changed in recent years. Almost 50% of schools[4] now offer a two-year KS3, mainly as a consequence of the view that the new GCSE is seen as extremely 'crowded' and it is difficult to get all the content in within a two-year framework. Also, many schools have changed the way they teach KS3 to provide **background knowledge** to GCSE topics and provide new understanding of history skills such as source/interpretation analysis[4]. In addition, there is clear evidence[5] of a significant **word gap** in UK schools: this is an increasing problem which is holding back children's learning. This OUP course has been ambitiously designed to reflect the new landscape by ensuring that each suggested topic in the KS3 History National Curriculum is covered, but we have also made sure that our content supports literacy and vocabulary development, and progression towards study beyond KS3. We have carefully designed the content and assessments to match the needs of students who will go on to study any of the GCSE History specifications (all of which offer vastly different question types and are different in scope of content).

Curriculum planning

Key question	How OUP can help you:
How is the course sequenced (and why is it sequenced this way)?	Topics are sequenced chronologically, from pre-1066 to the present day, and the chapters are themed. This ensures that schools can teach both chronologically and thematically in order to help students grapple with the demands of History content at KS3 and beyond. Every chapter and every lesson follow a consistent approach, with features that have been successfully trialled and tested such as Objectives, Fact boxes, Key Words, Over to You activities, and History Skills activities. Activities and assessments progress in difficulty as students work through the chapters and through the three textbooks.
How is progression built into the course?	This is done through a gradual ramping of level of activities for each lesson, as well as end-of-chapter assessment questions. Also, there are History Skills activities that deal with progressively more difficult question types through each book (and through all books). There are also regular low-stakes knowledge quizzes to check students' knowledge acquisition, and carefully designed literacy activities that support development in extended writing in History.
How does the course help ensure students make progress?	The series does this by offering accessible, engaging content that builds into a solid body of historical knowledge and understanding; by supporting the acquisition of key history skills; and by offering a consistent mixture of low- and high-stakes assessment opportunities that allow students to demonstrate progress.
What assessments does the course offer and how do they help form part of the process of evaluating progress and identifying next steps?	**Summative**: Quick Knowledge Quizzes; Literacy Focus activities; interactive auto-marked end-of-lesson self-assessments. Also, as stated, there is a set of activities at the end of each chapter that become progressively more challenging. **Formative**: end-of-chapter assessment questions with mark schemes and differentiated assessment worksheets (core and foundation). Teachers can also track performance.
How does this course ensure that students will know more?	This is done by presenting accessible, engaging content with regular progress checks (via the low- and high-stakes assessments) to assess knowledge and understanding.
How can/will this course be developed over time (includes adaptability)?	The *Kerboodle* package is continually reviewed and updated, likely with further assessment and auto-marked materials.
How can the resources in this course help teachers present subject matter clearly?	The *Student Books* are engaging and accessible, and easy to navigate. The accompanying *Curriculum and Assessment Planning Guides* map the course out with schemes of work, and support History departments with planning their assessments.
How can this course help reduce teacher workload (including how does it help teachers with their subject knowledge and knowledge of the course)?	The *Student Books* are clearly organised with a contents list and index, and they are supported by accompanying *Curriculum and Assessment Planning Guides* (in print and digital format). These teacher guides support curriculum planning, assessment planning and subject knowledge (including 'a brief history' and timeline features), and is ideal for non-specialists and NQTs. Answers guidance for *Student Books* activities and sample answers for assessment questions are available too, to help reduce teacher workload. The digital *Kerboodle* product provides the activities from the *Student Books* as printable and photocopiable differentiated worksheets and an assessment package that supports every lesson of every chapter.

[4] *data based on **Historical Association** survey (2018)*
[5] *based on the **Oxford Language Report** (2018), which surveyed over 1300 primary and secondary school teachers about their experiences of the word gap in schools*

Curriculum planning: building a historical vocabulary and closing the word gap

One of the curriculum principles in this *KS3 History* series is to build a historical vocabulary and close the word gap. This principle follows on from research from the *Oxford Language Report* (2018)[6], which found evidence of a significant word gap in UK schools. You may find the suggested activities and classroom strategies here and on pages 40–42 useful.

1 Building knowledge-rich vocabulary across year groups

Plan how you will teach key concepts and build them over time. Decide what students need to know by the end of KS3 or even GCSE, and work backwards to inform how you teach throughout Key stages 3 and 4. Substantive knowledge and second-order concepts can therefore be planned throughout the five years. Here's an example:

Year 7	Year 8	Year 9 / GCSE
• Monarch – Norman invasion and medieval monarchs • Changes in Tudor and Stuart periods • Church – medieval England	• Introduce the concept of empire and how this had an effect on the monarchy in Victorian Britain.	• **Power and the people** – challenges to royal authority • Elizabethan systems of government
• Reformation • Revolution – English Civil War	• Use the Reformation for the context of the Troubles in Northern Ireland.	• **Elizabethan Church** and religious change
• French Revolution	• Apply the definition to a completely different kind of revolution – Industrial Revolution.	• **Germany in revolution** • American Revolution (context) • Revolution in 19th-century policing

This activity can be done as a department or with your classes. Share the bigger picture of what students are learning across the key stages – what is it leading to? Then try to break it down into big questions and then small questions. The learning is then mutually agreed, and students understand the context of their written work, which is more coherent and sustained as a result.

Our experience as a school of sharing knowledge-rich, big-picture planning with students is that it helps to democratise the learning process. Students become increasingly confident when articulating their ideas and their developing historical vocabulary is evident in their speaking, listening and writing.

---

[6] report based on a survey of over 1,300 primary and secondary school teachers about their experiences of the word gap in schools

Curriculum planning

2 Using word banks

Teacher notes

A word bank can be so much more than words on the wall; it can be a way to consolidate, test, apply and revisit knowledge. Research supports the idea that you need to teach vocabulary in the context of students' learning rather than in isolation.

Start with your KS3 curriculum, and group key words into themes such as academic words, question words or words that feature across topics. Try to avoid producing word banks with far too many words as this can be overwhelming for students.

You could adopt a knowledge-rich approach, and use knowledge organisers to embed and revisit key words (*Kerboodle* contains knowledge organisers for each chapter, to help save you time). The knowledge organisers can function as word banks which relate to the bigger picture – what students need to learn.

We were mindful that knowledge organisers could be a 'fad'. As Christine Counsell (2017) has observed, when we adopted them we did not expect or want them to be the full extent of students' learning, but to support their learning. Students use them at home to support their online homework or in class.

Also, try to provide an opportunity for students to hear the words spoken aloud, which can help to embed new vocabulary. Research suggests that students need to hear a word ten times before they become confident in understanding and applying it to different contexts (Schmitt, 2008).

Reference:
Counsell, C. (2017) 'I would call knowledge organisers a fad' in *Schools Week*, 28 November 2017.
Schmitt, N. (2008) Review article: Instructed second language vocabulary learning. *Language Teaching Research*, 12(3), 329–363.

Using the template below, students can test themselves or friends by folding the page over. Encouraging students to use the concept/term will help to push their responses into higher bands in the end-of-chapter *Student Book* assessments.

Content	Concept/term I expect to see
Royal authority	execution, Bill of Rights
Challenges to power	revolution, rebellion, plot
Tudor England	vagrant, nobility, empire

This word bank could be used to introduce new vocabulary or as part of a knowledge organiser. Encourage students to write their own definitions or annotate existing definitions so that the words are meaningful on a personal level:

Key term	Definition
Republic	a country with no monarch
Roundhead	nickname for the soldiers who fought for Parliament during the English Civil War. Most famously the New Model Army under Cromwell.

Suggested strategies for using word banks

- **Highlight key words.** Use word banks to help students to assess their own written responses by highlighting key vocabulary in their work. This is a powerful visual tool to enable them to see how often they use key words, and to track their learning as they work.

- **Collaborate and compete.** Break a unit down into three parts and have three teams of students compete with each other to collate the most comprehensive word bank. For example, a unit on religion in Tudor and Stuart England could be broken into: threats, policies, and key figures. These word banks could then be evaluated and adapted by everyone. Consider using window crayons for easy reference when writing or discussing.

3 Model key vocabulary to all abilities

As teachers, we differentiate for our classes. I (Lindsay) had considered myself reasonably good at it: I stretched those who needed a challenge and supplied extra information for those needing more support. I later spoke to a friend who is developing literacy in his school, and he mentioned the Matthew effect (Cunningham & Stanovich, 2001). A little research revealed that I had not been helping the students who needed the most support: I had instead been depriving them of literacy and knowledge.

To interrogate how you model key vocabulary, record yourself teaching the same content to different ability levels. I found that I gave rich explanations to my higher-attaining students but simple, generic explanations to my lower-attaining students. I was in fact widening the word gap!

I now make a concerted effort to expose lower-attaining students to more advanced vocabulary in advanced texts and sources. I can emphasise and explain these as I read. Here are some suggestions:

- Annotate Big Questions (open-ended for exploratory discussion) to break down language without dumbing it down.

- Allow students to highlight and explore tier 2 words (skills words, many of which are command words) and tier 3 words (subject-specific, academic words), and use root words to decode meanings.

- Give students access to background knowledge and substantive knowledge, allowing them to build understanding.

Reference:
Cunningham A. E., & Stanovich, K. (2001) 'What Reading Does for the Mind' in *Journal of Direct Instruction*, Vol. 1 No. 2.

4 Knowledge-rich: the football net of words

To engage with the knowledge-rich approach to teaching, you can use the philosophy of building substantive knowledge over the course of your curriculum, giving students the chance to build on their subject knowledge and develop their vocabulary. A sensible departmental approach would include mapping out what key concepts, knowledge, and vocabulary students need to know by Year 11, and where this can be taught and revisited, starting from Year 7.

In *Why Closing the Word Gap Matters*, Jean Gross's football net analogy shows the importance of this in relation to vocabulary: some students can connect new words with words in their existing word net, whereas others struggle to do this because they have far fewer words available to them.

It is so important that first-order concepts (such as empire, parliament, war, monarchy, revolution) are taught and revisited to show that words/concepts can have multiple meanings. Giving time to building an understanding of concepts through knowledge should prevent students from feeling that they are repeatedly starting again.

- Expect students to make links and recall content from the previous unit, year, or key stage. By continually revisiting substantive knowledge, students will be able to retain a word's meaning.

- Allow students to discuss differences in key concepts and terms. Help them to make sense of how a word can mean the same thing in different contexts, but also to realise that this is not always the case.

Reference:
Oxford University Press (2018) *Why Closing the Word Gap Matters*, available online at: oxford.ly/wordgap

Curriculum planning: Sample curriculum plans

Sample curriculum plans for KS3

We know that History teachers want their KS3 curriculum to be ambitious and designed to give *all* students the opportunity to build substantive knowledge and develop the skills to progress at a higher level. We also understand that many History departments are planning KS3 with GCSE in mind, so what we provide on the following pages are suggested 'routes' through Oxford's *KS3 History* series that will help support progression towards all GCSE specifications. Each route takes into account both the requirements of the KS3 History National Curriculum *and* the demands of each of the main GCSE examination boards.

General note on curriculum planning

There are some issues to be taken into consideration when planning and constructing your KS3 History course so that it progresses seamlessly to your GCSE History specification. You can use the guidance and questions suggested in the *Curriculum planning: Ofsted inspection framework* section of this guide (pages 17–20) to help inform your planning.

Sample two-year and three-year routes

The sample curriculum plans in this section are intended purely as illustrations of possible course structures. Remember, there are many combinations for each GCSE History specification, so you have lots of flexibility to cater to the needs of both your staff and your students.

Visit these websites for more information on the specifications:

AQA www.aqa.org.uk
Edexcel qualifications.pearson.com
OCR www.ocr.org.uk
Eduqas www.eduqas.co.uk
WJEC www.wjec.co.uk

Curriculum planning

For AQA: a possible two-year route:

Year 7 Term 1		Term 2		Term 3	
Invasion, Plague and Murder (BOOK 1): Chapter 1 *1066 and all that* BOOK 1: Chapter 2 *The Norman Conquest*	BOOK 1: Chapter 4 *Life in the Middle Ages*	BOOK 1: Chapter 6 *Health and medicine* BOOK 1: Chapter 8 *Here come the Tudors*	BOOK 1: Chapter 9 *Medieval Britain: what changed?* **Revolution, Industry and Empire (BOOK 2):** Chapter 1: *Queen Elizabeth*	BOOK 2: Chapter 2 *Life in Tudor times* This might be a good place to include the study of a **historic environment** such as the Globe Theatre or an Elizabethan country house. You can introduce the place's location, function, and design, the people connected with the site, and how important developments from the Tudor era are connected to the site.	BOOK 2: Chapter 5 *The Restoration: the Merry Monarch* BOOK 2: Chapter 7 *The Industrial Revolution: from farming to factories*

Year 8 Term 1		Term 2		Term 3	
BOOK 2: Chapter 8 *Terrible towns* BOOK 2: Chapter 11 *India: a British Empire case study*	BOOK 2: Chapter 12 *From Tudor to Victorian Britain: what changed?*	**Technology, War and Independence (BOOK 3):** Chapter 1 *A new century* BOOK 3: Chapter 2 *The First World War (depth study)*	BOOK 3: Chapter 2 *The First World War* (depth study) continued BOOK 3: Chapter 4 *Power in the early twentieth century*	BOOK 3: Chapter 4 *Power in the early twentieth century* continued BOOK 3: Chapter 5 *The Second World War* (depth study)	BOOK 3: Chapter 8 *Into the modern world*

Many schools are now moving towards a two-year KS3. This route through the three textbooks helps to pick out some of the key content and themes for a school that has chosen the following topics from the AQA GCSE History specification:

- **Period study:** Germany 1890–1945: Democracy and Dictatorship
- **Wider world depth study:** Conflict and Tension 1918–1939: The Inter-War Years
- **Thematic study:** Britain: Health and the People: c1000–Present Day
- **British depth study:** Elizabethan England c1568–1603.

It is important that KS3 is not viewed purely as a 'feed' for KS4 – it is a programme of study in its own right and is vital in ensuring that schools deliver a coherently planned and sequenced curriculum that provides students with knowledge of the 'history of these islands as a coherent, chronological narrative, from the earliest times to the present day' (*DfE History Programmes of study: Key stage 3 National curriculum in England*).

This KS3 route begins in 'earliest times' and works through the Norman Conquest and the Middle Ages, towards the Tudors and Elizabethan England (as a focus point for this AQA specification route). The topic of Health is also highlighted in several places through this route when students focus on the Black Death (Year 7 Term 2), the Great Plague (Year 7 Term 3) and disease and public health in the topics covered in each of the terms in Year 8 (e.g. in Year 8 Term 1 when studying the 'public health heroes'). The rise of empire in the nineteenth century (something that students doing the Germany 1890–1945 topic will find helpful when studying the Kaiser's ambitions), the First World War and its impact, the rise of dictatorships in the 1930s, Hitler's Germany and the onset of the Second World War are also covered in Year 8, and will certainly help prepare those students studying Conflict and Tension 1918–1939 and Germany 1890–1945.

Curriculum planning

For AQA: a possible three-year route:

Year 7 Term 1		Term 2		Term 3	
BOOK 1: Chapter 1 *1066 and all that*	BOOK 1: Chapter 3 *How religious were people in the Middle Ages?*	BOOK 1: Chapter 4 *Life in the Middle Ages continued*	BOOK 1: Chapter 7 *England at war*	BOOK 1: Chapter 9 *Medieval Britain: what changed?*	BOOK 2: Chapter 3 *Exit the Tudors, enter the Stuarts*
BOOK 1: Chapter 2 *The Norman Conquest*	BOOK 1: Chapter 4 *Life in the Middle Ages* This might be a good place to include the study of a **historic environment** such as a Norman castle or battle site.	BOOK 1: Chapter 5 *Power in the Middle Ages*	BOOK 1: Chapter 8 *Here come the Tudors*	BOOK 2: Chapter 1 *Queen Elizabeth*	BOOK 2: Chapter 4 *From Civil War to Commonwealth*

Year 8 Term 1		Term 2		Term 3	
BOOK 2: Chapter 5 *The Restoration: the Merry Monarch*	BOOK 2: Chapter 7 *The Industrial Revolution: from farming to factories*	BOOK 2: Chapter 8 *Terrible towns*	BOOK 2: Chapter 10 *Britain versus France*	BOOK 2: Chapter 12 *From Tudor to Victorian Britain: what changed?*	BOOK 3: Chapter 1 *A new century*
BOOK 2: Chapter 6 *Exit the Stuarts, enter the Georgians*		BOOK 2: Chapter 9 *The slave trade*	BOOK 2: Chapter 11 *India: a British Empire case study*		BOOK 3: Chapter 2 *The First World War* (depth study)

Year 9 Term 1		Term 2		Term 3	
BOOK 3: Chapter 2 *The First World War* (depth study) continued	BOOK 3: Chapter 4 *Power in the twentieth century*	BOOK 3: Chapter 5 *The Second World War* (depth study) continued	BOOK 3: Chapter 7 *From Empire to Commonwealth*	Many schools that have a three-year KS3 use the last term as a means of completing topics that have 'run over' a little – or as a place to introduce the GCSE topics/course, or even complete a depth study.	
BOOK 3: Chapter 3 *Between the wars*	BOOK 3: Chapter 5 *The Second World War* (depth study)		BOOK 3: Chapter 8 *Into the modern world*		

This route through the three textbooks helps to pick out some of the key content and themes from a school that has chosen the following topics from the AQA specification:

Period study: America 1920–1975: Opportunity and Inequality

Thematic study: Britain: Power and the People c1170–Present

Wider world depth study: Conflict and Tension: The First World War 1894–1918

British depth study: Norman England c1066–c1100.

The links to the AQA Norman England topic are obvious – this route ensures that students have a basic understanding of the Norman Conquest and life in England at that time if they are to go on and study at a higher level. This route also puts slightly more emphasis on preparing students for the power Thematic study by, for example, covering topics such as Magna Carta, the Peasants' Revolt and the development of Parliament (Year 7 Term 2), the English Civil War (Year 7 Term 3), Chartism (Year 8 Term 3), the anti-slavery movement (Year 8 Term 2) and factory reform (Year 8 Term 1). There are also opportunities to do some vital groundwork in highlighting the development of America in preparation for a Period study of the USA (Year 7 Term 3 and Year 8 Term 2, for example). This route also covers the First World War as a distinct topic (Year 8 Term 3 and Year 9 Term 1) as well as subtly introducing some of the themes you will need to cover in that topic, such as empire (Year 8 Term 2, for example). As well as the beginnings of the British Empire and the contribution of it during the First World War, this route also explores the end of empire (Year 9 Term 2).

For Edexcel: a possible two-year route:

Year 7 Term 1		Term 2		Term 3	
BOOK 1: Chapter 4 *Life in the Middle Ages*	BOOK 1: Chapter 5 *Power in the Middle Ages*	BOOK 1: Chapter 8 *Here come the Tudors* continued	BOOK 2: Chapter 1 *Queen Elizabeth*	BOOK 2: Chapter 3 *Exit the Tudors, enter the Stuarts*	BOOK 2: Chapter 5 *The Restoration: the Merry Monarch*
	BOOK 1: Chapter 8 *Here come the Tudors*	BOOK 1: Chapter 9 *Medieval Britain: what changed?*	BOOK 2: Chapter 2 *Life in Tudor times*	BOOK 2: Chapter 4 *From Civil War to Commonwealth*	BOOK 2: Chapter 7 *The Industrial Revolution: from farming to factories*

Year 8 Term 1		Term 2		Term 3	
BOOK 2: Chapter 8 *Terrible towns* *This might be an opportunity to introduce students to the **historic environment** of Whitechapel, London. You might explore local sources relevant to the site.*	BOOK 2: Chapter 9 *The slave trade* BOOK 2: Chapter 10 *Britain versus France*	BOOK 2: Chapter 12 *From Tudor to Victorian Britain: what changed?* BOOK 3: Chapter 1 *A new century*	BOOK 3: Chapter 2 *The First World War* (depth study) BOOK 3: Chapter 3 *Between the wars*	BOOK 3: Chapter 4 *Power in the twentieth century* BOOK 3: Chapter 5 *The Second World War* (depth study)	BOOK 3: Chapter 5 *The Second World War* (depth study) continued BOOK 3: Chapter 8 *Into the modern world*

This route through the three textbooks helps to pick out some of the key content and themes from a school that has chosen the following topics from the Edexcel specification:

- **Thematic study:** Crime and punishment in Britain c1000–Present *and* Whitechapel c1870–c1900
- **Period study:** British America 1713–1783
- **British depth study:** Early Elizabethan England 1558–1588
- **Modern depth study:** Weimar and Nazi Germany 1918–1939.

The focus of the route means that slightly more emphasis has been placed on preparing students for the changes (and continuities) relating to the crime and punishment Thematic study – from crime detention, trial and punishment in the Middle Ages (Year 7 Term 1) through to the infamous case of Jack the Ripper and more modern policing methods (Year 8 Term 1). This route also encompasses the coming of the Tudors and Elizabethan England through to British involvement in America from Elizabethan times to the late eighteenth century (Year 7 Term 3 and Year 8 Term 1, for example), as well as the rise the rise of dictatorships in the 1930s and Hitler's Germany, for example (Year 8 Terms 2 and 3).

Curriculum planning

For Edexcel: a possible three-year route:

Year 7 Term 1		Term 2		Term 3	
BOOK 1: Chapter 1 *1066 and all that*	BOOK 1: Chapter 3 *How religious were people in the Middle Ages?*	BOOK 1: Chapter 4 *Life in the Middle Ages* continued	BOOK 1: Chapter 7 *England at war*	BOOK 2: Chapter 1 *Queen Elizabeth*	BOOK 2: Chapter 3 *Exit the Tudors, enter the Stuarts*
BOOK 1: Chapter 2 *The Norman Conquest*	BOOK 1: Chapter 4 *Life in the Middle Ages*	BOOK 1: Chapter 5 *Power in the Middle Ages*	BOOK 1: Chapter 8 *Here come the Tudors*	BOOK 2: Chapter 2 *Life in Tudor times*	BOOK 2: Chapter 4 *From Civil War to Commonwealth*
Year 8 Term 1		**Term 2**		**Term 3**	
BOOK 2: Chapter 5 *The Restoration: the Merry Monarch*	BOOK 2: Chapter 7 *The Industrial Revolution: from farming to factories*	BOOK 2: Chapter 10 *Britain versus France*	BOOK 3: Chapter 2 *The First World War* (depth study)	BOOK 3: Chapter 3 *Between the wars*	BOOK 3: Chapter 5 *The Second World War* (depth study)
BOOK 2: Chapter 6 *Exit the Stuarts, enter the Georgians*	BOOK 2: Chapter 9 *The slave trade*	BOOK 2: Chapter 11 *India: a British Empire case study*		BOOK 3: Chapter 4 *Power in the twentieth century*	This might be an opportunity to introduce students to the **historic environment** of London during the Second World War. You might explore local sources relevant to the site.
Year 9 Term 1		**Term 2**		**Term 3**	
BOOK 3: Chapter 6 *The post-war world*	BOOK 3: Chapter 8 *Into the modern world* continued	This time might be used to complete topics that have 'run over' a little.		This might be a place to introduce the GCSE topics/course, or complete a KS3 depth study.	
BOOK 3: Chapter 8 *Into the modern world*	BOOK 3: Chapter 9 *The modern world: what changed?*				

This route through the three textbooks helps to pick out some of the key content and themes from a school that has chosen the following topics from the Edexcel specification:

- **Thematic study:** Warfare and British society c1250–Present and London and the Second World War 1939–1945
- **Period study:** Superpower relations and the Cold War 1941–1991
- **British depth study:** Anglo-Saxon and Norman England c1060–1088
- **Modern depth study:** Weimar and Nazi Germany 1918–1939.

The route begins with a direct link to the Edexcel Anglo-Saxon and Norman England c1060–1088 topic. This route also puts slightly more emphasis on preparing students for the warfare Thematic study by, for example, covering topics such as the Hundred Years War (Year 7 Term 2), the English Civil War (Year 7 Term 3), the Napoleonic Wars (Year 8 Term 2), and the First and Second World Wars (Year 8 Terms 2 and 3). This route also covers the rise of dictatorships in the 1930s and Nazi Germany (Year 8 Term 3) and the Cold War (Year 9 Term 1).

Curriculum planning

For OCR B (SHP): a possible three-year route:

Year 7 Term 1		Term 2		Term 3	
BOOK 1: Chapter 1 *1066 and all that*	BOOK 1: Chapter 3 *How religious were people in the Middle Ages?*	BOOK 1: Chapter 4 *Life in the Middle Ages* continued	BOOK 1: Chapter 7 *England at war*	BOOK 1: Chapter 9 *Medieval Britain: what changed?*	BOOK 2: Chapter 3 *Exit the Tudors, enter the Stuarts*
BOOK 1: Chapter 2 *The Norman Conquest*	BOOK 1: Chapter 4 *Life in the Middle Ages*	BOOK 1: Chapter 5 *Power in the Middle Ages*	BOOK 1: Chapter 8 *Here come the Tudors*	BOOK 2: Chapter 1 *Queen Elizabeth*	BOOK 2: Chapter 4 *From Civil War to Commonwealth*
Year 8 Term 1		**Term 2**		**Term 3**	
BOOK 2: Chapter 5 *The Restoration: the Merry Monarch*	BOOK 2: Chapter 7 *The Industrial Revolution: from farming to factories*	BOOK 2: Chapter 8 *Terrible towns* continued	BOOK 2: Chapter 10 *Britain versus France*	BOOK 2: Chapter 12 *From Tudor to Victorian Britain: what changed?*	BOOK 3: Chapter 2 *The First World War* (depth study)
BOOK 2: Chapter 6 *Exit the Stuarts, enter the Georgians*	BOOK 2: Chapter 8 *Terrible towns*	BOOK 2: Chapter 9 *The slave trade*	BOOK 2: Chapter 11 *India: a British Empire case study*	BOOK 3: Chapter 1 *A new century*	
Year 9 Term 1		**Term 2**		**Term 3**	
BOOK 3: Chapter 3 *Between the wars*	BOOK 3: Chapter 4 *Power in the twentieth century* continued	BOOK 3: Chapter 5 *The Second World War* (depth study) continued	BOOK 3: Chapter 7 *From Empire to Commonwealth*	BOOK 3: Chapter 8 *Into the modern world* continued	The final term might be an ideal opportunity to introduce the idea of the 'History Around Us' unit. Placing this at the end of KS3 gives you greater scope to select a historical site relevant to one of the topics you have covered.
BOOK 3: Chapter 4 *Power in the twentieth century*	BOOK 3: Chapter 5 *The Second World War* (depth study)	BOOK 3: Chapter 6 *The post-war world*	BOOK 3: Chapter 8 *Into the modern world*	BOOK 3: Chapter 9 *The modern world: what changed?*	

This route through the three textbooks helps to pick out some of the key content and themes from a school that has chosen the following topics from the OCR B specification:

- **Thematic study:** Migrants to Britain c1250–Present
- **Period study:** The Making of America 1789–1900
- **British depth study:** The Norman Conquest 1065–1087
- **Wider world depth study:** Living under Nazi Rule 1933–1945.

This route places slightly more focus on preparing students for a study of the Norman Conquest and life in England at that time (Year 7 Terms 1 and 2), early US history (Year 7 Term 3 and Year 8 Term 2), Migration (Year 9 Term 2), and Living under Nazi Rule (Year 9 Terms 1 and 2).

Revolution, Industry and Empire: Britain 1558–1901   31

Curriculum planning

For Eduqas: a possible two-year route:

Year 7 Term 1		Term 2		Term 3	
BOOK 1: Chapter 4 *Life in the Middle Ages*	BOOK 1: Chapter 8 *Here come the Tudors*	BOOK 2: Chapter 1 *Queen Elizabeth*	BOOK 2: Chapter 4 *From Civil War to Commonwealth*	BOOK 2: Chapter 7 *The Industrial Revolution: from farming to factories*	BOOK 2: Chapter 8 *Terrible towns* continued
BOOK 1: Chapter 6 *Health and medicine*	BOOK 1: Chapter 9 *Medieval Britain: what changed?*	BOOK 2: Chapter 2 *Life in Tudor times*	BOOK 2: Chapter 5 *The Restoration: the Merry Monarch*	BOOK 2: Chapter 8 *Terrible towns*	BOOK 2: Chapter 12 *From Tudor to Victorian Britain: what changed?* This might be an opportunity to introduce students to a **historic environment** such as a seaside resort.
Year 8 Term 1		**Term 2**		**Term 3**	
BOOK 3: Chapter 1 *A new century*	BOOK 3: Chapter 2 *The First World War (depth study)* continued	BOOK 3: Chapter 4 *Power in the twentieth century*	BOOK 3: Chapter 5 *The Second World War (depth study)* continued	BOOK 3: Chapter 6 *The post-war world* continued	BOOK 3: Chapter 8 *Into the modern world*
BOOK 3: Chapter 2 *The First World War (depth study)*	BOOK 3: Chapter 3 *Between the wars*	BOOK 3: Chapter 5 *The Second World War (depth study)*	BOOK 3: Chapter 6 *The post-war world*	BOOK 3: Chapter 7 *From Empire to Commonwealth*	BOOK 3: Chapter 9 *The modern world: what changed?*

This route through the three textbooks helps to pick out some of the key content and themes from a school that has chosen the following topics from the Eduqas specification:

- **British depth study:** The Elizabethan Age 1558–1603
- **Period study:** The Development of the UK 1919–1990
- **Non-British studies in depth:** Germany in Transition 1919–1939
- **Thematic study:** Changes in Entertainment and Leisure in Britain c500–Present Day.

The Entertainment and Leisure in Britain topic is highlighted in several places through this route when students focus on leisure and entertainment in, for example, medieval times (Year 7 Term 1), the Tudor and Stuart era (Year 7 Term 2), the industrial age (Year 7 Term 3) and modern times (Year 8 Term 3). The Elizabeth Age (in Year 7 Term 2, for example), Germany in Transition (in Year 8 Terms 1 and 2) and the Development of the UK (in Year 8) are also key components of this route.

Assessment and progression to GCSE

Assessment and progression to GCSE

The teaching and learning landscape at KS3 and KS4 has changed in recent years. According to the **Historical Association** survey (2018):

- 55% of secondary schools indicated that KS3 has been or was going to be shortened due to the new GCSE specifications, mainly as a consequence of the view that it is difficult to fit all the GCSE content in within a two year framework.
- 56% of schools have changed the way they teach KS3 to provide background knowledge to GCSE topics and provide new understanding of history skills such as source or interpretation analysis.

In addition, there is clear evidence from the *Oxford Language Report* (2018) of a significant word gap in UK schools, which can impede students' learning and success at KS3 and beyond.

As a result, we designed this *KS3 History* series to reflect the new landscape by ensuring that each suggested topic in the KS3 History National Curriculum is covered, but we have also made sure that our content supports literacy development and progression towards any of the GCSE History specifications.

This section provides: 1) a brief introduction to each of the GCSE exam board specifications and their key content; and 2) charts to show how our *Student Book* provides background context to the contents of different specifications.

AQA GCSE History specification

Introduction

The AQA GCSE History specification allows students to explore key themes in History, such as conflict and religion. AQA have included new topics to allow students to analyse the change and continuity of these themes – these topics can help students understand the world today. However, they have kept some of the more popular courses, for example Medicine through time (now known as Health and the People). The specification offers a good balance between political and social history, and there are no prohibited combinations, which allows departments to play to their strengths. Moreover, it builds nicely from well-established KS3 topics, and offers a firm foundation for further study in History.

AQA content	How *KS3 History: Revolution, Industry and Empire* (Book 2) matches
Period study	
America 1840–1895: Expansion and Consolidation	*This topic is referenced in* **Chapter 3** Exit the Tudors, enter the Stuarts
Germany 1890–1945: Democracy and Dictatorship	*Book 3 provides a good foundation for this topic*
Russia 1894–1945: Tsardom and Communism	*Book 3 provides a good foundation for this topic*
America 1920–1973: Opportunity and Inequality	*Book 3 provides a good foundation for this topic*
Wider world depth study	
Conflict and Tension 1894–1918	*Book 3 provides a good foundation for this topic*
Conflict and Tension 1918–1939	*Book 3 provides a good foundation for this topic*
Conflict and Tension between East and West 1945–1972	*Book 3 provides a good foundation for this topic*
Conflict and Tension in Asia 1950–1975	*Book 3 provides a good foundation for this topic*
Conflict and Tension 1990–2009	*Book 3 provides a good foundation for this topic*

Assessment and progression to GCSE

Thematic study	
Health and the People c1000–Present	✓ **Chapter 5** The Restoration: the Merry Monarch ✓ **Chapter 6** Exit the Stuarts, enter the Georgians ✓ **Chapter 8** Terrible towns ✓ **Chapter 12** From Tudor to Victorian England: what changed? *Book 1 and Book 3 also provide a good foundation for this topic*
Power and the People c1170–Present	✓ **Chapter 4** From Civil War to Commonwealth ✓ **Chapter 5** The Restoration: the Merry Monarch ✓ **Chapter 7** The Industrial Revolution: from farming to factories ✓ **Chapter 9** The slave trade ✓ **Chapter 10** Britain versus France ✓ **Chapter 12** From Tudor to Victorian England: what changed? *Book 1 and Book 3 also provide a good foundation for this topic*
Migration, Empires and the People c790–Present	✓ **Chapter 1** Queen Elizabeth ✓ **Chapter 3** Exit the Tudors, enter the Stuarts ✓ **Chapter 7** The Industrial Revolution: from farming to factories ✓ **Chapter 9** The slave trade ✓ **Chapter 11** India: a British Empire case study *Book 1 and Book 3 also provide a good foundation for this topic*
British depth studies including the historic environment	
Norman England c1066–c1100	*Book 1 provides a good foundation for this topic*
Medieval England: the Reign of Edward I 1272–1307	*Book 1 provides a good foundation for this topic*
Elizabethan England c1568–1603	✓ **Chapter 1** Queen Elizabeth ✓ **Chapter 2** Life in Tudor times *Book 1 and Book 3 also provide a good foundation for this topic*
Restoration England 1660–1685	✓ **Chapter 1** Queen Elizabeth ✓ **Chapter 4** From Civil War to Commonwealth ✓ **Chapter 5** The Restoration: the Merry Monarch ✓ **Chapter 6** Exit the Stuarts, enter the Georgians

The Over to You activities and the History Skills activities in each *Student Book* lesson, as well as the end-of-chapter History Skills and Assessments, are carefully mapped to command words from different exam boards, to help students familiarise themselves with the specialist vocabulary needed to succeed in further studies beyond KS3. You can also find in each chapter of this guide a detailed breakdown of **AQA exam-style questions** covered within that chapter. For example, see page 45 for the Chapter 1 chart.

Assessment and progression to GCSE

Edexcel GCSE History specification

Introduction

Edexcel have built their GCSE specification on the feedback they have been given from the history subject community, combining the most popular modern topics, along with those favourites of the Schools History Project, and brand-new topics into a single specification. There are no prohibited options – you can pick any topic. Edexcel have made an effort to make their exam questions and mark schemes straightforward with the requirements for success made clear. They feel that their GCSE builds on KS3 content while giving students a chance to apply their contextual understanding to new topics.

Edexcel content	How *KS3 History: Revolution, Industry and Empire* (Book 2) matches
Thematic study and historic environment	
Crime and Punishment in Britain c1000–Present *and* Whitechapel c1870–c1900: Crime, Policing and the Inner City	✓ **Chapter 2** Life in Tudor times ✓ **Chapter 3** Exit the Tudors, enter the Stuarts ✓ **Chapter 7** The Industrial Revolution: from farming to factories ✓ **Chapter 8** Terrible towns *Book 1 and Book 3 also provide a good foundation for this topic*
Thematic study and historic environment	
Medicine in Britain c1250–Present *and* The British Sector of the Western Front 1914–1918: Injuries, Treatment and the Trenches	✓ **Chapter 5** The Restoration: the Merry Monarch ✓ **Chapter 6** Exit the Stuarts, enter the Georgians ✓ **Chapter 7** The Industrial Revolution: from farming to factories ✓ **Chapter 8** Terrible towns ✓ **Chapter 12** From Tudor to Victorian Britain: what changed? *Book 1 and Book 3 also provide a good foundation for this topic*
Warfare and British Society c1250–Present *and* London and the Second World War 1939–1945	✓ **Chapter 1** Queen Elizabeth ✓ **Chapter 4** From Civil War to Commonwealth ✓ **Chapter 6** Exit the Stuarts, enter the Georgians ✓ **Chapter 10** Britain versus France ✓ **Chapter 11** India: a British Empire case study *Book 1 and Book 3 also provide a good foundation for this topic*
Period study	
Anglo-Saxon and Norman England c1060–1088	*Book 1 provides a good foundation for this topic*
The Reigns of King Richard I and King John 1189–1216	*Book 1 provides a good foundation for this topic*
Henry VIII and his Ministers 1509–1540	*Book 1 provides a good foundation for this topic*
Early Elizabethan England 1558–1588	✓ **Chapter 1** Queen Elizabeth ✓ **Chapter 2** Life in Tudor times ✓ **Chapter 3** Exit the Tudors, enter the Stuarts *Book 1 also provides a good foundation for this topic*
British depth study	
Spain and the 'New World' c1490–c1555	*Book 1 provides a good foundation for this topic*
British America 1713–1783: Empire and Revolution	✓ **Chapter 9** The slave trade ✓ **Chapter 10** Britain versus France
The American West c1835–c1895	*This topic is referenced in* **Chapter 3** Exit the Tudors, enter the Stuarts
Superpower Relations and the Cold War 1941–1991	*Book 3 also provides a good foundation for this topic*
Conflict in the Middle East 1945–1995	*Book 3 also provides a good foundation for this topic*
Modern depth study	
Russia and the Soviet Union, 1917–1941	*Book 3 also provides a good foundation for this topic*
Weimar and Nazi Germany, 1918–1939	*Book 3 also provides a good foundation for this topic*
Mao's China, 1945–1976	*This topic is referenced in Book 3*
The USA, 1954–1975: Conflict at Home and Abroad	*This topic is referenced in Book 3*

Assessment and progression to GCSE

The Over to You activities and the History Skills activities in each *Student Book* lesson, as well as the end-of-chapter History Skills and Assessments, are carefully mapped to command words from different exam boards, to help students familiarise themselves with the specialist vocabulary needed to succeed in further studies beyond KS3. You can also find in each chapter of this guide a detailed breakdown of **Edexcel exam-style questions** covered within that chapter. For example, see page 45 for the Chapter 1 chart.

OCR A GCSE History specification

Introduction
The key aim of the OCR A specification is to bring the subject to life and inspire students. Their specification is accessible and based on engagement with those in the History teaching community. OCR have a clear idea of what kind of students their specification produces: independent, articulate, and engaged. To assist teachers with this they offer a wide-range of support from the preparation stage to the delivery. As with previous exam boards, this Modern World option offers some of the old favourites and new exciting topics that are sure to engage students – moving away from a white, male dominated History.

OCR A content	How *KS3 History: Revolution, Industry and Empire* (Book 2) matches
Period study and non-British depth study	
International Relations: the Changing International Order 1918–2001	*Book 3 provides a good foundation for this topic*
China 1950–1981: The People and the State	*Book 3 provides a good foundation for this topic*
Germany 1925–1955: The People and the State	*Book 3 provides a good foundation for this topic*
Poland 1956–1990: The People and the State	
Russia 1928–1964: The People and the State	*This topic is referenced in Book 3*
South Africa 1960–1994: The People and the State	*This topic is referenced in Book 3*
The USA 1919–1948: The People and the State	*Book 3 provides a good foundation for this topic*
The USA 1945–1974: The People and the State	*Book 3 provides a good foundation for this topic*
British thematic study	
Migration to Britain c1000–c2010	✓ **Chapter 3** Exit the Tudors, enter the Stuarts *Book 1 and Book 3 also provide a good foundation for this topic*
Monarchy and Democracy in Britain c1000–2014	✓ **Chapter 1** Queen Elizabeth ✓ **Chapter 3** Exit the Tudors, enter the Stuarts ✓ **Chapter 4** From Civil War to Commonwealth ✓ **Chapter 5** The Restoration: the Merry Monarch ✓ **Chapter 6** Exit the Stuarts, enter the Georgians ✓ **Chapter 12** From Tudor to Victorian England: what changed? *Book 1 and Book 3 also provide a good foundation for this topic*
War and British Society c790–2010	✓ **Chapter 1** Queen Elizabeth ✓ **Chapter 3** Exit the Tudors, enter the Stuarts ✓ **Chapter 4** From Civil War to Commonwealth ✓ **Chapter 5** The Restoration: the Merry Monarch ✓ **Chapter 6** Exit the Stuarts, enter the Georgians ✓ **Chapter 10** Britain versus France *Book 1 and Book 3 also provide a good foundation for this topic*
British depth study and a study of the historic environment	
The Impact of Empire on Britain 1688–c1730 with Urban Environments: Patterns of Migration	✓ **Chapter 7** The Industrial Revolution: from farming to factories ✓ **Chapter 9** The slave trade ✓ **Chapter 10** Britain versus France ✓ **Chapter 11** India: a British Empire case study
The English Reformation c1520–c1550 with Castles: Form and Function c1000–1750	*Book 1 provides a good foundation for this topic*
Personal Rule to Restoration 1629–1660 with Castles: Form and Function c1000–1750	✓ **Chapter 4** From Civil War to Commonwealth ✓ **Chapter 5** The Restoration: the Merry Monarch

Assessment and progression to GCSE

The Over to You activities and the History Skills activities in each *Student Book* lesson, as well as the end-of-chapter History Skills and Assessments, are carefully mapped to command words from different exam boards, to help students familiarise themselves with the specialist vocabulary needed to succeed in further studies beyond KS3. You can also find in each chapter of this guide a detailed breakdown of **OCR exam-style questions** covered within that chapter. For example, see page 45 for the Chapter 1 chart.

OCR B GCSE History specification

Introduction

The ethos of OCR B echoes that of OCR A; however, this specification stays true to the principles of the Schools History Project by offering 'worthwhile and inspiring school history'. The course encourages students to ask questions of history through enquiry, and using pre-existing deep knowledge. The specification shows a commitment to diversity and the world around us. This specification offers new topics, but maintains some of the more popular courses from the Schools History Project. Improved teacher guidance aims to help with the implementation, delivery and results of the course.

OCR B content	How *KS3 History: Revolution, Industry and Empire* (Book 2) matches
Thematic study	
The People's Health c1250–Present	✓ **Chapter 5** The Restoration: the Merry Monarch ✓ **Chapter 7** The Industrial Revolution: from farming to factories ✓ **Chapter 8** Terrible towns ✓ **Chapter 12** From Tudor to Victorian England: what changed? *Book 1 and Book 3 also provide a good foundation for this topic*
Crime and Punishment c1250–Present	✓ **Chapter 2** Life in Tudor times ✓ **Chapter 3** Exit the Tudors, enter the Stuarts ✓ **Chapter 7** The Industrial Revolution: from farming to factories ✓ **Chapter 8** Terrible towns *Book 1 and Book 3 also provide a good foundation for this topic*
Migrants to Britain c1250–Present	✓ **Chapter 1** Queen Elizabeth *Book 3 also provides a good foundation for this topic*
British depth study	
The Norman Conquest 1065–1087	*Book 1 provides a good foundation for this topic*
The Elizabethans 1580–1603	✓ **Chapter 1** Queen Elizabeth ✓ **Chapter 2** Life in Tudor times ✓ **Chapter 3** Exit the Tudors, enter the Stuarts
Britain in Peace and War 1900–1918	✓ **Chapter 11** India: a British Empire case study
Period study	
Viking Expansion c750–c1050	*Book 1 provides a good foundation for this topic*
The Mughal Empire 1526–1707	*This topic is referenced in* **Chapter 11** India: A British Empire case study
The Making of America 1789–1900	✓ **Chapter 10** Britain versus France
World depth study	
The First Crusade c1070–1100	*Book 1 provides a good foundation for this topic*
Aztecs and the Spanish Conquest 1519–1535	
Living under Nazi Rule 1933–1945	*Book 3 provides a good foundation for this topic*

The Over to You activities and the History Skills activities in each *Student Book* lesson, as well as the end-of-chapter History Skills and Assessments, are carefully mapped to command words from different exam boards, to help students familiarise themselves with the specialist vocabulary needed to succeed in further studies beyond KS3. You can also find in each chapter of this guide a detailed breakdown of **OCR exam-style questions** covered within that chapter. For example, see page 45 for the Chapter 1 chart.

Assessment and progression to GCSE

Eduqas GCSE History specification

Introduction

The Eduqas specification makes clear links with the aims of the History National Curriculum by focusing on what kind of student the specification will produce. By the end of the GCSE course students will be able to ask questions, make judgements, and explain links between events, people, and outcomes. The specification focuses on key second order concepts while offering topics from across three compulsory time periods.

Eduqas content	How *KS3 History: Revolution, Industry and Empire* (Book 2) matches
British study in depth	
Conflict and Upheaval: England 1337–1381	*Book 1 provides a good foundation for this topic*
The Elizabethan Age 1558–1603	✓ **Chapter 1** Queen Elizabeth ✓ **Chapter 2** Life in Tudor times *Book 1 provides a good foundation for this topic*
Empire, Reform and War: Britain 1890–1918	✓ **Chapter 12** From Tudor to Victorian England: what changed? *Book 3 provides a good foundation for this topic*
Austerity, Affluence and Discontent: Britain 1951–1979	*Book 3 provides a good foundation for this topic*
Non-British study in depth	
The Crusades c1095–1149	*Book 1 provides a good foundation for this topic*
The Voyages of Discovery and the Conquest of the Americas 1492–1522	*Book 1 provides a good foundation for this topic*
Germany in Transition 1919–1939	*Book 3 provides a good foundation for this topic*
The USA: A Nation of Contrasts 1910–1929	*Book 3 provides a good foundation for this topic*
Period study	
The Development of the USA 1929–2000	*Book 3 provides a good foundation for this topic*
The Development of Germany 1919–1991	*Book 3 provides a good foundation for this topic*
The Development of the USSR 1924–1991	*Book 3 provides a good foundation for this topic*
The Development of the UK 1919–1990	*Book 3 provides a good foundation for this topic*
Thematic study	
Changes in Crime and Punishment in Britain c500–Present	✓ **Chapter 2** Life in Tudor times ✓ **Chapter 7** The Industrial Revolution: from farming to factories ✓ **Chapter 8** Terrible towns *Book 1 and Book 3 also provide a good foundation for this topic*
Changes in Health and Medicine in Britain c500–Present	✓ **Chapter 5** The Restoration: the Merry Monarch ✓ **Chapter 6** Exit the Stuarts, enter the Georgians ✓ **Chapter 7** The Industrial Revolution: from farming to factories ✓ **Chapter 8** Terrible towns ✓ **Chapter 12** From Tudor to Victorian England: what changed? *Book 1 and Book 3 also provide a good foundation for this topic*
The Development of Warfare in Britain c500–Present	✓ **Chapter 1** Queen Elizabeth ✓ **Chapter 4** From Civil War to Commonwealth ✓ **Chapter 10** Britain versus France *Book 1 and Book 3 also provide a good foundation for this topic*
Changes in Entertainment and Leisure in Britain c500–Present	✓ **Chapter 2** Life in Tudor times *Book 1 and Book 3 also provide a good foundation for this topic*

The Over to You activities and the History Skills activities in each *Student Book* lesson, as well as the end-of-chapter History Skills and Assessments, are carefully mapped to command words from different exam boards, to help students familiarise themselves with the specialist vocabulary needed to succeed in further studies beyond KS3. You can also find in each chapter of this guide a detailed breakdown of **Eduqas exam-style questions** covered within that chapter. For example, see page 45 for the Chapter 1 chart.

Assessment and progression to GCSE

WJEC GCSE History specification

Introduction

WJEC have developed a specification that allows teachers to develop their students as independent students who question and make links between the different topics studied. The specification builds on common KS3 topics and skills and concepts. As the course is linked to the Welsh Baccalaureate, there are opportunities to develop literacy and other skills that are being assessed through the Skills Challenge Certificate. The focus on the Welsh perspective, where possible, gives students the chance to see where they fit in to the wider UK, EU and world history.

WJEC content	How *KS3 History: Revolution, Industry and Empire* (Book 2) matches
Wales/wider perspective study in depth	
The Elizabethan Age 1558–1603	✓ **Chapter 1** Queen Elizabeth ✓ **Chapter 2** Life in Tudor times
Radicalism and Protest 1810–1848	✓ **Chapter 7** The Industrial Revolution: from farming to factories ✓ **Chapter 10** Britain versus France ✓ **Chapter 12** From Tudor to Victorian England: what changed?
Depression, War and Recovery 1930–1951	*Book 3 provides a good foundation for this topic*
Austerity, Affluence and Discontent 1951–1979	*Book 3 provides a good foundation for this topic*
European/wider world study in depth	
Russia in Transition 1905–1924	*Book 3 provides a good foundation for this topic*
The USA: A Nation of Contrasts 1910–1929	*Book 3 provides a good foundation for this topic*
Germany in Transition 1919–1939	*Book 3 provides a good foundation for this topic*
Changes in South Africa 1948–1994	*This topic is referenced in Book 3*
Thematic study	
Changes in Crime and Punishment c1500–Present	✓ **Chapter 2** Life in Tudor times ✓ **Chapter 7** The Industrial Revolution: from farming to factories ✓ **Chapter 8** Terrible towns ✓ **Chapter 12** From Tudor to Victorian England: what changed? *Book 3 also provides a good foundation for this topic*
Changes in Health and Medicine c1340–Present	✓ **Chapter 5** The Restoration: the Merry Monarch ✓ **Chapter 8** Terrible towns ✓ **Chapter 12** From Tudor to Victorian England: what changed? *Book 1 and Book 3 also provide a good foundation for this topic*
The Development of Warfare c1250–Present	✓ **Chapter 4** From Civil War to Commonwealth ✓ **Chapter 10** Britain versus France *Book 1 also provides a good foundation for this topic*
Changes in Patterns of Migration c1500–Present	✓ **Chapter 3** Exit the Tudors, enter the Stuarts *Book 3 also provides a good foundation for this topic*

The Over to You activities and the History Skills activities in each *Student Book* lesson, as well as the end-of-chapter History Skills and Assessments, are carefully mapped to command words from different exam boards, to help students familiarise themselves with the specialist vocabulary needed to succeed in further studies beyond KS3. You can also find in each chapter of this guide a detailed breakdown of **WJEC exam-style questions** covered within that chapter. For example, see page 45 for the Chapter 1 chart.

Progression to GCSE: closing the word gap

Progression to GCSE: closing the word gap

As mentioned in the Curriculum planning section of this guide (see pages 19–32), the research from the *Oxford Language Report* (2018) found evidence of a significant word gap in UK schools, which is holding back students' learning. As a result, we have included suggested activities and effective classroom strategies here that could help your school to close the word gap and support your students to succeed in progressing through KS3 and beyond.

1 Understanding vocabulary for exams/assessments

Teacher notes

The increased content demands of the current History GCSE specification has left us scrabbling for time to get students through the different units, and many schools have started to teach the KS3 curriculum over two years to allow more time for GCSE. In this context, it is easy to forget that students need time to practise applying their knowledge and skills to assessments, starting from KS3. We have all taught students who instinctively understand the demands of an exam-style question, but they are not in the majority.

We must help students to access the examination questions by making them become familiar with command words and giving them the confidence to break down unfamiliar vocabulary.

Consult with your exam board's examiner reports for more detail about the key words which specifically pose difficulties for students.

Work bank of command words

Command words used in GCSE History exams	AQA	Edexcel	OCR A	OCR B	WJEC Eduqas
account*	✓	✓	✓	✓	
accurate					✓
analyse	✓	✓	✓	✓	✓
change and continuity	✓	✓	✓	✓	✓
compare*		✓		✓	
connection			✓	✓	✓
convincing*	✓		✓	✓	
describe	✓	✓	✓	✓	✓
enquiry		✓			✓
evaluate		✓	✓	✓	
explain	✓	✓	✓	✓	✓
extent					✓
identify			✓	✓	✓
impact/change	✓		✓	✓	✓
importance*	✓		✓	✓	
inference		✓			✓
investigate			✓	✓	
judgement	✓	✓	✓	✓	✓
outline					✓
purpose					✓
significance	✓	✓			✓
summary			✓	✓	
utility*	✓	✓	✓	✓	✓

*Words identified in recent examiner reports as posing difficulties for students.

Defining key words

Encourage students to engage with exam key words by creating their own annotated table of definitions and prompts:

Word	Definitions/prompts
infer	What can you learn from the information or what does it suggest?
critical/opposes	Against something
change	What impact or effect did it have?
similar	Can you find anything (features or reasons) that are the same, despite the time difference?
supports	In favour of something
account	A story or narrative that flows chronologically

Checking confidence in key words

You could create a template similar to the one below to check students' confidence in using key words, using a scale from 1 to 5 (5 is most confident). Record the dates they use the words verbally or in their written work to show how their confidence rating changes:

Word	Confidence rating 1 to 5	Date used
Parliament	2	01/10/19
	4	09/01/20
Commonwealth	1	01/11/19
	5	20/01/20
empire	1	09/01/20
rebellion	4	20/01/20

2 Mining history articles and academic texts

Both academic and anecdotal research shows that for young people to develop their vocabulary and understand how to apply new vocabulary to their writing, they need time to read. When students read for pleasure, they develop a confidence that means they can make what they read 'mean something' to them; this is what gives them the confidence to give a tough question 'a go' in exams. This can help us in the History classroom when it comes to analysing and comprehending historical interpretations. Confident readers will be able to identify different opinions and attach those opinions to their contextual understanding, which is a skill vital for success at GCSE.

To promote reading in your classroom, gather different articles and books about a topic. For higher-tier vocabulary, you could make use of *BBC History* magazine, the Historical Association's articles, and *History Today*.

- Reading to students allows you to emphasise meaning and model how words can be used.
- Reading with students can lead to discussions about how vocabulary can be applied in their writing. This is a good exercise for identifying more advanced connecting words.

You can also use academic texts to help to extend students' vocabulary choices. For example, texts such as *The Age of Extremes: The Short Twentieth Century, 1914–1991* by Eric Hobsbawm (Abacus, 1995) can be used to teach how to compare arguments and to help students to widen their use of connectives to introduce new ideas. Students can highlight vocabulary used to compare historical concepts. They can then present the vocabulary they have chosen and explain what they thought of Hobsbawm's analysis, using his vocabulary. This activity can help students to be more able to compare arguments and ideas in exam settings.

- Give students a number of texts: GCSE, A Level, academic, or review articles. Give them a mind-map template (see page 42, and ask them to complete the mind-map in groups.
- Allow students several opportunities to read the academic texts, and make mind-maps with vocabulary as well as connections with prior vocabulary knowledge, before you expect to see any impact in their writing. This is about learning different writing styles – they need a chance to observe and understand a way of writing before they can apply it.
- Share good examples of new vocabulary to agree on ways that words, phrases, or style in general can be applied, and then get students to redraft their work.
- Develop low-stakes quizzes for matching definitions to new advanced vocabulary.
- As an alternative to classroom texts, share details of interesting broadsheet newspaper articles or satirical TV shows with your students.
- KS3 students might find the **Teachit History** resource *Handling challenging texts in history (19517)* a helpful starting point for looking at academic texts.

Mind-map template for analysing vocabulary in articles and academic texts

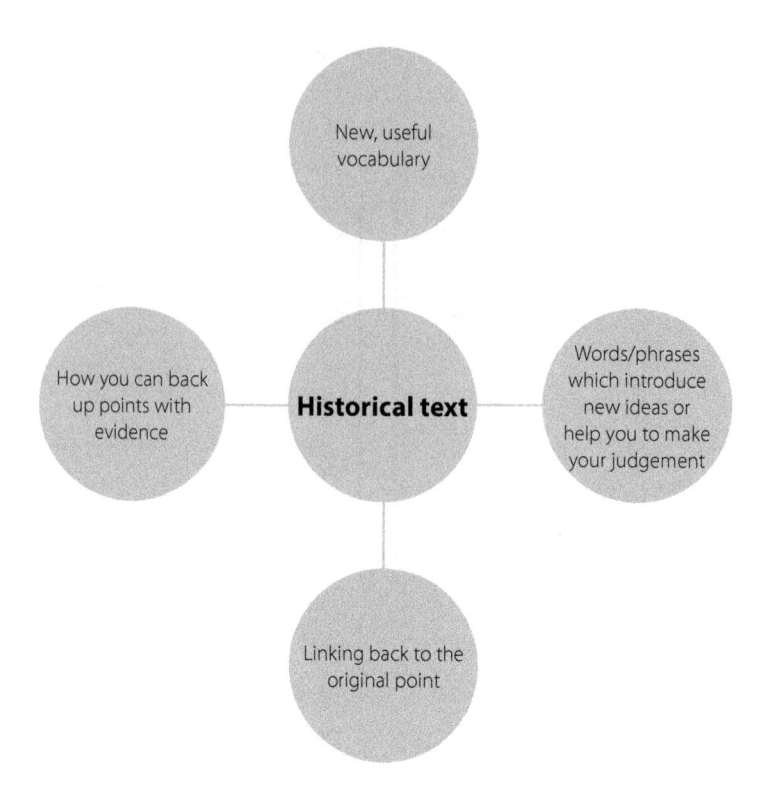

```
                    New, useful
                    vocabulary
                         |
How you can back ——— Historical text ——— Words/phrases
up points with                             which introduce
evidence                                   new ideas or
                                           help you to make
                                           your judgement
                         |
                   Linking back to the
                   original point
```

3 Organised writing

When analysing the demands of GCSE mark schemes, the top band always requires a clear, organised response with sustained judgements throughout. Some students will require writing frames and paragraph structures as a starting point for learning how to do this at the start of GCSE, while for others it is a skill they will have developed by the end of KS3, partly as a result of having a wide vocabulary.

- Modelling the use of connecting words such as conjunctions and tier three vocabulary (subject-specific academic words) can help students to incorporate more sophisticated language into their written work. We have built this modelling into this Oxford *KS3 History* series: for example, in the **Revolution, Industry and Empire 1558–1901 (Book 2) Chapter 3: Literacy Focus** section, a linking words activity is included with a word bank to familiarise students with connectives.
- Using a visualiser, you can quickly model good language use before, during, and after writing tasks.
- Annotate articles to show where connections have been made, judgements given, and comparisons explained. When students have done this in their homework, you can use their work as a model of good practice.
- Use academic texts to show students how tier three language can be incorporated into their written work.
- Gradually remove essay-writing structures as students develop confidence in their own vocabulary range and writing style.

Chapter 1 Queen Elizabeth

Links to KS3 History National Curriculum

Chapter 1 is a depth study of Elizabethan England that sets the scene for what Britain was like at the start of Elizabeth's reign. It recaps the social, religious and political history of the Tudor period. It then offers the opportunity to study the development of Church, state and society in Britain between 1509 and 1745 – as required by the latest Key Stage 3 History National Curriculum – by focusing on the Elizabethan period 1558–1603. Throughout the chapter Elizabeth's rocky road to monarchy is charted, as well as the conflict she encountered both at home from Catholic plots and from foreign Catholic powers, particularly Spain.

The concept of empire is developed as the foundations are laid for what will become the British Empire. Students will be challenged with a wide range of historical skills, such as evaluating the causes of events and their consequences. The incorporation of inference skills when looking at sources and interpretations will encourage students to mine material for information while attaching it to contextual understanding; this is particularly evident in **1.7** What did Queen Elizabeth look like? when looking at portraits of Elizabeth I.

Skills and processes covered in this chapter

		Lesson/activity in the Student Book
History Skills	Knowledge and understanding	1.1 Over to You: 1, 2
		1.2 Over to You: 1, 3a, 3b, 3c
		1.3 Over to You: 1, 2, 3a
		1.4 Over to You: 1, 3a, 4
		1.5A Similarity and Difference: 1
		1.5B Over to You: 1
		1.6 Over to You: 1
		1.7 Over to You: 1b, 2
		Have you been learning? Quick Knowledge Quiz: 1, 2, 3, 4, 5, 6, 7, 8, 9, 10
	Interpretations	1.3 Interpretation Analysis: 1
		1.5B Interpretation Analysis: 1, 2
		1.6 Over to You: 2a, 2b
		1.7 Over to You: 4
	Sources	1.2 Source Analysis: 1, 2
		1.4 Source Analysis: 1a, 1b, 2
		1.7 Over to You: 1a, 3a, 3b, 3c, 4a, 4b, 4c
		1 Assessment: Making inferences (source analysis): 1, 2
	Significance	
	Cause and consequence	1.3 Over to You: 3b
		1.4 Over to You: 2, 3b
		1.5A Over to You: 1, 2; Similarity and Difference: 2
		1.5B Over to You: 2a, 2b, 2c, 3
		1.6 Over to You: 1; Cause and Consequence: 1, 2
		1.7 Over to You: 1, 3

Chapter 1 Queen Elizabeth

		Lesson/activity in the Student Book
	Diversity/Similarity and difference	1.5A Similarity and Difference: 3
	Change and continuity	1.1 Change and Continuity: 1, 2
		1.2 Over to You: 2a, 2b
Literacy and Numeracy	Literacy	1.2 Over to You: 3a, 3b, 3c
		Have you been learning? Literacy Focus: 1, 2
	Numeracy	1.1 Over to You: 2

Lesson sequence

Lesson title	Student Book pages	Objectives
1.1 What was Britain like in 1558?	pp 8–9	• Examine what Britain was like in 1558. • Summarise England's relationship with its neighbouring countries. • Compare Britain in 1558 with Britain today.
1.2 Young Elizabeth: what was she like?	pp 10–11	• Identify why Princess Elizabeth was such an able student. • Examine the circumstances in which she became queen.
1.3 Queen Elizabeth's 'middle way'	pp 12–13	• Analyse how Elizabeth tried to end religious chaos in Tudor England. • Explain the consequences of Elizabeth's 'middle way'.
1.4 Why did Queen Elizabeth kill her cousin?	pp 14–15	• Examine the threat posed by Mary, Queen of Scots. • Discover the events surrounding the Babington Plot.
1.5A Match of the day: England versus Spain	pp 16–17	• Examine why the King of Spain decided to invade England in 1588.
1.5B Match of the day: England versus Spain	pp 18–19	• Compare the strengths and weaknesses of England and Spain's navies. • Judge key reasons why the Spanish Armada failed.
1.6 Britain begins to build an empire	pp 20–21	• Discover how and why the British Empire began. • Examine the significance of key individuals in the growth of the British Empire.
1.7 What did Queen Elizabeth look like?	pp 22–23	• Identify why it is so hard to know what Queen Elizabeth really looked like. • Examine why Elizabeth controlled her royal portraits so carefully.
Chapter 1 Have you been learning?	pp 24–25	• Choose the correct answer from the given options for a quick recap. • Improve sentences by adding specific factual detail. • Ensure correct chronological order of events.
Chapter 1 History skill: Making inferences (source analysis)	pp 26–27	• Identify different ways that historians use sources. • Understand the difference between source comprehension and source inference.
Chapter 1 Assessment: Making inferences (source analysis)	pp 28–29	• Describe the inferences that can be made about Elizabeth I from written and visual sources. • Support inferences with accurate detail.

Chapter 1 Queen Elizabeth

Links to the GCSE curriculum

This chapter provides some historical context to the following:

AQA: Elizabethan England c1568–1603

AQA: Migration, Empires and the People c790–Present

AQA: Restoration England 1660–1685

Edexcel: Early Elizabethan England 1558–1588

OCR A: Monarchy and Democracy in Britain c1000–2014

OCR A: War and British Society c790–c2010

OCR B: The Elizabethans 1580–1603

OCR B: Migrants to Britain c1250–Present

Eduqas: The Elizabethan Age 1558–1603

Eduqas: The Development of Warfare in Britain c500–Present

WJEC: The Elizabethan Age 1558–1603

Exam-style questions covered in this chapter

Exam board	Lesson/activity question location	Command words	History skills/concepts
AQA	1.1 Change and Continuity: 2	Explain two ways… different	Change and continuity
	1.4 Source Analysis: 2	How useful…	Source analysis
	1.5A Similarity and Difference: 3	Explain two ways… different	Similarity and difference
Edexcel	1.2 Source Analysis: 2	Give two…infer…	Source analysis
	1.4 Source Analysis: 2	How useful…	Source analysis
	1.5B Interpretation Analysis: 2	How far do you agree…	Interpretation analysis
	1.5B Over to You: 3	Explain two consequences of…	Cause and consequence
OCR A	1.4 Source Analysis: 2	How useful…	Source analysis
OCR B	1.3 Interpretation Analysis: 1	Identify and explain…	Interpretation analysis
	1.4 Source Analysis: 2	How useful…	Source analysis
Eduqas	1.6 Cause and Consequence: 2	Explain connections…	Cause and consequence

Revolution, Industry and Empire: Britain 1558–1901

Chapter 1 Queen Elizabeth

A brief history

1.1 What was Britain like in 1558?

This chapter opens where Chapter 9 in Book 1: *Invasion, Plague and Murder 1066–1558 Student Book* left off: what is life like for people in the sixteenth century? This focus on the lives of ordinary people will enable students to picture Elizabethan society by attaching content to their understanding of England at this time. The different aspects of Tudor society explored set the scene for the main themes of Elizabethan England: power, the Church, government and the struggle with Scotland. Students will be given the opportunity to explore the growing tension between Catholics and Protestants.

1.2 Young Elizabeth: what was she like?

This is a fantastic focus on Elizabeth as a person and offers a human angle to someone who is often just remembered as the Virgin Queen. Students learn about her difficult childhood while also seeing her as an intelligent, sociable girl who won her father's respect. A great activity to revisit and test knowledge and understanding would be to link the details of her timetable to Tudor society and the Renaissance. The inference activities build on the skills used when analysing portraits of Henry in Chapter 8 of Book 1: *Invasion, Plague and Murder 1066–1558 Student Book* – more able students could compare the purpose of Henry's and Elizabeth's portraits.

1.3 Queen Elizabeth's 'middle way'

New terminology, such as religious settlement, is an important part of this lesson. It would be advisable to recap learning about the difference between Catholics and Protestants to ensure that students understand the features of the Church of England after the 'middle way'. This will help them to correctly explain who was happy and who was unhappy with the settlement. Understanding cause and consequence in this way is vital for understanding extremism from both denominations. This could be a good opportunity to work with your RE, Citizenship, Geography or Politics department to investigate reasons for religious extremism and intolerance. Historical interpretation work is developed in this lesson.

Timeline

1533
Elizabeth Tudor is born to Anne Boleyn and Henry VIII.

1547
Elizabeth's half-brother Edward VI becomes king. He is a strict Protestant and makes lots of changes to the Church.

1553
Mary I becomes queen and changes the Church back to Catholic. She keeps her half-sister Elizabeth in prison.

1558
Elizabeth I becomes queen. She develops a 'middle way' to try to keep both Catholics and Protestants happy.

1568
Elizabeth's cousin Mary, Queen of Scots arrives in England after running away from Scotland. Elizabeth lets her stay, but imprisons her.

1587
Mary, Queen of Scots is executed after evidence is found to link her to the Babington Plot.

1587
Frances Drake 'singes the King of Spain's beard' when he sets fire to around 30 ships in Cadiz.

1588
England wins against the Spanish Armada due to a better fleet, sailors and tactics; bad weather also helps.

1600
British first start trading in India.

A brief history

1.4 Why did Queen Elizabeth kill her cousin?

Students will love learning about this rivalry that ends with Mary's execution. Classes with more able students or those with more time may want to offer more context of Mary's involvement in previous plots, but reinforce that the Babington Plot is the first one with hard evidence that she was involved in. For the first time in this chapter students will use their own knowledge to explain the utility of a source. A good tip is to get them to think: In what ways is the source *useful*? This will stop them focusing on what is missing, which could be a lot!

1.5A/B Match of the day: England versus Spain

Cause and consequence have been key concepts of Chapter 1 so far and this lesson offers students an opportunity to show off their learning. Higher ability students should be encouraged to think about the short and long term, while lower ability students should be given a chance to link the key people to events, such as Philip II, Drake and Elizabeth. When mapping out the key events students could have two maps, one for Philip's plan and the other for the reality of the Armada. The causation question about the reasons for the failure of the Spanish Armada is a time for students to shine with content they will love.

1.6 Britain begins to build an empire

Building history around the individual is key again but this lesson looks at the people who made Elizabeth powerful by bringing her money, taking over new land, and getting the better of powerful countries such as Spain. Students must understand the context of Elizabethan England from previous lessons and, importantly, how difficult travel was at the time. Furthermore, this was the foundation for the British Empire. To develop this lesson further while still focusing on the individual, you could bring in the role of Black Tudors in the voyages of discovery and in the colonies – this would enrich students' understanding of the period.

1.7 What did Queen Elizabeth look like?

The sky is the limit with this lesson as it can become just about anything you want it to be: portraits as propaganda, a lesson on body image, selfies and identity, or even a comparison with Henry's portraits. The matching exercise is a subtle way of getting students to focus on the details of the portraits and using the inference skills they developed earlier in the chapter. The historical interpretation links to religion, and is a great way to get students to revisit and consolidate the key concepts of Elizabethan England.

Further reading and links

For teachers:

- The BBC 4 documentary *Elizabeth I's Battle for God's Music* by Lucy Worsley (2017) is an insight into the religious settlement and choral evensong. Clips are available on YouTube.
- Miranda Kaufman's popular book *Black Tudors: The Untold Story* (Oneworld, 2017) sheds new light on the many influential black people in the Tudor period.
- Radio 4's *In Our Time* episode on the Spanish Armada (2010) is a great way to find out about key individuals and the power of both Spain and England. A transcript could be used as an academic text for higher ability students.

For students:

- BBC Bitesize has numerous media clips dramatising the events surrounding Elizabeth. Search the website for 'KS3 History Elizabeth I' to find them.
- Students could listen to historian Miranda Kaufman's 2017 podcast on the lives of black Tudors on www.historyextra.com. Go to Period > Tudor.

Beyond the classroom

- As Elizabethan England is one of the GCSE historic environment topics, many sites run school tours. Take your students to the Globe Theatre, Hardwick Hall, Kenilworth or the other historic sites to bring the period to life.
- Students could imagine they have been asked by Henry VIII to write a school report about Elizabeth. They could think about the lessons she studied, her strengths and her attitudes towards learning. They could even set it out like one of their school reports. This will help them relate to Elizabeth the schoolgirl.
- Work with the Art department so students can create self-portraits to show power and strength. Art staff can explain the use of colour and symbols to convey a particular impression, while History teachers can ensure the symbols used match those from Tudor content.
- Take students to visit the local Anglican church and interview the minister about the 'middle way' and how the features are still evident today.

Revolution, Industry and Empire: Britain 1558–1901

Chapter 1 Answers guidance

Answers guidance

The answers provided here are examples, based on the information provided in the Student Book. There may be other factors which are relevant to each question, and students may draw on as much of their own knowledge as possible to give detailed and precise answers. There are also many ways of answering questions, including exam-style questions (for example, of structuring an essay). However, these exemplar answers should provide a good starting point.

Timeline from 1558–1901
STUDENT BOOK PAGES 6–7

Over To You

1a They are named after the royal family, or the kings or queens, who ruled during that period.
b Student answers will vary.
2a Reading from left to right:
- seventeenth century
- eighteenth century
- sixteenth century
- nineteenth century

b
- seventeenth century
- seventeenth century
- twentieth century
- seventeenth century
- sixteenth century

c Defeat of the Spanish Armada > James I/VI unites Scotland and England > The Great Fire of London > The Glorious Revolution > Death of Queen Victoria

1.1 What was Britain like in 1558?
PAGES 8–9

Over To You

1 Elizabeth; Wales; Scotland; farming; woodland; ten; countryside; more; market.
2 Students' bar charts will reflect populations: England 3,500,000; Scotland 500,000; Ireland 800,000; Wales 250,000.

Change and Continuity

1 Student answers will vary, but will be based on the categories in the spider diagram. For example, the 'Britain in 1558' column will say that people travelled on foot, on horseback or by cart, and roads were in poor condition. However, the 'Britain today' column will list the different types of transport today (car, train, aeroplane etc.) and include that we have an excellent road and motorway system.
2 Student answers will focus on the differences between the two eras and include lots of examples. For example, in 1558, the diet was very basic but today we have a wide variety of foods imported from all over the world.

1.2 Young Elizabeth: what was she like?
PAGES 10–11

Over to You

1 Answers might include: mother executed; loneliness; tough father who died when she was 13; not trusted by brother.
2a Students could mention:
- Bible study – important to be a good Christian as a member of the royal family to a foreign Christian prince as a potential bride.
- Conversation – royals should be able to converse with other upper classes and foreign powers, also to attract a foreign prince.
- Learning and translating foreign languages – royals should be able to converse with foreign powers, also to attract a foreign prince.
2b Student answers may vary, but they may say PE to understand the importance of good health and nutrition, or ICT to live in our modern world.
3 Students' answers should cover the three areas in detail. For example, Elizabeth speaks five languages – English, French, Italian, Greek and Latin – which will be useful and impressive when talking with rich powerful friends and foreign powers. Students should also write about her strengths and attitude to learning, using Robert Ascham's report to help them.

Source Analysis

1 Student descriptions will vary, but should make reference to the dress, jewellery and books.
2 Answers will vary but students may infer from the expensive jewellery that she is rich and from the books that she is an able student/keen reader.

1.3 Queen Elizabeth's 'middle way'
PAGES 12–13

Over to You

1a A priest hole was a place where Catholic priests hid to avoid capture/punishment, when officials came looking for them.
1b They were needed because new laws meant that Catholic priests could now be tried and executed for treason.
2 Suggested answers:
Actions that please Catholics:
- Elizabeth made herself Governor of the Church of England.
- Bishops allowed to stay in their jobs.
- Edward VI's prayer book replaced.
- Recusants allowed to miss church services.

Actions that please Protestants:
- Priests allowed to get married.
- Church services and the Bible kept in English.

3a 'Middle' tends to refer to a centre path that is not on one side or the other – the 'middle way' refers to the fact that Elizabeth tried to find a religious settlement that followed neither the Protestant nor the Catholic way too closely.

48 Chapter 1 Queen Elizabeth

Chapter 1 Answers guidance

3b Student answers will vary, but they may say: Worked to some extent – it pleased many people, but extremists on both sides were left unhappy. Very strict Protestants didn't want to compromise with Catholics, while strict Catholics believed that Protestants were a danger to religion. In the end, Elizabeth decided to make life tougher for Catholics – so it could be argued that the 'middle way' failed.

Interpretation Analysis

1 The author does this by saying that everyone was going to be on the 'same team' and they would be 'working together' for a 'common goal'. The author also uses words like 'united' and 'unite'.

1.4 Why did Queen Elizabeth kill her cousin?
PAGES 14–15

Over to You

1 Key events include:
- 1542 – Mary born, became Queen of Scotland
- 1558 – Married French king (who died tragically young)
- 1565 – Married an English lord (who was strangled to death and blown up)
- 1567 – Married Earl Bothwell
- 1568 – Scots rebelled and she fled to England. Kept prisoner for 19 years
- 1586 – Babington Plot
- 1587 – Executed

2 Mary was a problem for Elizabeth – she was Catholic, and made no secret of the fact that she thought she should be Queen of England if Elizabeth died. Some English Catholics agreed with Mary, so Elizabeth tried to reduce this threat by putting her in jail.

3a Babington got Mary's servants to hide secret coded letters in beer barrels. Mary wrote back saying she agreed to his plans but the servants worked for England's chief spy, Sir Francis Walsingham, who took the letters to Elizabeth.

3b Students may say that Elizabeth didn't want to upset Catholics (which would turn Mary into a martyr) or that she was a family member.

4 Students answers will vary.

Source Analysis

1a Answers will vary, but the scene shows Mary on a small scaffold with her head on a block, people around watching, with an executioner about to execute her. She is blindfolded and kneeling down.

1b Answers will vary but might include: brave, courageous, scared, religious, forgiving.

2 Answers should reflect the fact that the sources are useful because they are contemporary accounts that give vivid insight into the execution. We know that the person who wrote Source C was present, which gives the account some validity. The source allows us to get an idea of the location, process etc.

1.5A Match of the day: England versus Spain
PAGES 16–17

Over to You

1 Student answers may include: Long term: For many years, English sailors had been stealing gold and silver from Spanish ships; or that rebels in the Spanish Netherlands were being helped by English soldiers. Short term: This was Philip's response to the news that Sir Francis Drake had just sailed into Cadiz harbour in southern Spain and set fire to 30 of Spain's royal warships; or that he had heard that Mary, Queen of Scots had been executed by Queen Elizabeth. He thought that the people who had killed a Catholic queen should be punished.

2 After invasion, his plan was to remove Elizabeth from the English throne. Philip would then become King of Spain and England.

Similarity and Difference

1 Answers will vary, but may include: **English:** Their experienced sailors would steer their ships parallel to the Spanish about 150m away and use their superior guns to fire huge solid 20kg cannonballs through the side of the enemy ships. Then smaller cannons known as 'man killers' would fire 8kg balls at the sailors. When the Spanish ships were floating wrecks packed with battered and tired soldiers, the English would hop on board and finish them off.
Spanish: Spanish galleons would sail next to the enemy ships and tie themselves alongside with ropes and hooks. Then soldiers would jump onto the enemy ships and fight with swords, daggers and muskets. Heavy guns below decks would almost touch the other ships and blow holes in their sides.

2 Student answers will vary, but most will go for the nimbleness and firepower of English ships.

3 English: smaller ships, nimble/agile/easier to manoeuvre; very accurate guns. Spanish: larger ships, harder to manoeuvre, different tactics to try to sink the enemy too.

1.5B Match of the day: England versus Spain
PAGES 18–19

Over to You

1 Student maps will reflect the route taken by the Armada.

2a Students may add that the Spanish leader was a poor commander.

Revolution, Industry and Empire: Britain 1558–1901   49

Chapter 1 Answers guidance

2b Student answers will vary.

2c Answers should be backed up with reasons. For example, many will put the faster English ships as the reason for the failure, because most of the other factors may have been overcome, but the English ships were so superior that this was decisive.

3 Answers may include: that the defeat of the Spanish showed that Elizabeth could govern England in times of war as well as peace; it made Elizabeth believe she should always have a strong navy to protect England; she began to build up the navy and soon it would begin to venture out in search of valuable land all over the world – this led to the creation of colonies and trading companies that began the age of the British Empire; for many Protestants in England (and other places around the world), it made them believe that God was on their side; Catholicism became increasingly unpopular and was viewed as anti-English; Spain's failure proved that Spain was beatable and Spanish kings could no longer do as they wished.

Interpretation Analysis

1 The author says that the English won because they were better sailors, their ships had greater firepower and they had good leaders, while the Spanish had a poor leader.

2 Students will generally agree with the interpretation, citing that the information it contains backs up what they know.

1.6 Britain begins to build an empire
PAGES 20–21

Over to You

1
- 1583 – Sir Humphrey Gilbert claims land in North America
- 1587 – Walter Raleigh sets up a colony in North America, which fails
- 1600 – British first start trading in India
- 1607 – first successful British colony is started in North America
- 1642 – sugar is first grown in the British colony of Barbados
- 1655 – British defeat the Spanish and take Jamaica
- 1664 – British seize New Amsterdam from the Dutch, renaming it New York after Charles II's brother, the Duke of York
- 1713 – British take over much of Canada

2a Sir Gilbert is cutting earth in North America in August 1583, which symbolises that the land was now English.

2b Despite failing to set up a colony and dying on his way back from an unsuccessful voyage, Gilbert claimed hundreds of miles of land for the queen. The area around where he landed is regarded as the first part of the British Empire.

Cause and Consequence

1
- Trade – the British set up trading stations in areas of the world and gained influence there.
- Wars – sometimes Britain went to war in an area, beat the opponents and took the land that the defeated nation previously ruled.
- New crops – these were very popular in Britain, such as sugar, which meant that the British wanted to seize land where it was grown.

2 Student answers will vary, but an example might be that Britain's desire to open trading stations in different parts of the world is linked to war because it might be that this means they come into contact (and possible conflict) with rival nations that also want to set up trading stations.

1.7 What did Queen Elizabeth look like?
PAGES 22–23

Portraits and descriptions of Queen Elizabeth match up as follows: B = 2, C = 4, D = 3 E = 1, F = 5

Over to You

1 Student answers will include that portraits were a chance for Elizabeth to show her power and wealth.

1a Student answers will vary, but be based on the portrait and the description attached.

1b Student answers will vary, depending on the description. A positive description of a younger Elizabeth would probably please her, while a description that describes her as old would not.

2 Because she did not like to be shown as anything less than her best. She wanted people to view her as desirable, strong and elegant. There may be some vanity in this too.

3a The writers agree that her face was long, she had bad teeth and false red hair (a wig).

3b The writers disagree about the colour of her teeth and her height.

3c Students may say that in the later source, the teeth are black, so they may have got worse. It might also be related to the circumstances in which they met – she may have been seated for one meeting, not the other, one visitor may have seen her close up, whereas the other might not have.

4 The portrait shows her religious brother that she too is religious and clever.

50 Chapter 1 Queen Elizabeth

Chapter 1 Have you been learning?

Answers guidance

Chapter 1 Have you been learning?

Quick Knowledge Quiz

PAGE 24

1 a Anne Boleyn
2 b Mary and Edward
3 b 1558
4 c Religious Settlement
5 a Mary, Queen of Scots
6 b Anthony Babington
7 b 1588
8 b Philip II
9 a 1578
10 c empire

Literacy Focus

PAGE 25

Writing in detail

1 Student answers will vary, but they will use the tips given in the Student Book to help them write the second paragraph.

Here is an example: There were several reasons why the Spanish king, Philip II, wanted to attack England in 1588. In the previous year Mary, Queen of Scots had been executed for her part in the Babington Plot, which angered Philip because Mary was Catholic, and this was viewed as an attack on Catholicism. Furthermore, the English had supported Protestant rebels in the Spanish Netherlands, which was a direct challenge to Philip II of Spain. Another reason was because the English had been attacking Spanish ships as the Spanish were very rich and they could get lots of gold for Elizabeth (and themselves!). The English fleet then went to Cadiz in the south of Spain and attacked Spain's royal warships by setting fire to them. They were led by Francis Drake.

Chronology

2
- Henry Tudor defeats Richard III to become the first Tudor monarch, Henry VII
- Henry VII's son, Arthur, dies, leaving his younger son (also called Henry) as heir to the throne
- Henry VIII becomes king
- Nine-year-old Edward VI becomes king. He is a strict Protestant
- Mary Tudor, Henry VIII's eldest daughter, becomes queen – she is a strict Catholic
- Elizabeth I becomes queen. She tries to find a 'middle way' in religion

Revolution, Industry and Empire: Britain 1558–1901   51

Chapter 1 Assessment: Making inferences (source analysis)

Assessment summary

The assessments in this textbook have been carefully designed and tested with History teachers to support student progression throughout the course. This specific assessment is written to support Year 8 or Year 9 students in tackling questions relating to making inferences from sources.

1. Give two things you can infer from **Source C** about how Queen Elizabeth wanted to be portrayed. (10)
2. Give two things you can infer from **Source D** about Queen Elizabeth and her views of her reign as queen. (10)

▼ **SOURCE C** A portrait of Elizabeth I, painted around 1600. Many people think it was painted by Isaac Oliver, a well-known painter. It is known as the 'Rainbow Portrait' because of the rainbow Elizabeth holds in her right hand. She was around 60 years old when this was painted, but looks much younger.

▼ **SOURCE D** Adapted from Queen Elizabeth's last speech to Parliament on 30 November 1601. It is known as the 'Golden Speech'. At this time, she had been queen for 43 years. When Elizabeth talks about her 'subjects', she is referring to the people she rules over.

> 'I do assure you there is no prince that loves his subjects better, or whose love can beat our love. And, though God has raised me high, this is what I think is the glory of my crown, that I have reigned with your love. Of myself I must say this: I never was any greedy, selfish or wasteful queen. My heart was never set on any worldly goods, but only for my subjects' good. There will never be a Queen who sits in my seat with more love for my country, care for my subjects, and that will sooner dedicate her life for your good and safety, than myself.'

Chapter 1 Assessment: Making inferences (source analysis)

Students are encouraged to look at the visual source and pick out examples of what they can infer about Elizabeth from the portrait. Then they describe the relevant details from which they are making their inferences, backing this up with their own knowledge. They repeat this process with the text source.

To support Year 8s or Year 9s with this inference question they have been given sentence starters, points from the sources to focus on, scaffolded statements, and tips about the difference between comprehension and inference.

For the mark scheme, see page 55.

A note about the end-of-chapter assessments

There is an assessment for each Student Book chapter. Each is structured like a GCSE exam-style question, with scaffolding steps to support KS3 students. Each assessment has a total of 20 marks, and is designed to be completed in a typical lesson – each has been written with a time allowance of about 30 minutes.

There is a mark scheme for each assessment. You can choose how to give student outcomes: a mark out of 20; a percentage; a performance indicator (we use a three-stage indicator – 'Developing', 'Secure', 'Extending' – but you could adapt to match any performance indicators used in your school); or a GCSE grade indicator. To convert raw marks to a performance or GCSE grade indicator, use this table:

Raw marks			
0	1–6	7–13	14–20
GCSE grade (9–1) indicators*			
U	1–3	4–6	7–9
Performance indicator			
Ungraded	Developing	Secure	Extending

* Please appreciate that these are approximate grades based on grade boundaries from recent GCSE exam papers. If a student achieves a Grade 7 in one of these assessments, it is not the equivalent of a Grade 7 at GCSE. Instead it is an indicator of the grade the student could expect to get if they continue on their flight path through KS3 and GCSE. Please note:
  - the raw-mark boundaries are based on but do not match precisely those for recent GCSE exam papers: this is because our assessments are focused around one exam-style question, likely to be done at the end of a chapter (topic) rather than at the end of the course. Secondly, we provide carefully considered scaffolded steps to allow KS3 students to tackle high level questions and gain confidence through the deliberate practice of building up detailed answers.
  - the assessments for Student Book 3 are progressively more demanding in that they use higher-order command words and provide less scaffolded support – if you set one of them for Year 8 students, please take that into account when awarding GCSE grade indicators.

Entering student outcomes into the Kerboodle Markbook

The Kerboodle Markbook records scores and percentages to allow for quick comparison of performance. If you want to use the Markbook to record student outcomes, you will need to enter the appropriate values given in the raw marks row of the table above.

Chapter 1 Assessment: Making inferences (source analysis)

Links to GCSE

By the end of KS3, students should be familiar with the History skill of analysing sources to make inferences. At GCSE, most exam boards specifically ask students to make inferences. For example:

Edexcel:

- Give two things you can infer from Source A about… Complete the table below to explain your answer. (4)

| What I can infer: | Details in the source that tell me this: |
| What I can infer: | Details in the source that tell me this: |

OCR B:

- What can Source A tell us about…? Use the source and your own knowledge to support your answer. (7)

Eduqas:

- What was the purpose of Source B? Use details from Source B and your own knowledge and understanding of the historical context to answer the question. (8)

Links to KS3 History resources

Student Book

This assessment question links to these lessons:

1.2 *Young Elizabeth: what was she like?*
1.4 *Why did Queen Elizabeth kill her cousin?*
1.5B *Match of the day: England versus Spain*
1.6 *Britain begins to build an empire*
1.7 *What did Queen Elizabeth look like?*

Kerboodle

Support for this assessment question on Kerboodle:

RIE 1 *Assessment presentation: Making inferences (source analysis)*
RIE 1 *Assessment worksheet (Core): Making inferences (source analysis)*
RIE 1 *Assessment worksheet (Foundation): Making inferences (source analysis)*

Curriculum and Assessment Planning Guide

Support for this assessment question in this guide:

1 *Assessment mark scheme – page 55*
1 *Assessment sample student answers – pages 56–57*

Chapter 1 Assessment: Making inferences (source analysis)

Student name: _____   Date: _____

Mark scheme

Assessment bands	Marks	GCSE grade indicators*	I have...
	0	Ungraded	
Developing	1–6	1–3	☐ written a valid inference on each of the sources. ☐ included some supporting details to back up the inferences made.
Secure	7–13	4–6	☐ written one or two valid inferences on each source. ☐ included relevant supporting detail, showing some knowledge and understanding of the topic.
Extending	14–20	7–9	☐ written two valid inferences on both sources. ☐ included accurate and relevant supporting detail backing up the inference, showing excellent knowledge and understanding of the topic.

* IMPORTANT: These are approximate indicators devised using publicly available information on the new GCSE grades. They are designed to assist in the process of tracking and monitoring. They cannot and should not be used to replace teachers' professional judgement. Teachers should use their own discretion in applying them, taking into account the cumulative test scores of an individual student (rather than just one assessment point), and should refer to their institution's assessment policy.

Mark: _____

Comment:

Chapter 1 Assessment: Making inferences (source analysis)

Sample student answers

Assessment: Making inferences (source analysis)

STUDENT BOOK PAGES 26–27

1. Give two things you can infer from **Source C** about how Queen Elizabeth wanted to be portrayed. (10)
2. Give two things you can infer from **Source D** about Queen Elizabeth and her views of her reign as queen. (10)

Sample Developing band answer

In Source C Elizabeth wants to be portrayed as a smart and wise queen. A detail in the source that shows me this is the snake on her dress, which symbolises wisdom. This could be because of her age as, at the time of the painting, she was 60 years old.

Source D shows that Queen Elizabeth views her reign as a success because she states that she has reigned with the love of Parliament. This suggests she has been a good queen.

Sample Secure band answer

I can infer from Source C that Elizabeth I wants to be portrayed as a good queen. A detail from the source that support this is that it shows her holding a rainbow, a sign of a storm having cleared. Elizabeth faced many threats during her reign but dealt with them all. Another inference from Source C is that Elizabeth wanted to be portrayed as a queen who knows what is going on in her country. The source supports this as it shows her with eyes and ears all over her dress. Elizabeth had a spy network that helped her defeat plots and rebellions like the Babington Plot.

I can infer from Source D that Queen Elizabeth considers her reign a success. A detail from the source that support this is that she states that she has had the support of both God and Parliament. After the English victory during the Armada of 1588, the English believed that this was proof that God was on their side.

Another inference from Source D is that Queen Elizabeth believes she has served her country and Parliament well. I can see this as she says she was never greedy or selfish but that she thought of her subjects.

Chapter 1 Assessment: Making inferences (source analysis)

⭐ Sample Extending band answer

I can infer from Source C that Elizabeth wanted to be portrayed as young. A detail in the source that supports this is that the painter Isaac Oliver has made her look very young, when she was actually 60 and coming towards the end of her reign. Portraits were used to send messages to subjects and foreign powers – this would be a way of making Elizabeth still seem strong and able so people don't try to take the throne. I can also infer that Elizabeth wanted to be portrayed as a successful queen. The source supports this by showing her holding a rainbow and with the Latin message, 'no rainbow without the sun'. This suggests that England is a happy, peaceful country that Elizabeth is in control of – this was the case in 1588, after the English victory over the Spanish Armada. The portrait will send the message that she is still a strong queen despite her age and plots and rebellions against her – for example she dealt with the Babington Plot of 1586, which led to the execution of Mary, Queen of Scots.

One inference from Source D relating to how Queen Elizabeth viewed her reign is that she thinks she has been the best queen England has had or could have. One detail from the source to support this is where she states that there is no-one who could love England more or dedicate their life to it. Another inference would be that she believes she has made life better for the people of England. The source supports this where it says, 'My heart was never set on worldly goods, but only for my subjects' good'. During her reign, there were numerous voyages of discovery that brought new goods and wealth to England – for example, Walter Raleigh's attempted colonies in North America in 1584. It seems that after a long reign she wants to remind people what she did for them, and gives the impression that she was unselfish and only cared for her people and not for herself.

Chapter 2 Life in Tudor times

Links to KS3 History National Curriculum

This chapter shows the diverse history of the Elizabethan period by looking at not only the changes within a time period but also those that happen across time periods. The poor are a key focus, especially looking at the Poor Law of 1601; this key legislation changed how the poor were seen and was not amended until the 1800s. Another contributing factor to the changing view of the poor was the building of theatres after actors were given licences. Theatre is a great vehicle for looking at the interests of both the poor and the wealthy – the AQA GCSE historic environment for 2019 was the Globe Theatre so there are lots of resources available to study that. Students will build their contextual understanding of the period, but this chapter also ensures that your curriculum is cumulatively sufficient as the idea of the poor and the feudal system changes, along with free time, diet and houses. Students will feel more connected to the Elizabethan period after this focus on social and class history, especially the sections on education and crime and punishment.

Throughout the chapter your students will have the opportunity to develop their inference and analysis skills by using sources and interpretations.

Skills and processes covered in this chapter

		Lesson/activity in the Student Book
History Skills	Knowledge and understanding	2.1A Over to You: 1a, 1b, 3
		2.1B Over to You: 1a, 1b, 1c, 1d; Significance: 1, 2
		2.2 Over to You: 1a, 1b, 1c, 1d, 3
		2.3 Over to You: 1a; Knowledge and Understanding: 3
		2.4 Over to You: 1a, 1b, 2
		2.5 Over to You: 2a, 2b; Change and Continuity: 1a, 1b
		2.6 Over to You: 1a, 2
		2.7A Over to You: 2
		2.7B Over to You: 1, 3a; Knowledge and Understanding: 1, 2
		Have you been learning? Quick Knowledge Quiz: 1, 2, 3, 4, 5, 6, 7, 8, 9, 10
	Interpretations	2.4 Interpretation Analysis: 1, 2
	Sources	2.3 Knowledge and Understanding: 1, 2a, 2b, 3
		2.6 Over to You: 2
	Significance	2.1B Significance: 3
	Cause and consequence	2.1A Over to You: 2
		2.2 Over to You: 2, 4b
		2.3 Over to You: 1b, 2
		2.4 Over to You: 1a, 1b
		2.5 Over to You: 1
		2.7A Over to You: 1
		2.7B Over to You: 2a, 2b, 3a, 3b

Chapter 2 Life in Tudor times

		Lesson/activity in the Student Book
	Diversity/Similarity and difference	2.1B Over to You: 2a, 2b
		2.2 Change and Continuity: 1
		2.6 Similarity and Difference: 1
		2 Assessment: Similarity and difference: 1, 2, 3
	Change and continuity	2.2 Over to You: 4a; Change and Continuity: 1, 2
		2.5 Change and Continuity: 2
		2.6 Over to You: 1b
Literacy and Numeracy	Literacy	2.2 Over to You: 3
		2.7A Over to You: 2
		Have you been learning? Literacy Focus: 1a, 1b, 2a, 2b, 2c, 2d, 2e, 2f, 2g, 2h, 2i

Lesson sequence

Lesson title	Student Book pages	Objectives
2.1A Who's who?	pp 30–31	• Define the main groups that made up Tudor society. • Examine how the poor were treated in Tudor society.
2.1B Who's who?	pp 32–33	
2.2 What were Tudor schools like?	pp 34–35	• Recall a typical day in a Tudor school. • Compare today's schools with those in Tudor times.
2.3 How did people have fun in Tudor times?	pp 36–37	• Recall different types of Tudor entertainment. • Examine how and why Tudor entertainment differed from the types of entertainment we enjoy today.
2.4 And now for your Shakespeare lesson…	pp 38–39	• Discover Tudor theatres and the plays performed in them. • Examine why William Shakespeare became one of the most famous English writers in the world.
2.5 Fashion victims	pp 40–41	• Describe what some rich Tudor women did to their skin to create the 'perfect face' and why.
2.6 Tudor Masterchef	pp 42–43	• Examine Tudor daily routines and meals. • Compare these routines with modern daily routines.
2.7A Tudor crime and punishment	pp 44–45	• Discover how some of the poorer people in Tudor times tried to make money. • Examine how Tudor society dealt with sturdy beggars. • Analyse why and how torture was used during the Tudor period.
2.7B Tudor crime and punishment	pp 46–47	
Chapter 2 Have you been learning?	pp 48–49	• Choose the correct answer from the given options for a quick recap. • Use correct spelling, punctuation and grammar to improve a paragraph. • Categorise historical vocabulary and check understanding.
Chapter 2 History skill: Similarity and difference	pp 50–51	• Understand the concept of similarity and difference. • Compare the diets of rich and poor people.
Chapter 2 Assessment: Similarity and difference	pp 52–53	• Categorise areas of life in Tudor times to compare. • Compare and contrast the lives of the upper and lower classes in Tudor times.

Chapter 2 Life in Tudor times

Links to the GCSE curriculum

This chapter provides some historical context to the following:

AQA: Elizabethan England c1568–1603

Edexcel: Early Elizabethan England 1558–1588

Edexcel: Crime and Punishment in Britain c1000–Present

OCR B: Crime and Punishment c1250–Present

OCR B: The Elizabethans 1580–1603

Eduqas: The Elizabethan Age 1558–1603

Eduqas: Changes in Entertainment and Leisure in Britain c500–Present

Eduqas: Changes in Crime and Punishment in Britain c500–Present

WJEC: The Elizabethan Age 1558–1603

WJEC: Changes in Crime and Punishment c1500–Present

Exam-style questions covered in this chapter

Exam board	Lesson/activity question location	Command words	History skills/concepts
AQA	2.2 Change and Continuity: 2	In what ways...	Change and continuity
	2.3 Knowledge and Understanding: 3	How far do you agree...	Knowledge and understanding
	2.6 Similarity and Difference: 1	Explain two ways... different	Similarity and difference
	2.7B Knowledge and Understanding: 2	Describe...	Knowledge and understanding
Edexcel	2.3 Knowledge and Understanding: 3	How far do you agree...	Knowledge and understanding
	2.4 Interpretation Analysis: 2	What is the main difference...	Interpretation analysis
	2.5 Change and Continuity: 2	Explain one way...	Change and continuity
OCR A	2.1B Significance: 3	How significant...	Significance
	2.3 Knowledge and Understanding: 3	How far do you agree...	Knowledge and understanding
	2.7B Knowledge and Understanding: 2	Describe...	Knowledge and understanding
OCR B	2.3 Knowledge and Understanding: 3	How far do you agree...	Knowledge and understanding

A brief history

2.1 A/B Who's who?

Now students have a clear understanding of Elizabethan England they must add the context of life in the Tudor period for different classes. You could take this lesson further by asking students to compare the feudal system from the medieval period to society in the sixteenth century. They can do this by looking at people's houses – changing architecture is a key theme of the Elizabethan period as a time of peace and a move away from fortified castles. Students are introduced to the key factor of population increase during the Elizabethan era and the reasons why the number of poor people increased in particular. Finally, they will evaluate the significance of the Poor Law.

2.2 What were Tudor schools like?

Students will love comparing their school day to that of an Elizabethan child in a grammar school. A good question to ask would be: How different was Elizabeth's school day to others at the time? The comparison of education in the towns and countryside, along with the different homes from the previous lesson, really build an understanding of life in this period. This lesson has the capacity for lots of fun when students look at how children were punished and how that compares to their school's conduct policy!

2.3 How did people have fun in Tudor times?

How people in different historical periods spent their leisure time is an excellent way of analysing the diverse history that one period can contain. When looking at the medieval period it was clear that the rich and the poor spent their time differently. Can students say the same for the Elizabethan period? Something extra that students will find interesting would be to compare today's pastimes and entertainments with those of the Elizabethans.

2.4 And now for your Shakespeare lesson...

A study of the development of Elizabethan theatre really shows the change in attitudes during the later 1500s. Changing attitudes to the poor and the grammar school system all led to the creation of the first public theatre, and then the Globe – this is an opportunity to help students understand the historic environment element of all GCSE History specifications. For higher ability students you may want to introduce the concept of patronage and the role of key individuals. Students evaluate interpretations of Shakespeare and the development of theatre. A nice link to the Elizabeth portraits lesson in Chapter 1 would be to look at the role of theatre as propaganda.

Timeline

1531
The poor are given a licence to beg.

1562
Queen Elizabeth catches smallpox, which leaves her face scarred.

1576
James Burbage opens the first successful permanent theatre.

1588
William Shakespeare starts to write plays. He will be remembered as the greatest English playwright.

1590s
Nearly every large town has a grammar school.

1601
Queen Elizabeth introduces her Poor Law. This will not be amended until the 1800s.

Chapter 2 Life in Tudor times

A brief history continued

2.5 Fashion victims

Elizabeth I is one of the most important English monarchs, so why are we obsessing about the way she looked when we didn't consider this for the kings? The reason is the extreme lengths to which she went to keep her looks. Furthermore, because she was the queen, rich women copied her. Poorer women, however, could not afford to spend time on their looks – they had work to do. When students analyse the sources they should be encouraged to consider the aims of Elizabeth's portraits and how this contradicts the reality. This lesson could also be a great change and continuity lesson looking at the risks women take today to look young.

2.6 Tudor Masterchef

If you want to understand society, look at the food that is eaten. The similarities and differences between the diets of the rich and the poor, and in their daily routines, adds further context to life in Elizabethan England. You could take the activities further by making links with Chapter 1 – this would add context to the exciting new foods for the rich by showing how the voyages of discovery led to cocoa, tea and coffee becoming part of daily life for some.

2.7 A/B Tudor crime and punishment

Students will thoroughly enjoy learning about all the different crimes, their names and Tudor punishments. It would be advantageous to link back to the closing of the monasteries under Henry VIII – importantly the impact this had on the poor – and then the population increase that occurred during Elizabeth's reign. This will allow richer explanations of the rise of poverty in the period. The key concept of law and order at this time was community policing – this will be a well-trodden path at GCSE so there are lots of case studies available for study. Students get the chance to think about why punishments today are so different from those in the Elizabethan period.

Further reading and links

For teachers:

- The historian Ruth Goodman's *Tudor Monastery Farm* programme (2013) offers some great examples of life in the Tudor period. Search for clips on the BBC website.
- The Historic Royal Palaces website has fantastic information about the Tudor court at Hampton Court Palace.
- English Heritage's website categorises Tudor history and then links it to different sites around the country. Go to 'Learn', then 'Tudors' under 'Story of England'.

For students:

- BBC Bitesize has excellent videos on specific aspects of the Tudor period. Students can search for 'Tudors BBC Bitesize' and find the video for the area they are interested in.
- Encourage students to find the historical fiction section in the school or local library. Reading a book set in the Tudor period (such as Philippa Gregory's *The Other Queen* (HarperCollins, 2008) about Mary, Queen of Scots or Jean Plaidy's *Queen of this Realm* (Hale, 1984) would be a good way for them to test their understanding of the period. Perhaps they might find some big mistakes!

Beyond the classroom

- As part of the latest KS3 History National Curriculum, students have to complete a local history study. There could be an ideal opportunity to complete this requirement by studying a local Tudor home.
- Students could design a poster advertising a performance of a Shakespeare play in London in the 1590s. They should remember to include the venue, date and time of the production, the entry cost, the name of the play and even a few lines from it to encourage people to attend.
- Students could research the different types of tricksters and 'sturdy beggars' and present their findings in a 'police briefing' to the rest of the class. They could think about how to advise people to avoid them and what punishments someone could expect to receive if they got involved in such crimes.
- Some Tudor torture equipment is kept on display in the Tower of London. Students could design an information leaflet for a young schoolchild on a torture chamber tour. They should include:
  - colourful pictures of torture instruments
  - facts about how they worked
  - background information on torture
  - an imaginative title, for example, 'The Tower's Terrible Torture Guide'.

Chapter 2 Answers guidance

Answers guidance

The answers provided here are examples, based on the information provided in the Student Book. There may be other factors which are relevant to each question, and students may draw on as much of their own knowledge as possible to give detailed and precise answers. There are also many ways of answering questions, including exam-style questions (for example, of structuring an essay). However, these exemplar answers should provide a good starting point.

2.1A Who's who?
STUDENT BOOK PAGES 30–31

Over to You

1a labourers
1b yeomen
2 Students may give one of the following: to show their wealth; they could afford larger homes; they needed servants so needed accommodation for them.
3 A = 3; B = 4; C = 1; D = 2

2.1B Who's who?
PAGES 32–33

Over to You

1a Gentleman: rich man who lived in a huge country house with lots of rooms. Owned lots of land and people paid him rent to farm it. Some gentlemen helped the monarch run the country. Although 'gentlemen' was the term used by William Harrison in his description, there were some women who had the same social status as gentlemen.
1b Citizen: person who lived in a town; in Tudor times this referred to a wealthy town person – often called merchants.
1c Yeoman: a farmer who owned or rented land; most were relatively wealthy although some were quite poor
1d Labourer: person who does manual work such as working in the fields.

2a
Class	Home	Picture	Description
Lady	B	B	3
Citizen	A	A	1
Yeoman	C	C	4
Labourer	D	D	2

2b Possible student answers:
- I think Picture B shows a lady because she looks very wealthy. For example, she is wearing very expensive clothing.
- I think Home B would belong to a lady or gentleman because the home is large and luxurious. Peasants lived in small huts and yeomen and citizens lived in slightly larger houses, but not of the same luxury as this.
- I think Description 3 is that of a lady because I know they owned lots of land and people paid them rent to farm it. Some ladies and gentlemen helped the king or queen to run the country – and this description clearly describes a rich person.

Significance

1 A pauper was someone who had no job and relied on charity.
2 Answers may include: The poor were put into four categories according to the 1601 Poor Law: pauper children (given work and taught a trade), sick paupers (looked after in special homes), fit paupers (given work – received food and drink as payment), lazy, idle paupers (whipped, then sent to a House of Correction). Also, poor people had to stay in their own town or village and not wander about. Each town or village had to appoint people to be 'Overseers of the Poor'. Their job was to collect money from people (a local tax, known as the 'poor rate') and make sure it was given to those in need.
3 Student answers will vary, but may include: The new Poor Law clearly made an impact on paupers at the time; for example, they were classified and treated according to their category. They had to stay in their own town or village and not wander about. The Poor Law also affected the people in the town – each town or village had to appoint people to be 'Overseers of the Poor' whose job was to collect money from people and make sure it was given to those in need. The community was also taxed. This system of helping the poor remained largely unchanged for around 200 years, so it shows it was a significant law that affected a lot of people for a long time.

2.2 What were Tudor schools like?
PAGES 34–35

Over to You

1a Birch: bundle of birch twigs or even a whip used to hit children.
1b Quill pen: pen made from a feather; dipped in ink to write.
1c Hornbook: flat, double-sided paddle, shaped like a table-tennis bat; used to help students read and write.
1d Grammar school: school that taught mainly Latin and Greek grammar.
2 Poor children were too busy working and couldn't afford to go to school.
3 Student answers will vary but should follow the basic outline of a school day shown in A and mention some of the key words and activities in the diagram.
4a Student answers will vary, but will probably mention not learning a passage from the Bible off by heart or losing your school cap.
4b Student answers will vary, but, for example, they may not get punished for learning the Bible off by heart because it is not something we do in schools today.

Revolution, Industry and Empire: Britain 1558–1901   63

Chapter 2 Answers guidance

Change and Continuity

1 Student answers will vary, depending on the school, but common similarities include being taught in classrooms, sitting at tables, learning maths and the teacher being in control. Differences might include more subject choice, larger, more inclusive schools and not being physically beaten.
2 Student answers will focus on the 'differences' element of Q1.

2.3 How did people have fun in Tudor times?
PAGES 36–37

Over to You

1a Shin-hacking, cudgels, blood sports, going to executions.
1b Cruel (blood sports), too dangerous (e.g. cudgels), no executions any more.
2 New, different type of entertainment – and they brought news from other places.

Knowledge and Understanding

1 Source A: Sword-fighting, playing shin-hacking, throwing javelins. Source B: horse races, hunting, fishing, hawking, duck-hunting, cock-fighting, tennis, bowling, billiards, chess, draughts, cards, dice, quizzes, stage plays, dancing, singing, handball, football, skittles, golf, cudgels, bear-baiting, bull-baiting, bow and arrow, throwing, bowling, leaping, wrestling and ringing of bells.
2a Examples include: cock-fighting, bull-baiting, bear-baiting, shin-hacking.
2b Examples include: stage plays, dancing, singing, handball, football, skittles, golf, bell ringing, chess.
3 Student answers will vary, but broadly speaking they should write that while many sports were indeed cruel and dangerous (and give an example), there were other sports that were not (and give examples).

2.4 And now for your Shakespeare lesson...
PAGES 38–39

Over to You

1a Burbage built the first successful permanent theatre, in Shoreditch, just north-east of London.
1b Students answers will vary, but may mention that theatre is expensive today (cheap enough for poorer people to go in Tudor times), more forms of entertainment available.
2 Students answers will vary, but may mention theatregoers would have had access to food and drink (pies, beer, fruit and soup), seen plays about human emotions (love, hate and jealousy), rich and poor mixed, open air theatre etc.

Interpretation Analysis

1 B says how useful Shakespeare is, how he helps us understand ourselves in the same way that science helps us understand the world. C says Shakespeare does not help us understand ourselves – and his plays can be 'baffling, tiring, frustrating'.
2 B is very positive about Shakespeare and think he helps humans understand more about themselves. C thinks this is not the case, is negative about him and finds him 'baffling, tiring and frustrating'.

2.5 Fashion victims
PAGES 40–41

Over to You

1 Rich Tudor women wanted to show their wealth and didn't want anyone to think that they had to spend time outside working and getting a tanned face.
2a Student answers will reflect the information on the page.
2b Student answers will reflect their own beauty regime.

Change and Continuity

1a Cochineal: crushed beetles mixed with egg, used to colour the cheeks and lips red. White lead: caused the skin to whiten in the day, which was the desired colour for a rich woman. Brick dust: mixed with honey and used to clean the teeth. Sulphur: chemical that lightened the hair. Mercury: silvery liquid metal that took off the top layer of skin for a smoother face.
1b Belladonna damaged vision; cochineal did little damage (but wasn't very nice); white lead poisoned the body; brick dust damaged teeth; sulphur made hair fall out; mercury also poisoned the body.
2 Student answers will vary but will explain one key difference – for example, in the modern world we don't use harmful chemicals such as mercury or lead in make-up.

2.6 Tudor Masterchef
PAGES 42–43

Over to You

1a An established pattern of behaviour that people follow most of the time.
1b Answers will vary but might mention that a difference might be the time they get up, and a similarity might be they still have several breaks – and their main meal of the day is in the evening, like country workers.
2 Answers will vary, but should describe the things they see in the picture (the way the table is set up, the children, the walls etc.) and the foods they eat. They will also mention some of the 'rules' and foods from Sources A and B.

Chapter 2 Answers guidance

Similarity and Difference ⭐

1 Answers will vary, but examples might include the fact that the rich ate more meat (beef, pork, mutton and fish would be offered, but more unusual foods such as roasted pigeon, seagulls, lobster and peacock might appear as well) and that the country workers ate a simple meal of bread, cheese and ale around 11am, while the rich ate a more substantial meal at 12pm.

2.7A Tudor crime and punishment
PAGES 44–45

Over to You

1 Henry VII banned rich barons from keeping private armies – lots of men lost their jobs as soldiers. Many large landowners started to keep sheep on their land rather than allow farmers to rent it and grow crops. This meant there were fewer jobs, so farmers and their families had to fend for themselves. Henry VIII closed monasteries, so an increasing number of poor people couldn't go to the local monks for handouts. Also, during Queen Elizabeth's reign there were bad harvests, so there were fewer jobs working in the fields.

2 Student leaflets will vary, but will reflect the information on pages 44–45.

2.7B Tudor crime and punishment
PAGES 46–47

Over to You

1 A watchman looked out for criminals, a Justice of the Peace investigated crimes, gathered information and held trials – but also looked after roads and bridges, checked alehouses and reported people who continually failed to attend church.

2a Answers will vary.

2b Answers will vary but may focus on the fact that we help the poor in today's society.

3a Spies were costly and took time to gather information.

3b Answers will vary.

Knowledge and Understanding ⭐

1 Answers will vary, but may include increasing numbers of sturdy beggars and they were thought to be behind all sorts of crimes.

2 Answers could include: Henry VII put beggars in stocks for three days, then sent them back to their birthplace or previous residence, whereas Edward VI also whipped them and branded them with a V (for vagabond) on the forehead. They were also made a slave for two years. If they offended again or tried to escape, they were executed (this law remained in force for three years before it was changed back to the 1531 law because it was viewed as too severe).

Chapter 2 Have you been learning?

Answers guidance

Chapter 2 Have you been learning?

Quick Knowledge Quiz

PAGE 48

1 **c** labourers
2 **a** paupers
3 **b** a quill pen
4 **c** cudgels
5 **a** strolling players
6 **c** James Burbage
7 **a** galleries
8 **a** cochineal
9 **b** pottage
10 **a** a Tudor con-artist or trickster

Literacy Focus

PAGE 49

Spelling, punctuation and grammar

1
- In Tudor society the poor people were known as paupers.
- Paupers were the most feared group in Tudor times.
- In 1601, a Poor Law was introduced that tried to help them.
- The law said that poor people had to stay in their own town or village and not wander from one place to another.
- Each town or village had to appoint people to be responsible for the poor.
- Their job was to collect money from people (a local tax, known as the 'poor rate') and make sure it was given to those in need.
- This job was the best job in Tudor society.
- This system of helping the poor remained largely unchanged for around 200 years.

Vocabulary check

2 **b** engineers
   c Business Studies
   d Blood Sports
   e Fortune
   f Shakespeare
   g lipstick
   h ale
   i vagabond

Revolution, Industry and Empire: Britain 1558–1901 **65**

Chapter 2 Assessment: Similarity and difference

Assessment summary

The assessments in this textbook have been carefully designed and tested with History teachers to support student progression throughout the course. This specific assessment is written to support Year 8 or Year 9 students in tackling questions relating to similarities and differences (diversity):

> ⭐ Explain two ways in which the lives of the upper and lower classes in Tudor times were similar. Explain two ways in which they were different. (20)

The task starts with students making notes on the features of upper and lower classes in Tudor society (Question 1). These notes will be used to categorise features for different groups of people (Question 2). This will then lead students to collate their notes and write an answer to the question explaining both similarities and differences (Question 3).

Students will be given prompts of what areas of life to look at and what groups of people to compare and contrast. They are also given sentence starters.

For the mark scheme, see page 68.

A note about the end-of-chapter assessments

There is an assessment for each Student Book chapter. Each is structured like a GCSE exam-style question, with scaffolding steps to support KS3 students. Each assessment has a total of 20 marks, and is designed to be completed in a typical lesson – each has been written with a time allowance of about 30 minutes.

There is a mark scheme for each assessment. You can choose how to give student outcomes: a mark out of 20; a percentage; a performance indicator (we use a three-stage indicator – 'Developing', 'Secure', 'Extending' – but you could adapt to match any performance indicators used in your school); or a GCSE grade indicator. To convert raw marks to a performance or GCSE grade indicator, use this table:

Raw marks			
0	1–6	7–13	14–20
GCSE grade (9–1) indicators*			
U	1–3	4–6	7–9
Performance indicator			
Ungraded	Developing	Secure	Extending

*Please appreciate that these are approximate grades based on grade boundaries from recent GCSE exam papers. If a student achieves a Grade 7 in one of these assessments, it is not the equivalent of a Grade 7 at GCSE. Instead it is an indicator of the grade the student could expect to get if they continue on their flight path through KS3 and GCSE. Please note:
- the raw-mark boundaries are based on but do not match precisely those for recent GCSE exam papers: this is because our assessments are focused around one exam-style question, likely to be done at the end of a chapter (topic) rather than at the end of the course. Secondly, we provide carefully considered scaffolded steps to allow KS3 students to tackle high level questions and gain confidence through the deliberate practice of building up detailed answers.
- the assessments for Student Book 3 are progressively more demanding in that they use higher-order command words and provide less scaffolded support – if you set one of them for Year 8 students, please take that into account when awarding GCSE grade indicators.

Entering student outcomes into the Kerboodle Markbook

The Kerboodle Markbook records scores and percentages to allow for quick comparison of performance. If you want to use the Markbook to record student outcomes, you will need to enter the appropriate values given in the raw marks row of the table above.

Chapter 2 Assessment: Similarity and difference

Links to GCSE

By the end of KS3, students should be familiar with the History skill of considering similarity and difference. At GCSE, some exam boards specifically ask students to explain and analyse change and continuity over and within time periods. For example:

AQA:
- Explain two ways in which… and… were similar/different. (8)

Edexcel:
- Explain one way in which… was/were different from/similar to… (4)

Links to KS3 History resources

Student Book

This assessment question links to these lessons:

2.1A/B Who's who?
2.2 What were Tudor schools like?
2.3 How did people have fun in Tudor times?
2.5 Fashion victims
2.6 Tudor Masterchef

Kerboodle

Support for this assessment question on Kerboodle:

RIE 2 Assessment presentation: Similarity and difference
RIE 2 Assessment worksheet (Core): Similarity and difference
RIE 2 Assessment worksheet (Foundation): Similarity and difference

Curriculum and Assessment Planning Guide

Support for this assessment question in this guide:

2 Assessment mark scheme – page 68
2 Assessment sample student answers – pages 69–70

Chapter 2 Assessment: Similarity and difference

Student name: _____   Date: _____

Mark scheme

Assessment bands	Marks	GCSE grade indicators*	I have...
	0	Ungraded	
Developing	1–6	1–3	☐ written a basic, very general comment about similarities or differences. ☐ included some information, but this is limited – and the key words are not used correctly.
Secure	7–13	4–6	☐ written a detailed comment about similarities *and* differences. ☐ included some accurate and relevant information, showing some knowledge and understanding of the topic. Most key words are used correctly. ☐ made some links between points.
Extending	14–20	7–9	☐ written a well-developed answer in which features of upper class and lower class lives in Tudor times are analysed to explain *both* similarities and differences. ☐ included specific, accurate information about the different areas of life to support the comparison, showing excellent knowledge and understanding. All key words are used correctly. ☐ clearly and logically structured my answer and made links between my points.

* IMPORTANT: These are approximate indicators devised using publicly available information on the new GCSE grades. They are designed to assist in the process of tracking and monitoring. They cannot and should not be used to replace teachers' professional judgement. Teachers should use their own discretion in applying them, taking into account the cumulative test scores of an individual student (rather than just one assessment point), and should refer to their institution's assessment policy.

Mark: _____

Comment:

68   Chapter 2 Life in Tudor times

Chapter 2 Assessment: Similarity and difference

Sample student answers

Assessment: Similarity and difference

STUDENT BOOK PAGES 52–53

> Explain two ways in which the lives of the upper and lower classes in Tudor times were similar. Explain two ways in which they were different. (20)

☆ Sample Developing band answer

There were many differences in Tudor classes and the way people lived at the time. One difference is the types of houses people lived in. For example, the lower classes lived in huts, but in towns the richer people lived in big houses with lots of rooms and servants. Poorer people mostly worked on the land or as carpenters while richer people got money from people.

☆ Sample Secure band answer

There were many differences in class and the way people lived in Tudor times. One of the main differences is the type of home people lived in. For example, people in the lower classes, such as ordinary labourers, lived in cottages made with straw roofs and mud, with only a little land to grow their own food. However, people in the upper classes lived in different types of homes. For example, a gentleman would live in a massive country house with plenty of land.

Another difference was the types of jobs that people did. For example, many people in the lower classes worked on the land as labourers or as skilled workers in the towns. The lower classes could make money if they were part of the yeoman class. The upper classes made money from people renting their land to farm on. The merchant class made money buying and selling goods, such as wool, jewellery, food, wine or cloth.

There were also some similarities in the way different classes lived, for example, in the ways people spent their free time. Both the upper and lower classes took part in going to the theatre.

Chapter 2 Assessment: Similarity and difference

⭐ Sample Extending band answer

There were many similarities in the way different classes lived in the Tudor period. One similarity is with diet. Both rich and poor got up at the same time each day to eat their breakfast, which mostly consisted of bread and ale. Both groups also ate three meals a day. However, there were also some differences. The rich would often add meat or fish to their meals – even breakfast – but the poor could not afford this and only had meat if they were able to catch a rabbit or fish. The rich might also eat more unusual foods such as roasted pigeon and peacock. Another difference is that although both groups ate three meals a day, the rich would have their larger meal in the afternoon while the poor would eat their large meal in the evening once they had finished their work – which was very physical – for the day.

The differences in diet link with the differences in how people spent their free time in the Tudor period. Hunting was still an activity just for the rich, as it had been for hundreds of years. However, one of the similarities of the Tudor period is that both classes enjoyed the theatre, which grew in popularity. Theatres like the Globe in London were built so that they had cheap seats in the 'pit' that the poor could buy for a penny, about the same as a loaf of bread. The rich could have fancier seats in covered areas known as galleries, but regardless of the seats, both rich and poor went to the same theatres and enjoyed the same plays as each other.

A key difference in this period was housing. Although people could enjoy the same pastimes, they went home to very different homes. The poorer classes lived in huts in the countryside with mud and straw roofs, with a small patch of land to grow their own food on. In the towns, the poorer skilled workers would live in small, cramped houses. However, the rich lived in big houses. If they were gentlemen or ladies, like Bess of Hardwick, they would live in country manors with lots of land and rooms. If they were part of the merchant class, they would live in spacious town houses with servants. It would be hard for someone in the Tudor period to work their way out of poverty and into one of the large country or town houses because the poor did not receive an education. Education was available only to the children of gentlemen or merchants.

Chapter 3 Exit the Tudors, enter the Stuarts

Links to KS3 History National Curriculum

This chapter introduces students to the Stuarts, another of Britain's most famous ruling dynasties, and introduces the idea of a United Kingdom. This content supports the compulsory area of the development of Church, state and society in Britain 1509–1745 in the latest KS3 History National Curriculum. There are a number of key historical terms highlighted in the chapter, such as the 'Divine Right of Kings', that are essential for students to learn. There are some wonderful sources for students to analyse, and a source-based enquiry encourages students to question accepted versions of events – such as the Gunpowder Plot – and make judgements based on evidence. By the end of the chapter students will also have had the opportunity to analyse causes of events (specifically the colonisation of America), argue for and/or against a particular point of view, use key historical terminology appropriately, and increase their knowledge and understanding of key historical events.

Skills and processes covered in this chapter

		Lesson/activity in the Student Book
History Skills	Knowledge and understanding	3.1 Over to You: 2a, 2b, 2c, 3a, 3b
		3.2 Over to You: 2, 4a, 4b
		3.3 Over to You: 1, 4
		3.4 Over to You: 1, 2
		3.5A Over to You: 1, 2a
		3.5B Over to You: 1a, 1b, 1c, 1d, 2a, 3
	Interpretations	3.1 Interpretation Analysis: 1, 2
	Sources	3.1 Over to You: 3a, 3b
		3.2 Over to You: 3; Source Analysis: 1, 2
		3.3 Over to You: 1, 2, 3, 4
		3.4 Source Analysis: 1, 2, 3, 4
		3.5B Over to You: 2a, 2b, 2c
		3 Assessment: Source analysis: 1, 2, 3, 4
	Significance	3.2 Over to You: 5
	Cause and consequence	3.1 Over to You: 1
		3.2 Over to You: 1, 4b
		3.3 Over to You: 2, 3
		3.4 Over to You: 3
		3.5A Over to You: 2b
		3.5B Over to You: 2b, 2c; Causation: 1
	Diversity/Similarity and difference	
	Change and continuity	
Literacy and Numeracy	Literacy	3.2 Over to You: 4b
		3.4 Over to You: 2
		3.5B Over to You: 3
		Have you been learning? Literacy Focus: 1

Revolution, Industry and Empire: Britain 1558–1901

Chapter 3 Exit the Tudors, enter the Stuarts

Lesson sequence

Lesson title	Student Book pages	Objectives
3.1 King James I: the scruffy Stuart!	pp 54–55	• Explain why the throne of England passed to the Scottish royal family. • Identify what England's new Scottish king believed about his 'Divine Right'.
3.2 Remember, remember the fifth of November!	pp 56–57	• Recall at least five accepted facts about the Gunpowder Plot. • Identify the role of key individuals in the story of the Gunpowder Plot.
3.3 History Mystery: Were the gunpowder plotters framed?	pp 58–59	• Assess evidence related to the Gunpowder Plot. • Justify whether you think Robert Cecil knew about the plot all along.
3.4 Which witch is which?	pp 60–61	• Outline why witchcraft was so widely believed in. • Identify how people were accused of witchcraft.
3.5A Why do Americans speak English?	pp 62–63	• Describe the early days of European settlement in America.
3.5B Why do Americans speak English?	pp 64–65	• Explain why the English settled in North America during the Stuart period.
Chapter 3 Have you been learning?	pp 66–67	• Choose the correct answer from the given options for a quick recap. • Use connectives to improve a historical narrative.
Chapter 3 History skill: Source analysis	pp 68–69	• Understand what the usefulness of a source is. • Recognise how to judge how useful a source is to a historian.
Chapter 3 Assessment: Source analysis	pp 70–71	• Assess the content and usefulness of two sources when exploring the views of James VI of Scotland/James I of England.

Links to the GCSE curriculum

This chapter provides some historical context to the following:

AQA: Migration, Empires and the People c790–Present
Edexcel: Crime and Punishment in Britain c1000–Present
Edexcel: Early Elizabethan England 1558–1588
OCR B: Crime and Punishment c1250–Present
OCR B: The Elizabethans 1580–1603
WJEC: Changes in Patterns of Migration c1500–Present

Exam-style questions covered in this chapter

Exam board	Lesson/activity question location	Command words	History skills/concepts
AQA	3.2 Source Analysis: 2	How useful…	Source analysis
	3.4 Source Analysis: 4	How useful…	Source analysis
Edexcel	3.2 Source Analysis: 2	How useful…	Source analysis
	3.4 Source Analysis: 4	How useful…	Source analysis
	3.5B Causation: 1	Explain two causes…	Cause and consequence
OCR A	3.1 Interpretation Analysis: 2	Explain why…	Interpretation analysis
	3.2 Source Analysis: 2	How useful…	Source analysis
	3.4 Source Analysis: 4	How useful…	Source analysis
OCR B	3.2 Source Analysis: 2	How useful…	Source analysis
	3.4 Source Analysis: 4	How useful…	Source analysis
WJEC	3.5B Over to You: 1	Complete the sentences…	Knowledge and understanding

A brief history

3.1 King James I: the scruffy Stuart!

The first order concepts of power and monarchy have been developed throughout the series and this lesson offers students an opportunity to build their knowledge by looking at James I. Religion is another concept that is developed throughout this chapter: in this lesson students will look at James's Bible and the reactions of some Protestants and Catholics to his actions. This lesson introduces the key term 'Divine Right of Kings'.

3.2 Remember, remember the fifth of November!

Students will enjoy learning about the Gunpowder Plot and the key people involved. The utility question will allow students to test their understanding and make a judgement about how useful the sources are. To help develop their judgements for the utility exercises an extra step could be to get students to record their opinion of the plot on a continuum or tension graph; this will help to explain judgements. A link back to Chapter 1 and Catholic plots against Elizabeth would be a good way to develop the concept of religion and extremism.

3.3 History Mystery: Were the gunpowder plotters framed?

This lesson gives students responsibility for their learning by using historical evidence. The questions provided will get them thinking and challenging evidence to come to a judgement. This could be a great time to build on the lesson by focusing on literacy, either through oracy, or by giving students some academic texts to read with judgements about the Gunpowder Plot and who may really have been behind it. The enquiry would lend itself well to presentations, an assembly or a class court. When students present their findings, they should try to show links between the different evidence. The activities provided are fantastic for consolidating learning.

Timeline

1584
Queen Elizabeth gives the explorer Walter Raleigh permission to start a colony in North America, but it is not successful.

1587
Raleigh starts a second colony in North America.

1603
Elizabeth dies.

1606
The Union Flag is adopted to symbolise James's rule over England and Scotland.

1604
James I commissions a new translation of the Bible, which is published in 1611 and is known as the King James Bible.

1604
Witchcraft becomes punishable by hanging.

1605
The Gunpowder Plot is successfully stopped after Robert Cecil uncovers the plan.

1607
Jamestown in Virginia, America is colonised.

1620
Puritans arrive in America. They had left England because James I refused to accept their religious views. They became known as the Pilgrim Fathers.

1625
James I dies and his son Charles I becomes king.

1640s
Matthew Hopkins, the 'Witch Finder General', starts witch hunts in East Anglia.

Revolution, Industry and Empire: Britain 1558–1901

Chapter 3 Exit the Tudors, enter the Stuarts

A brief history continued

3.4 Which witch is which?

Looking at James's rule with a focus on witches is sure to engage students. The superstitious nature of society under James and how this translates for women is grim but exciting to learn. As with Chapter 2 this lesson focuses on class differences as it was normally working or single women who would be accused of being witches. Some students may be able to link back to the punishments lesson in Chapter 2 and give a judgement on the nature of punishments for women accused of witchcraft. Using testimonies and accounts from witch trials would be a good way to put ordinary people back at the centre of history.

3.5A/B Why do Americans speak English?

This lesson, which provides great context for many aspects of British and American history, acts as one of the building blocks for new knowledge about empire, religion, conflict and revolution. It would be wise to revisit the content from Chapter 1 about the foundations of the British Empire under Elizabeth. The introduction of push and pull factors for immigration to America also builds on religion, economy and government as concepts. Therefore, it would be useful to encourage students to start keeping 'factor files' – this will be helpful later for GCSE Thematic studies. Students will undoubtedly enjoy considering the diverse history of American Indians and the impact colonisation had on them.

Further reading and links

For teachers:

- The History Extra website has two useful articles on witch-hunting. Suzannah Libscomb outlines some facts and myths about witch-hunting in the 1600s, while Tracy Borman discusses James's obsession with witchcraft. Search for both under 'witches'.

- Look through the history department cupboards to find some A Level resources on James I. Use them to find out more about his spending and his relationship with the people of Scotland. Consider what they think about his religious policies.

- Read about the use of the Guy Fawkes mask in today's popular uprisings. This could be a good way to develop cultural capital by sharing information about current protest groups and their methods, giving students more context on current affairs and how they link with the history they study.

For students:

- An article from the History Extra website on *Macbeth* and James's witch hunts will help students make links between English and History lessons and develop context in their writing. Search for 'Macbeth King James'.

- Students could read Tracey Borman's *The King's Witch* (Hodder & Stoughton, 2018), a novel about a female healer who serves Elizabeth and gets caught up in the political events at James's court.

Beyond the classroom

- Students could design their own flag to represent the union of England and Scotland under one king. Remind them, though – both the English and the Scots would have to like it!

- Students could imagine that Witch Finder General Matthew Hopkins is visiting their town. They should design a booklet detailing the town's efforts to find witches, and include information about spotting witches, successful convictions and drawings of their witch trials.

- After researching the US holiday of Thanksgiving, students could create a cartoon or Thanksgiving cards, explaining the real meaning of the holiday. They could consider the accuracy of historical interpretations of early settlers in North America and American Indians by watching a film such as Disney's *Pocahontas* (1995).

- Students could research Catholic interpretations of Bonfire Night and create a presentation to explain why not everyone celebrates it. They could then make a judgement about whether we should celebrate something that has – for some – anti-Catholic feeling.

- Have a day with the English and Drama departments where students create presentations about the importance of the witch trials on literature and theatre. As good historians they should make sure they support their presentations with evidence.

Chapter 3 Answers guidance

Answers guidance

The answers provided here are examples, based on the information provided in the Student Book. There may be other factors which are relevant to each question, and students may draw on as much of their own knowledge as possible to give detailed and precise answers. There are also many ways of answering questions, including exam-style questions (for example, of structuring an essay). However, these exemplar answers should provide a good starting point.

3.1 King James I: the scruffy Stuart!
STUDENT BOOK PAGES 54–55

Over to You

1. He was Elizabeth's nearest blood relative (third cousin).
2a. The belief that God has chosen the king, and that the king was answerable to no one except God.
2b. Answers may vary but, for example, it meant that James could use God as his reason for all his decisions and he was not answerable to Parliament.
2c. It meant Parliament had no say in the running of the country so long as the king used his 'divine right' and ruled as he wished. And if Parliament went against the king, it may be accused of going against God's wishes.
3a. Answers will vary but should focus on the beautiful clothing and jewels, crown etc.
3b. Answers will vary but should focus on the fact that kings wanted to portray a particular image of themselves, so they closely controlled what was painted, and the portrait painter wished to please the king etc. Some students might draw on their previous knowledge of Elizabeth's portraits.

Interpretation Analysis

1. Answers may include James has poor manners, is fat and foolish, for example.

2. Answers may vary but, for example, the writer has met him, so may be reflecting what he saw/thinks – or he may not like James (he was sacked by him) so wishes to portray a negative view of him. Also, the Stuarts were no longer in power at this time, so he may be trying to please the new regime – or simply being honest with his views.

3.2 Remember, remember the fifth of November!
PAGES 56–57

Over to You

1. They hoped to seize James's young daughter, Elizabeth, and place her on the throne instead, and bring her up as a Catholic.
2. King James – the king they tried to assassinate; Robert Catesby – strict Catholic leader of plot; Thomas and Robert Winter, Christopher and John Wright, Thomas Percy – fellow plotters; Guido Fawkes – was going to set off the gunpowder; Lord Monteagle – warning note sent to him; Robert Cecil – king's chief adviser who received note.
3. Answers may include: Don't attend Parliament, devise an excuse because it will receive a terrible blow.
4a. As a warning for others – and to punish their wrongdoing.
4b. Answers will vary but will mention the detail of them being dragged through the streets of London, hanged until they were nearly dead, cut down, cut open, and their insides pulled out and burned on a fire in front of them.
5. On 5 November many people attend bonfires, sometimes burning models of Guy Fawkes (often made of clothing stuffed with straw) to remember the Gunpowder Plot. There are also displays of fireworks.

Source Analysis

1. A shows the main plotters, all in conversation, probably planning the assassination of James. C shows the punishments of the surviving plotters: they are being hung, drawn and quartered.
2. Answers will vary, but students may write that both are useful because they give some factual detail – for example, A gives us names and C shows us the punishments/consequences for the plotters. A is not so useful on how the plotters looked because the artist never saw them, but the fact that it was created by a Dutch publisher and appeared in the Netherlands shows that there was wide interest in this story.

3.3 History Mystery: Were the Gunpowder Plotters framed?
PAGES 58–59

Over to You

1. Answers will vary but evidence of the plotters being framed might include, for example: John Whynniard, a friend of Robert Cecil, renting out the cellar – and then Whynniard dying suddenly and unexpectedly on the morning of 5 November. Also, the gunpowder records for 1604 being missing might indicate a 'cover up' as to who let the plotters have gunpowder.
2. Answers will vary but may include that the cellars weren't searched straight away, but it was left until the last minute – which is more dramatic. Also, evidence H indicated that Cecil knew all along because the other plotters were captured *before* Fawkes confessed to their existence.

Revolution, Industry and Empire: Britain 1558–1901   75

Chapter 3 Answers guidance

3 Answers will vary but might point out that Fawkes's confession was obtained under torture, so he was more likely to say what was needed to stop the pain. Also, Thomas Winter's confession was written out by Cecil.

4 Answers will vary, but will weigh up the evidence from their investigation.

3.4 Which witch is which?
PAGES 60–61

Over to You

1 Student facts will vary, but may include Hopkins's name, main profession, location where he mainly worked, who he targeted, results.

2 Student booklets will include the criteria detailed in the question.

3 Because the king believed in witchcraft, so they were interested in what the king was interested in. Also, there were things about their world they couldn't explain, so blamed witches and evil spirits.

Source Analysis

1 A woman's hands were tied and she was thrown into a pond that would have been 'blessed' by a priest. It was thought that if the accused floated, they must be a witch because the 'pure' water didn't want them. They would be hanged. If they sank, the 'pure' water wanted them so they must be pure themselves and couldn't possibly be a witch – they were declared innocent.

2 Students will not think it was a fair test because the accused died in both outcomes.

3 They are familiars so they have been drawn to illustrate what to look out for.

4 Students will mention the fact that A is useful for illustrating the technique of 'swimming', but also the fact that this was accepted at the time so shows the level of suspicion and fear of witches. B, again, is useful because it shows information about witch-hunting, but students may point to the fact that it was a book, which shows how serious people were about witchcraft – and might link it to the fact that books like this sold really well.

3.5A Why do Americans speak English?
PAGES 62–63

Over to You

1 1492 – Christopher Columbus becomes first recorded European to reach the Americas. He was an Italian who was sponsored by Spain
1584 – Queen Elizabeth gives permission to Walter Raleigh to start a colony in North America
1585 – First attempted settlement in North America fails
1587 – Second settlement established
1590 – Support ships arrive at second settlement, but settlers had disappeared
1607 – Jamestown colony established
1620 – Pilgrim Fathers settlement

2a Pilgrim Fathers or Founding Fathers are sometimes referred to as the founding fathers of America – the people who established America as a strong English colony.

2b Answers will vary, but may include: A father is often viewed as a figure that begins something – so this group is seen as fathers because they established a strong colony, and pilgrims because they were making a religious journey.

3.5B Why do Americans speak English?
PAGES 64–65

Over to You

1a Squanto.
1b Thanksgiving.
1c 13.
1d Tobacco, cotton, sugar.
2a Food: meal, beef, pork, butter, cheese. Clothing: shoes, boots, stockings (socks), shirts, handkerchiefs. Tools: hammer, spade, shovel, axe, wood hook.
2b Some couldn't afford the items.
2c They were building their own settlement, needed food to survive.
3 Answers will vary but students should mention the opportunities there to make money (growing tobacco, cotton and sugar, which will be imported to Britain); religious freedom; chance for a new life; abundance of resources – students might refer to Source A here.

Causation

1 Answers will vary but may mention the economic opportunities in North America to make money (growing tobacco, cotton and sugar, which will be imported to Britain). Also the religious freedom some (such as the Puritans) had not experienced in Britain.

Chapter 3 Have you been learning?

Answers guidance

Chapter 3 Have you been learning?

Quick Knowledge Quiz

PAGE 66

1 **b** 1603
2 **c** James VI
3 **b** Divine Right of Kings
4 **a** Robert Catesby
5 **c** Lord Monteagle
6 **b** Holbeche House
7 **a** witchcraft
8 **b** Walter Raleigh
9 **a** Pilgrim Fathers
10 **b** New Amsterdam

Literacy Focus

PAGE 67

Linking things together

1 Answers will vary, but they may write: In October 1605, a man called Lord Monteagle received a note warning him not to attend Parliament. Monteagle took the note to Robert Cecil, the king's chief advisor, **and then** Cecil took the letter to the king. **Consequently**, in the early hours of 5 November, the cellars below Parliament were searched. Guy Fawkes was found there next to the gunpowder. **Firstly**, he was brought before King James. **Then** he refused to answer any questions. **Subsequently**, the king ordered Fawkes to be taken to the Tower of London and tortured. The other plotters ran away to Holbeche House in the Midlands. They tried to dry out some of their wet gunpowder near a fire **and** it blew up. The noise from the explosion alerted the king's troops. **This led to** a shoot-out. Catesby and Percy were killed by the same bullet. The surviving plotters were arrested **and** they were taken to London.

Revolution, Industry and Empire: Britain 1558–1901

Chapter 3 Assessment: Source analysis

Assessment summary

The assessments in this textbook have been carefully designed and tested with History teachers to support student progression throughout the course. This specific assessment is written to support Year 8 or Year 9 students in tackling questions relating to analysing sources.

> 1. What can Source A tell us about the views of James VI of Scotland/James I of England? (10)
> 2. What can Source B tell us about the views of James VI of Scotland/James I of England? (10)

▼ **SOURCE A** Adapted from a speech by King James VI of Scotland (also King James I of England), at Whitehall Palace, London in March 1609.

> 'Monarchy is the greatest thing upon earth. Kings are rightly called gods since, just like God, they have power of life and death over all their people in all things. They are accountable to God only... so it is a crime for anyone to argue about what a king can do.'

▼ **SOURCE B** An image from a book written in 1597 by King James VI of Scotland/James I of England called *Daemonologie*. The book covers James' ideas on magic, sorcery and witchcraft. The image shows four suspected witches kneeling in front of the king at a witch trial in Scotland in 1590.

78 Chapter 3 Exit the Tudors, enter the Stuarts

Chapter 3 Assessment: Source analysis

After considering the content (Question 1), caption (Question 2) and context (Question 3) of each source about King James VI/I, students will come to a conclusion (Question 4) as to what each source tells us about the views of James VI of Scotland/James I of England.

Sample sentence starters are provided to support students in tackling this question.

For the mark scheme, see page 81.

A note about the end-of-chapter assessments

There is an assessment for each Student Book chapter. Each is structured like a GCSE exam-style question, with scaffolding steps to support KS3 students. Each assessment has a total of 20 marks, and is designed to be completed in a typical lesson – each has been written with a time allowance of about 30 minutes.

There is a mark scheme for each assessment. You can choose how to give student outcomes: a mark out of 20; a percentage; a performance indicator (we use a three-stage indicator – 'Developing', 'Secure', 'Extending' – but you could adapt to match any performance indicators used in your school); or a GCSE grade indicator. To convert raw marks to a performance or GCSE grade indicator, use this table:

Raw marks			
0	1–6	7–13	14–20
GCSE grade (9–1) indicators*			
U	1–3	4–6	7–9
Performance indicator			
Ungraded	Developing	Secure	Extending

*Please appreciate that these are approximate grades based on grade boundaries from recent GCSE exam papers. If a student achieves a Grade 7 in one of these assessments, it is not the equivalent of a Grade 7 at GCSE. Instead it is an indicator of the grade the student could expect to get if they continue on their flight path through KS3 and GCSE. Please note:
- the raw-mark boundaries are based on but do not match precisely those for recent GCSE exam papers: this is because our assessments are focused around one exam-style question, likely to be done at the end of a chapter (topic) rather than at the end of the course. Secondly, we provide carefully considered scaffolded steps to allow KS3 students to tackle high level questions and gain confidence through the deliberate practice of building up detailed answers.
- the assessments for Student Book 3 are progressively more demanding in that they use higher-order command words and provide less scaffolded support – if you set one of them for Year 8 students, please take that into account when awarding GCSE grade indicators.

Entering student outcomes into the Kerboodle Markbook

The Kerboodle Markbook records scores and percentages to allow for quick comparison of performance. If you want to use the Markbook to record student outcomes, you will need to enter the appropriate values given in the raw marks row of the table above.

Chapter 3 Assessment: Source analysis

Links to GCSE

By the end of KS3, students should be familiar with the History skill of analysing sources. At GCSE, most exam boards specifically ask students to analyse sources. For example:

AQA:

- How useful is Source A to a historian studying…? Explain your answer using Source A and your contextual knowledge. (8)
- How useful are Sources B and C to a historian studying…? Explain your answer using Sources B and C and your contextual knowledge. (12)

Edexcel:

- How useful are Sources A and B for an enquiry into…? Explain your answer, using Sources A and B and your knowledge of the historical context. (8)

OCR B:

- How useful are Source B and Interpretations C and D for a historian studying…? In your answer, refer to the source and the two interpretations as well as your own knowledge. (15)
- What can Source A tell us about…? (7)

Eduqas:

- What can be learnt from Sources A and B about…? (4)

WJEC:

- What can be learnt from Sources A and B about…? (4)

Links to KS3 History resources

Student Book

This assessment question links to these lessons:

3.1 *King James I: the scruffy Stuart!*
3.2 *Remember, remember the fifth of November!*
3.4 *Which witch is which?*
3.5A/B *Why do Americans speak English?*

Kerboodle

Support for this assessment question on Kerboodle:

RIE 3 *Assessment presentation: Source analysis*
RIE 3 *Assessment worksheet (Core): Source analysis*
RIE 3 *Assessment worksheet (Foundation): Source analysis*

Curriculum and Assessment Planning Guide

Support for this assessment question in this guide:

3 *Assessment mark scheme – page 81*
3 *Assessment sample student answers – pages 82–83*

Chapter 3 Assessment: Source analysis

Student name: _____   Date: _____

Mark scheme

Assessment bands	Marks	GCSE grade indicators*	I have...
	0	Ungraded	
Developing	1–6	1–3	☐ written one thing learned from each source from these categories: content, caption and context. ☐ given a basic description of what each source tells me about the king's views.
Secure	7–13	4–6	☐ written some (perhaps two of the three – but not all) of the boxes for each source relating to content, caption and context. ☐ summarised what each source tells me about the king's views, showing relevant supporting knowledge. NOTE: Marks can only be given to information about the limitations of a source (what the source does not tell you) if you have clearly explained how it limits your understanding of the topic.
Extending	14–20	7–9	☐ described two things learned from each source from each of these categories: content and caption, context. ☐ summarised what each source tells me about the king's views, with lots of accurate, relevant supporting knowledge. NOTE: Marks can only be given to information about the limitations of a source (what the source does not tell you) if you have clearly explained how it limits your understanding of the topic.

*IMPORTANT: These are approximate indicators devised using publicly available information on the new GCSE grades. They are designed to assist in the process of tracking and monitoring. They cannot and should not be used to replace teachers' professional judgement. Teachers should use their own discretion in applying them, taking into account the cumulative test scores of an individual student (rather than just one assessment point), and should refer to their institution's assessment policy.

Mark: _____

Comment:

Revolution, Industry and Empire: Britain 1558–1901

Chapter 3 Assessment: Source analysis

Sample student answers

Assessment: Source analysis

STUDENT BOOK PAGES 70–71

> 1 What can Source A tell us about the views of James VI of Scotland/James I of England? (10)
> 2 What can Source B tell us about the views of James VI of Scotland/James I of England? (10)

Sample Developing band answer

Source A: One thing I can learn from the content of Source A about the views of James VI/I is that he believed that he was put on the throne by God and only had to answer to God – not his subjects.

Source B: One thing I can learn from the content of Source B about James VI/I is that James believed in witches, and his view was that they should be punished.

Sample Secure band answer

Source A: One thing I can learn from the content of Source A about the views of James VI/I is that he believed that he was put on the throne by God and only had to answer to God – not his subjects. One thing I already know is that James believed in the Divine Right of Kings, and when Parliament did not do what he wanted, he sent them away for 10 years. This tells us that James's view was that he could do no wrong and only had to answer to God, not his subjects.

Source B: One thing I can learn from the content of Source B about James VI/I is that James believed in witches, and his view was that they should be punished. One thing I already know is that James passed strict laws in 1604 which made witchcraft a criminal offence, and the punishment was hanging. Another thing I know is that to find out if someone was a witch, the authorities would 'swim' them. This resulted in death either way.

Chapter 3 Assessment: Source analysis

⭐ Sample Extending band answer

Source A: The content of Source A tells us that James I believed in the Divine Right of Kings. He states that monarchy is the greatest thing on earth, and kings are viewed as gods. This was part of a speech James gave to Parliament in 1609, which is after the Gunpowder Plot – this could mean James was trying to remind Parliament who was boss. He also wanted to ask them for money, which they didn't want to give him. One thing I already know about James is that he needed money from Parliament, but when they refused he sent them away for 10 years. This matches what the source says about him being answerable to God only, because he did what he wanted when it came to ruling the country. He gave his friends important jobs and spent all the money, leaving the country bankrupt. Another thing I know about the view of James is that he wanted everyone to follow his religion, so he insisted that people worship using the Bible he translated.

Source B: One thing I learned from Source B about the views of King James is that he believed in witchcraft. Another thing I learned is that he believed witches should be punished. The source is the front cover of a book he wrote in 1597, when he was the King of Scotland only. It was written after witch trials in Scotland. Having this picture for the front cover sent a clear message that James disagreed with witchcraft. One thing I already know about the views of James is that he wanted the book to act as a guide on how to catch witches. He spoke about them having familiars. Another thing I know is that he believed that witches should be placed in water, to find out if they were a witch, and that if found guilty, they would be hanged. This doesn't match the source, as it only shows someone holding a stick to beat the witches, and the source was created before the 1604 law was passed, which made it a crime to be a witch. Source B tells us that James believed in witchcraft and that he believed it was something that should be punished.

Chapter 4 From Civil War to Commonwealth

Links to KS3 History National Curriculum

The causes and events of the English Civil War covered in this chapter were crucial in establishing the type of government we have today, and are mentioned in the latest KS3 History National Curriculum. The role of the military is a key aspect of this chapter with terminology central to learning. Establishing cause and consequence – a key History skill – is addressed through considering the outbreak of the Civil War and Charles's fate. By the end of the chapter, students should be aware that most events have several causes and consequences (short- and long-term).

The Interregnum (including Cromwell in Ireland) and the Restoration are example topics in the National Curriculum. The concepts, content and historical terminology can be quite challenging, so these lessons break the topics down simply and logically while giving students plenty of opportunity to demonstrate understanding and come to their own conclusions.

Skills and processes covered in this chapter

		Lesson/activity in the Student Book
History Skills	Knowledge and understanding	4.1 Over to You: 1a, 1b, 1c, 2
		4.2 Over to You, 1a, 1b, 1c, 1d, 2a, 2b, 3; Knowledge and Understanding: 1, 2
		4.3 Over to You: 2; Source Analysis: 1
		4.4 Over to You: 2, 3
		4.5 Over to You: 3c
		4.6 Over to You: 1a, 1b, 2a, 3a, 3b
		4.7 Over to You: 1a, 1b, 1c, 2, 3
		4.8 Over to You: 2a, 2b, 2c, 2d
		Have you been learning? Quick Knowledge Quiz: 1, 2, 3, 4, 5, 6, 7, 8, 9, 10
	Interpretations	4.3 Over to You: 3
		4.7 Interpretation Analysis: 1, 2
	Sources	4.3 Over to You: 1, 3; Source Analysis: 1, 2
		4.5 Over to You: 2a, 2b, 3a, 3b
	Significance	4.8 Significance: 1
	Cause and consequence	4.1 Over to You: 3a, 3b, 3c, 3d, 3e, 3f; Causation: 1, 2, 3
		4.3 Over to You: 1, 4
		4.4 Over to You: 1
		4.5 Over to You: 1a, 1b; Causation: 1a, 1b, 1c, 1d, 1e, 2
		4.6 Over to You: 2b, 2c
		4.8 Over to You: 1, 3
		4 Assessment: Write a narrative account (causation): 1, 2, 3, 4
	Diversity/Similarity and difference	
	Change and continuity	4.6 Change: 1a, 1b, 2
Literacy and Numeracy	Literacy	4.2 Over to You: 3
		4.4 Over to You: 2, 3
		4.7 Over to You: 3
		Have you been learning? Literacy Focus: 1

Chapter 4 From Civil War to Commonwealth

Lesson sequence

Lesson title	Student Book pages	Objectives
4.1 Why did the English start fighting each other?	pp 72–73	• Define the term 'civil war'. • Examine the causes of the English Civil War.
4.2 Match of the day: Roundheads versus Cavaliers	pp 74–75	• Examine which sections of society supported each side in the Civil War. • Describe the different types of soldiers and summarise how they fought.
4.3 What was new about the New Model Army?	pp 76–77	• Summarise why Parliament needed to improve its army. • Examine the impact of Parliament's new fighting force.
4.4 Why was King Charles I sentenced to death?	pp 78–79	• Discover how and why King Charles I was put on trial. • Analyse the key events of the trial.
4.5 Charlie for the chop!	pp 80–81	• Examine the details of Charles I's execution. • Evaluate sources relating to the execution.
4.6 Cromwell: the man who banned Christmas	pp 82–83	• Define the words 'republic' and 'interregnum'. • Discover how the country changed under Cromwell. • Explain why Christmas celebrations were banned.
4.7 Why does Cromwell divide opinion?	pp 84–85	• Examine a variety of opinions about Oliver Cromwell. • Justify the sort of reputation you think Cromwell deserves.
4.8 The monarchy returns – but what happened to Cromwell's head?	pp 86–87	• Explain how England became a monarchy once more. • Discover how and why King Charles II sought revenge after 1660.
Chapter 4 Have you been learning?	pp 88–89	• Choose the correct answer from the given options for a quick recap. • Write down the important words from sentences to practice note-taking.
Chapter 4 History skill: Write a narrative account (causation)	p 90	• Examine how to write a narrative account.
Chapter 4 Assessment: Write a narrative account (causation)	p 91	• Construct a narrative account that explains the key factors that caused the English Civil War.

Chapter 4 From Civil War to Commonwealth

Links to the GCSE curriculum

This chapter provides some historical context to the following:

AQA: Power and the People c1170–Present

AQA: Restoration England 1660–1685

Edexcel: Warfare and British Society c1250–Present

OCR A: Monarchy and Democracy in Britain c1000–2014

OCR A: War and British Society c790–c2010

OCR A: Personal Rule to Restoration 1629–1660

Eduqas: The Development of Warfare in Britain c500–Present

WJEC: The Development of Warfare c1250–Present

Exam-style questions covered in this chapter

Exam board	Lesson/activity question location	Command words	History skills/concepts
AQA	4.2 Knowledge and Understanding: 2	Describe…	Knowledge and understanding
	4.3 Source Analysis: 2	How useful…	Source analysis
	4.6 Change: 2	In what ways…	Change and continuity
Edexcel	4.1 Causation: 3	Explain why…	Cause and consequence
	4.2 Knowledge and Understanding: 2	Describe…	Knowledge and understanding
	4.3 Source Analysis: 2	How useful…	Source analysis
	4.5 Causation: 2	The main reason… How far do you agree…	Cause and consequence
	4.7 Interpretation Analysis: 2	How far do you agree… interpretation…	Interpretation analysis
	4.8 Over to You: 3	Explain why…	Cause and consequence
	4.3 Source Analysis: 2	How useful…	Source analysis
	4.8 Over to You: 3	Explain why…	Cause and consequence
	4.8 Significance: 1	How significant…	Significance
OCR B	4.3 Source Analysis: 2	How useful…	Source analysis
Eduqas	4.7 Interpretation Analysis: 2	How far do you agree… interpretation…	Interpretation analysis
	4.8 Over to You: 3	Explain why…	Cause and consequence
WJEC	4.2 Over to You: 1a, 1b, 1c, 1d	Complete the sentences…	Knowledge and understanding
	4.7 Interpretation Analysis: 2	How far do you agree… interpretation…	Interpretation analysis
	4.8 Over to You: 3	Explain why…	Cause and consequence

ps
A brief history

4.1 Why did the English start fighting each other?

This chapter has something for everyone. The first lesson introduces students to a cross-section of people and opinions to set the scene for this turbulent period. The key terms of 'civil war', 'Royalist' and 'Parliamentarian' are crucial in allowing students to build on the concepts of monarchy and government, and their changing relationship. To develop this further students should link back to their first encounter with the Divine Right of Kings in Chapter 3. Straight away students have to differentiate between varying opinions of Charles depending on the economy or religion. To consolidate they will define key words and categorise these opinions, eventually explaining why the Civil War started.

4.2 Match of the day: Roundheads versus Cavaliers

War and conflict have been a theme throughout this whole KS3 series but this is the first civil war that students have looked at. There are class and regional distinctions that can be made with regard to Royalists and Parliamentarians. The descriptions of the different soldiers such as pikemen and musketeers would suit a 'Top Trumps' style activity to test and consolidate the specifics, encouraging students to include detail in their work in preparation for GCSE. This lesson has a healthy focus on the use of key terms when writing about the Civil War.

4.3 What was new about the New Model Army?

This lesson focuses on the turning point of the Civil War – the creation of the New Model Army and its victories at Marston Moor and Naseby. Furthermore, students will consider the importance of the role of the individual in the outcome of the war with relation to the part played by Cromwell. Considering the laws of the New Model Army is a great way to reveal its discipline in comparison to the Cavaliers. The activities allow students to make a judgement about the New Model Army and then analyse the usefulness of sources about it.

4.4 Why was King Charles I sentenced to death?

For narrative history this lesson is hard to beat! Although students know that Charles is executed they will relish the detail of MPs being stopped from entering Parliament to vote on Charles's fate and the fact that so few judges attended his trial. Students will then be expected to draw inferences about Charles's attitude during the trial, thinking about why he behaved the way he did.

Timeline

1625
Charles I becomes king after James dies.

1629–1640
Charles rules without Parliament.

December 1641
Parliament sends a long list of complaints to the king.

1642
Charles raises his royal standard in Nottingham and starts the English Civil War.

1642
The Battle of Edgehill ends in a draw between the Parliamentarians and the Royalists.

1644
The Battle of Marston Moor is a major Parliamentarian victory thanks to the New Model Army.

1645
The Parliamentarians win the Battle of Naseby.

1646–47
Charles surrenders to the Scots who hand him over to Parliament. He later escapes from the New Model Army.

August 1648
Charles is recaptured after fighting the Second Civil War.

1649
Charles is put on trial and found guilty of treason. He is executed by having his head chopped off.

1653
Cromwell dismisses Parliament and becomes Lord Protector.

1660
The monarchy is restored when Charles II becomes king.

Chapter 4 From Civil War to Commonwealth

A brief history continued

4.5 Charlie for the chop!

Charles's execution is at the centre of this lesson but the focus is around using evidence and making judgements. A good way to build on this lesson, to ensure students are supporting opinions of Charles, is to get them to categorise all the causes for the Civil War using religion, economy and politics, then mark next to them whether they think Charles's actions were a crime against the country. This will help them decide what was the main reason for his execution and, importantly, if he was guilty of treason.

4.6 Cromwell: the man who banned Christmas

Cromwell is one of the most divisive figures in British history. This lesson gives students the chance to consider him as an individual and his impact. The focus on the second order concept of change is developed by looking at how people's lives change because of a change of government and religious policy. The new key words 'republic' and 'Interregnum' will be built upon at the end of the lesson when students evaluate Cromwell's role as Lord Protector and the creation of the role of Major-Generals.

4.7 Why does Cromwell divide opinion?

This lesson allows students to explore different opinions of Cromwell. They will use evidence to make their own opinions of him, drawing on the impact of his changes from the previous lesson. As this lesson deepens contextual understanding, students are introduced to a piece of academic writing and are then asked to analyse this interpretation. This could take the shape of a literacy lesson for some students: by using the word gap guidance in this Guide you could develop vocabulary, writing style, and inference skills. Getting students to explain how evidence is used and why contrasting arguments and interpretations of the past have been constructed supports the aims of the KS3 History National Curriculum.

4.8 The monarchy returns – but what happened to Cromwell's head?

The chapter ends with the gruesome story of Cromwell's head and its long journey to a final resting place. The fascinating events of the Restoration show the ever-changing relationship between the monarchy and Parliament (much like *4.1 Why did the English start fighting each other?*), allowing students to build on their understanding of the concepts. After they have written about the events of the Restoration students will be expected to explain the significance of the Interregnum.

Further reading and links

For teachers:

- The National Archives have excellent resources on women and the Civil War. Their sources and case studies bring the story to life by looking at ordinary people, not just the key (male) players. Navigate to 'Education' and then the 'Early modern 1485–1750' section and scroll to find resources about 'Women and the English Civil Wars'.

- To understand the different historiography surrounding Cromwell look on the History Today website for an article entitled 'Cromwell and the Historians' by D. H. Pennington (1958). This will give you more of an insight into interpretations and provide further details of Cromwell's actions. Search on the author's name.

For students:

- BBC Bitesize KS3 History section has many clips on Cromwell and the Civil War.

- Reading *Horrible Histories: Slimy Stuarts* by Terry Deary (Scholastic, 2016) will allow students to consolidate their knowledge and understanding of this topic.

- www.johndclare.net has some excellent sources, interpretations and visuals on the causes of the Civil War. Choose 'A United Kingdom' in the KS3 portal, and then 'A Kingdom Divided'.

Beyond the classroom

- Get students to research and create a map of local links to the Civil War.

- Students could research all of the statues in Parliament Square, including that of Cromwell – who do they think should be there? They could present this in a school assembly and then run a student poll about which figures should be there.

- Students could research a local battle and create a script for a tour guide. It should focus on causes, key events and consequences. They could use the National Trust or English Heritage sites to help them.

Chapter 4 Answers guidance

Answers guidance

The answers provided here are examples, based on the information provided in the Student Book. There may be other factors which are relevant to each question, and students may draw on as much of their own knowledge as possible to give detailed and precise answers. There are also many ways of answering questions, including exam-style questions (for example, of structuring an essay). However, these exemplar answers should provide a good starting point.

4.1 Why did the English start fighting each other?
STUDENT BOOK PAGES 72–73

Over to You

1a Royalist: supporter of the king.
1b Parliamentarian: supporter of Parliament.
1c Divine right: the idea that God has appointed the king and he can rule as he likes in God's name.
2 Answers may include: Ordinary war is usually fought between two nations, whereas a civil war is fought between two groups in the same nation.
3a–b Royalist.
3c–f Parliamentarian.

Causation

1 Answers may include:
King: I am king, divinely appointed, Parliament should not keep me short of money.
Cavendish: Charles is king and must be obeyed. They should not be telling him what to do. Hampden: Charles just uses Parliament to raise taxes and sends us home when we do not like what he asks of us. Vane: Puritan beliefs are becoming more popular – the king has married a Catholic, which worries us. Short: The ship tax is wrong, we are not at war and it is unfair. Farrall: If Parliament goes against Charles then they are going against God and must be stopped.

2 King: Royalist.
Cavendish: Royalist.
Hampden: Parliamentarian.
Vane: Parliamentarian.
Short: Parliamentarian.
Farrall: Royalist.
3 Answers will vary, but students should make sure they include an explanation of the ship tax and why it caused some people to be upset at the king, and also some of the actions of Parliament that upset the king (for example, the complaints that undermined his 'divine right'). Also, students can bring in other reasons – such as the invasion of a Scottish army as a result of the king's actions and his choice of wife.

4.2 Match of the day: Roundheads versus Cavaliers
PAGES 74–75

Over to You

1a 1641.
1b King.
1c Parliament.
1d Roundheads.
2a The soldier with the red sash fought for the king, while the soldier with the yellow sash fought for Parliament.
2b Answers will vary, but may include: Pikeman: stood at the front of the whole army with a pike – a five-metre-long pole tipped with steel. As the enemy approached, they dug one end into the ground and pointed the other at the charging enemy's horses. They wore heavy armour and also carried a sword. Musketeer: carried a gun (musket). The gun was fired by using a 'match' (a piece of burning rope) to light the gunpowder that had been poured into the barrel. A ball or shot would fly out and travel up to 400 metres.

3 Descriptions will focus on the criteria in the question.

Knowledge and Understanding

1a Cavalry: the part of an army that fought on horses.
1b Infantry: the part of an army that fought on foot.
1c Musketeer: soldier who fired a musket.
1d Pikeman: soldier who carried a pike to prevent the enemy from advancing.
2 Answers will vary but students could mention which areas generally supported which side (for example, Parliament was most popular in the south, especially in London and other large towns and ports. Most merchants, businessmen and Puritans also fought for Parliament.). Students might mention that one feature was the makeup of the armies in that the ordinary villagers tended to fight for their lord, or supported the side that got to their town or village first. Students might also mention the types of soldiers who fought.

4.3 What was new about the New Model Army?
PAGES 76–77

Over to You

1 Answers will vary, but may include: Parliament's troops were no match for the Royalists and were in danger of losing the war. They lacked discipline and skill.
2 Thomas Fairfax.
3 Answers may include: Men of great spirit (Source A); men of God who were strictly trained and strictly disciplined (Interpretation B).
4 Answers will include that the New Model Army was a success because it won the

Revolution, Industry and Empire: Britain 1558–1901   89

Chapter 4 Answers guidance

Battles of Marston Moor and Naseby and also defeated the Royalist army in the Second Civil War.

Source Analysis

1. Students may answer: It was to try to win widespread support, to show people they had nothing to fear from Parliament's soldiers, their reputation was poor because the actions of the armies had been poor in the past.
2. Answers may include: They are useful because they show us how the New Model Army was managed and disciplined, and its success increased after these changes were made. Source A shows us what were the issues with the army before, from someone who was there and fought in it.

4.4 Why was King Charles I sentenced to death?
PAGES 78–79

Over to You

1. To show he did not respect the court or the trial so did not treat it respectfully.
2. Letters will reflect both the events and the opinion of the writer. Students will have used the tips to help them.
3. Letters will reflect both the events and the opinion of the writer. Students will have used the tips to help them.

4.5 Charlie for the chop!
PAGES 80–81

Over to You

1a. Answers may include: People were worried about repercussions, thought it was morally wrong, didn't want to kill someone they may have believed was appointed by God.

1b. They would remain anonymous.

2a. Summary may include: I didn't start the war, Parliament started war on me, and future generations will see that – I die for what I believe in, so I am a martyr.

2b. He did not think he was guilty – 'They began war upon me', 'they began these unhappy troubles, not I', 'I am the martyr of the people'.

3a. Top left: Charles I. Bottom left: on his way to execution. Top right: Charles's head with executioner. Bottom right: people dipping handkerchiefs in blood.

3b. Reasons might include: shock, horror, disgust, sight of blood.

3c. Reasons might include: to sell, people thought he had been appointed by God so might think this was a holy relic.

Causation

Students' order and reasons will vary.

2. Students should outline how Charles upset Parliament (he ruled without Parliament, which upset the MPs; he would only reassemble Parliament when he wanted to raise funds because he ran out of money; he was disrespectful to Parliament and never seriously tried to make peace, which led many people to think him arrogant), but also outline other reasons (Charles married the Catholic Henrietta Maria, which offended many English Protestants; he joined forces with Scotland and invaded England in an attempt to win the war – many thought this was treason). Students should conclude with an answer to the question.

4.6 Cromwell: the man who banned Christmas
PAGES 82–83

Over to You

1a. Republic: country without a monarchy and that is run by Parliament or another elected group.

1b. Interregnum: period from the execution of Charles I in 1649 to when Charles II became king; when Oliver Cromwell ruled as Lord Protector.

2a. Lord Protector was in overall charge, while a Major-General ran one of the 11 areas.

2b. Cromwell didn't want to be called 'king'; he felt he was 'protecting' the nation.

2c. Answers will relate to the strict laws that were unpopular.

3a. Dead King Charles and Oliver Cromwell.

3b. It is dramatic. It makes you think about the events. The artist may have been trying to sell paintings – people like the 'what ifs' of History.

Change

1a. Churches: plain glass replaced stained glass, church bells were removed, candlesticks were melted down and organs smashed up.

1b. Entertainment: football banned, inns shut, bear-baiting stopped, theatres closed, maypole dancing stopped, gambling banned, Christmas celebrations stopped.

2. Answers should mention the removal of the monarchy, establishment of a Lord Protector and Major-Generals and the division of the country into 11 areas, changes to churches and entertainment.

Chapter 4 Answers guidance

4.7 Why does Cromwell divide opinion?
PAGES 84–85

Over to You

1a Answers will vary, but positive ones might include A, C, F, I.

1b Answers will vary, but negative ones might include D, G, H, K.

1c Answers will vary, but one example might be J. It is positive because Cromwell stopped Parliament restricting religious freedom, but negative because it led to him acting without Parliament (which is exactly what the executed king did).

2 Answers will vary, but opinions should be justified.

3 Captions will vary. An example might be: Cromwell was a brilliant soldier who helped improve the army. He promoted people based on their abilities. He supported the trial and execution of King Charles I. Cromwell wanted Parliament to rule the country, but when they couldn't agree, he ran the country as Lord Protector. During his reign, sports and entertainment that ordinary people thoroughly enjoyed were stopped. In Ireland, Cromwell slaughtered people who refused to surrender to him. He allowed Jews to come back into the country and worship how they wanted to.

Interpretation Analysis

1 Answers may include: Cromwell divides opinion – some see him as a hero, who loved freedom and did the best he could for the country, while others see him as a villain, who was cruel and power mad.

2 Answers will vary, but will most likely reflect the two views. Students should back up their opinion with examples of him as both a hero and a villain.

4.8 The monarchy returns – but what happened to Cromwell's head?
PAGES 86–87

Over to You

1 Answers may include: To set an example, and that even after death, you will be punished.

2a Answers may include: He was worried he might get into trouble, perhaps to get a reward if it was missing for a long time.

2b There was a hole in the top of the head where a spike had been, and axe marks on the neck.

2c It matched portraits of Cromwell.

2d To stop anyone taking it as a trophy.

3 Answers will vary but may include: After Cromwell's death, his son Richard was made Lord Protector, but he didn't want the job. Then Parliament and the army argued and Richard resigned after only a few months. After a few more months of confusion, Parliament asked Charles I's son to return to the country from abroad to become King Charles II.

Significance

1 Answers will vary but the Interregnum was clearly significant at the time (removal of the monarchy, establishment of a Lord Protector and Major-Generals and the division of the country into 11 areas, changes to churches and entertainment etc.) and the legacy is still felt today (hatred of what Cromwell did in Ireland during the Interregnum and the fact that the balance between monarch and Parliament is now firmly with Parliament).

Chapter 4 Have you been learning?

Answers guidance

Chapter 4 Have you been learning?

Quick Knowledge Quiz

PAGE 88

1 **a** Royalist
2 **b** 1642
3 **b** cavalry
4 **c** yellow
5 **a** Dunkirk
6 **c** New Model Army
7 **c** John Bradshaw
8 **b** 30 January 1649
9 **a** Lord Protector
10 **b** the Interregnum

Literacy Focus

PAGE 89

Note-taking

1 Student answers will vary, but notes may look like this:
   - Ordinary people, supported, town/village first, landowner, friends/family against each other (48 words down to 10).
   - Ordinary people, food/shelter, soldiers, homes, things and land destroyed, starvation (45 words down to 10).
   - King support: rich, countryside, Catholics, North, Wales, South-West (36 words down to 8).
   - Parliament support: big towns and ports, London, Puritans, business/trade (25 words down to 10).
   - Rich = horses (cavalry), steel breastplates, pistols, cutting with swords. Ordinary people = pikemen, musketeers, sashes red (Royalist) and yellow (Parliament) (57 words down to 19).

Chapter 4 Assessment: Write a narrative account (causation)

Assessment summary

The assessments in this textbook have been carefully designed and tested with History teachers to support student progression throughout the course. This specific assessment is written to support Year 8 or Year 9 students in tackling questions relating to writing a narrative account.

> ★ Write a narrative account of the events during the reign of Charles I (between 1625 and 1642) that led to the start of the English Civil War.
>
> You may use the following in your answer:
>
> - the Divine Right of Kings
> - the introduction of the Ship Tax.
>
> You must also use information of your own. (20)

Once students have planned the main events they would like to include (Question 1), they will put them in chronological order and add extra details (Question 2). Then they will use these events to write their version of what happened (Question 3). After students make links between the events (Question 4), they will have completed a narrative about the reasons (causes) the English Civil War started.

Students are given some causes of the English Civil War, along with sample sentence starters and connectives to help them link events together.

For the mark scheme, see page 95.

A note about the end-of-chapter assessments

There is an assessment for each Student Book chapter. Each is structured like a GCSE exam-style question, with scaffolding steps to support KS3 students. Each assessment has a total of 20 marks, and is designed to be completed in a typical lesson – each has been written with a time allowance of about 30 minutes.

There is a mark scheme for each assessment. You can choose how to give student outcomes: a mark out of 20; a percentage; a performance indicator (we use a three-stage indicator – 'Developing', 'Secure', 'Extending' – but you could adapt to match any performance indicators used in your school); or a GCSE grade indicator. To convert raw marks to a performance or GCSE grade indicator, use this table:

Raw marks			
0	1–6	7–13	14–20
GCSE grade (9–1) indicators*			
U	1–3	4–6	7–9
Performance indicator			
Ungraded	Developing	Secure	Extending

* Please appreciate that these are approximate grades based on grade boundaries from recent GCSE exam papers. If a student achieves a Grade 7 in one of these assessments, it is not the equivalent of a Grade 7 at GCSE. Instead it is an indicator of the grade the student could expect to get if they continue on their flight path through KS3 and GCSE. Please note:
  - the raw-mark boundaries are based on but do not match precisely those for recent GCSE exam papers: this is because our assessments are focused around one exam-style question, likely to be done at the end of a chapter (topic) rather than at the end of the course. Secondly, we provide carefully considered scaffolded steps to allow KS3 students to tackle high level questions and gain confidence through the deliberate practice of building up detailed answers.
  - the assessments for Student Book 3 are progressively more demanding in that they use higher-order command words and provide less scaffolded support – if you set one of them for Year 8 students, please take that into account when awarding GCSE grade indicators.

Entering student outcomes into the Kerboodle Markbook

The Kerboodle Markbook records scores and percentages to allow for quick comparison of performance. If you want to use the Markbook to record student outcomes, you will need to enter the appropriate values given in the raw marks row of the table above.

Chapter 4 Assessment: Write a narrative account (causation)

Links to GCSE

By the end of KS3, students should be familiar with the History skill of writing a narrative account. At GCSE, most exam boards specifically ask students to write an account. For example:

AQA:
- Write an account of… (8)

Edexcel:
- Write a narrative account analysing… (8)

OCR A:
- Outline… (5)

OCR B:
- Write a clear and organised summary that analyses… (9)

Eduqas:
- Outline how… changed. In your answer you should provide a written narrative discussing… (16) (SPaG 4)

Links to KS3 History resources

Student Book

This assessment question links to these lessons:

4.1 Why did the English start fighting each other?
4.2 Match of the day: Roundheads versus Cavaliers
4.3 What was new about the New Model Army?
4.4 Why was King Charles I sentenced to death?

Kerboodle

Support for this assessment question on Kerboodle:

RIE 4 Assessment presentation: Write a narrative account (causation)
RIE 4 Assessment worksheet (Core): Write a narrative account (causation)
RIE 4 Assessment worksheet (Foundation): Write a narrative account (causation)

Curriculum and Assessment Planning Guide

Support for this assessment question in this guide:

4 Assessment mark scheme – page 95
4 Assessment sample student answers – pages 96–97

Chapter 4 Assessment: Write a narrative account (causation)

Student name: _____   Date: _____

Mark scheme

Assessment bands	Marks	GCSE grade indicators*	I have...
	0	Ungraded	
Developing	1–6	1–3	☐ written a very general account which shows limited understanding and organisation of the sequence (correct order) of events. ☐ written some information, but this is limited – there is not a lot of detail and key words are not used correctly.
Secure	7–13	4–6	☐ written a detailed narrative, showing some organisation of material into a sequence (correct order) of events. The account of events shows some links between them, but some passages of the narrative may lack clear structure. ☐ added accurate and relevant information, showing some knowledge and understanding of the events. Some key words are used correctly. NOTE: Marks should only go above 10 if you have added extra detail that goes beyond the bullet points in the question.
Extending	14–20	7–9	☐ written a well-developed narrative that organises material into a clear sequence (correct order) of events that ends with the outbreak of war. The account of events analyses the links between them and is clearly and logically structured. ☐ included accurate and relevant information, showing excellent knowledge and understanding of the key features of the events. All key words are used appropriately. NOTE: You cannot get to this level if you have not included extra detail in addition to the two bullet points in the question.

* IMPORTANT: These are approximate indicators devised using publicly available information on the new GCSE grades. They are designed to assist in the process of tracking and monitoring. They cannot and should not be used to replace teachers' professional judgement. Teachers should use their own discretion in applying them, taking into account the cumulative test scores of an individual student (rather than just one assessment point), and should refer to their institution's assessment policy.

Mark: _____

Comment:

Chapter 4 Assessment: Write a narrative account (causation)

Sample student answers

Assessment: Write a narrative account (causation)

STUDENT BOOK PAGE 91

> Write a narrative account of the events during the reign of Charles I (between 1625 and 1642) that led to the start of the English Civil War.
>
> You may use the following in your answer:
> - the Divine Right of Kings
> - the introduction of the Ship Tax.
>
> You must also use information of your own. (20)

Sample Developing band answer

The English Civil War started in 1642 with Parliament fighting against those who supported the king. There were many reasons for the start of the war, the main one being the Divine Right of Kings. Another cause of the English Civil War was the Ship Tax that Charles introduced. Charles made everyone in the country pay the Ship Tax which made Parliament angry.

Sample Secure band answer

Charles I became king in 1625 and believed strongly in the Divine Right of Kings – he thought he was appointed by God and so he did not believe he had to listen to Parliament. Parliament had an important role helping monarchs make decisions, but Charles only called Parliament when he wanted to raise taxes, normally to help get money for wars that Parliament did not support. When Parliament refused to give Charles money, he sent it away for 11 years, and he ruled without Parliament during this entire time. Another cause of the English Civil War was when Charles raised the Ship Tax, which was normally only paid by those who lived by the coast. Charles raised these taxes without Parliament's permission.

Eventually, in 1641, Parliament sent Charles a list of their complaints about the way he was running the country. This resulted in Charles taking soldiers to London to arrest the Members of Parliament, but they had all escaped. Charles then travelled north to get his army together. Charles's belief in the Divine Right of Kings meant that he did not listen to Parliament, which caused tension and the Civil War to begin between Royalists (supporters of Charles) and Parliamentarians.

Chapter 4 Assessment: Write a narrative account (causation)

⭐ Sample Extending band answer

Charles I became king in 1625 after the death of his father James I. Both monarchs believed in the Divine Right of Kings, which meant they believed they did not need to listen to Parliament. They believed that they were appointed by God, so they felt that Parliament was there to serve them. On the other hand, Parliament felt it had a lawful right to be consulted over things relating to running the country. Charles was so stubborn that when Parliament refused to raise taxes for him, he sent it away for 11 years from 1629 to 1640. During this period, Charles ruled without Parliament, which angered many people. Charles recalled Parliament when the Scottish army invaded England – he needed money to raise an army to fight them. Parliament was reluctant to give him the money, so he sent it away again.

This links to another cause of the English Civil War – religion. The Scottish army invaded as Charles had introduced a new prayer book into Scotland which people believed to be more Catholic than their Protestant Church. Furthermore, Charles's wife, Henrietta Maria, was a Catholic, so this made people sure that Charles wanted to change Scotland and England to Catholic countries. As a result, Parliament needed to get more control over Charles, which caused tension between the king and his people.

Finally, Charles imposed a Ship Tax on the people of England. This was traditionally paid by those who lived by the coast to help defend the country from invasion. However, England was not at war at the time and he made everyone pay it regardless of where they lived. This resulted in Parliament sending Charles a list of complaints in 1641. This contradicted Charles's belief in the Divine Right of Kings, so eventually he went north to gather an army to fight Parliament. Parliament started to bring its own army together too. This led to the start of the English Civil War, between Royalists (supporters of the king) and Parliamentarians.

Chapter 5 The Restoration: the Merry Monarch

Links to KS3 History National Curriculum

There is no denying that the Restoration is important for the development of contextual understanding of the changing power of Church, state and society, as set out in the latest KS3 History National Curriculum. It may be a context chapter, but that does not mean it is boring – the Restoration era is filled with fascinating events, such as the Great Fire of London, and people, such as Samuel Pepys and Christopher Wren. Some niche terminology is used especially when exploring the Great Plague. This vocabulary will enhance students' understanding of the development of medicine and science as they progress through KS3 and beyond.

As students work through the activities, they will build their awareness of cause and consequence. Students will need to use sources to select and combine evidence in order to complete tasks and build their sequence of knowledge. They will develop their understanding of how towns and cities changed, in particular post-fire London, how religion changed, and how the power of the monarchy had been affected by the Civil War and Interregnum, setting them up to continue building on these concepts in Chapter 6.

Skills and processes covered in this chapter

		Lesson/activity in the Student Book
History Skills	Knowledge and understanding	5.1 Over to You: 2
		5.2A Over to You: 1, 3
		5.2B Over to You: 1, 3; Source Analysis: 1
		5.3 Over to You: 1, 2; Knowledge and Understanding: 1, 2
		5.4 Over to You: 1a, 1b, 1e, 3; Consequences: 1
		Have you been learning? Quick Knowledge Quiz: 1, 2, 3, 4, 5, 6, 7, 8, 9, 10
	Interpretations	5.4 Over to You: 2
	Sources	5.1 Over to You: 4
		5.2A Over to You: 2a, 2b, 2c
		5.2B Over to You: 3; Source Analysis: 2a, 2b, 2c, 2d, 3
		5 Assessment: Source analysis (historic environment): 1, 2, 3
	Significance	
	Cause and consequence	5.1 Over to You: 1, 3; Change and Continuity: 1
		5.2B Over to You: 2a, 2b, 4
		5.3 Over to You: 2
		5.4 Over to You: 1c, 1d; Consequences: 2
	Diversity/Similarity and difference	
	Change and continuity	5.1 Change and Continuity: 2
Literacy and Numeracy	Literacy	5.3 Over to You: 2
		Have you been learning? Literacy Focus: 1
	Numeracy	5.2B Source Analysis: 2c

Chapter 5 The Restoration: the Merry Monarch

Lesson sequence

Lesson title	Student Book pages	Objectives
5.1 Who was the Merry Monarch?	pp 92–93	• Explain how, when and why Charles II became king. • Compare Cromwell's nation with the 'Merry Monarch's'.
5.2A How deadly was the Great Plague?	pp 94–95	• Discover what people knew about the spread of plague and disease in seventeenth-century Britain. • Recall the symptoms of the Great Plague.
5.2B How deadly was the Great Plague?	pp 96–97	• Examine the impact of the plague.
5.3 Was the Great Fire of London an accident – or arson?	pp 98–99	• Describe how the Great Fire devastated London. • Explain why the fire spread so quickly.
5.4 London: a city reborn	pp 100–101	• Recall the impact of the Great Fire of London. • Examine how London was rebuilt after the Great Fire.
Chapter 5 Have you been learning?	pp 102–103	• Choose the correct answer from the given options for a quick recap. • Examine how to structure a paragraph using the PEEL writing approach.
Chapter 5 History skill: Source analysis (historic environment)	pp 104–105	• Define historic environment. • Consider questions relating to historic environment.
Chapter 5 Assessment: Source analysis (historic environment)	pp 106–107	• Describe features of London before the Great Fire. • Assess sources relating to the impact of the Great Fire.

Links to the GCSE curriculum

This chapter provides some historical context to the following:

AQA: Health and the People c1000–Present

AQA: Restoration England 1660–1685

Edexcel: Medicine in Britain c1250–Present

OCR A: Monarchy and Democracy in Britain c1000–2014

OCR A: Personal Rule to Restoration 1629–1660

OCR B: The People's Health c1250–Present

Eduqas: Changes in Health and Medicine in Britain c500–Present

WJEC: Changes in Health and Medicine c1340–Present

Exam-style questions covered in this chapter

Exam board	Lesson/activity question location	Command words	History skills/concepts
AQA	5.1 Change and Continuity: 2	Explain two ways… different	Change and continuity
AQA	5.2B Source Analysis: 3	How useful…	Source analysis
Edexcel	5.2B Source Analysis: 3	How useful…	Source analysis
Edexcel	5.4 Consequences: 2	Explain two consequences…	Cause and consequence
OCR A	5.2B Source Analysis: 3	How useful…	Source analysis
OCR A	5.3 Knowledge and Understanding: 2	Outline…	Knowledge and understanding
OCR A	5.2B Source Analysis: 3	How useful…	Source analysis

Chapter 5 The Restoration: the Merry Monarch

A brief history

5.1 Who was the Merry Monarch?

The chapter starts with much-needed context on Charles II – very quickly students can see who he is related to. Then the fun bit: how did Charles get the nickname, 'Merry Monarch'? Students will be able to explore the restoration of culture, but they will also evaluate the changing power of Parliament with the banning of non-Church of England services. There are plenty of opportunities to test comprehension and then analyse change and continuity comparing Cromwell and Charles II. This would be a good place to encourage students to categorise their comparisons.

5.2A/B How deadly was the Great Plague?

This lesson busts the myth that the plague happened in the 1300s and then only again in 1665. Students will thus build a picture of a period haunted by the plague. A good further testing exercise is to ask them to list features of the period to explain why and how disease spread so quickly. Using Samuel Pepys's diary is a fantastic way to track the disease's progress – an interesting extra activity would be to use the tension graph model to create a 'fear graph' to develop students' inference skills while reading the diary. The lessons also develop students' understanding of science and medicine during the period. The 'Later on' and 'Earlier on' features will help with the sequential learning required in a good curriculum.

5.3 Was the Great Fire of London an accident – or arson?

Students will relish the details of the Great Fire, and Pepys's diary again provides source material. This lesson is great practice for writing a narrative as it requires chronology, key people and key terms. This brings in social history with the issue of tightly-packed buildings and poor living conditions; religious history with the link to Catholic plots, allowing some excellent links with Elizabethan England and the Gunpowder Plot; and political history with the king and the Mayor of London working together to try to stop the fire spreading. Students will get a chance to focus on literacy by creating an exhibition for primary school students.

Timeline

29 May 1660
Charles II returns to London to become king.

1664
Parliament bans all religious services except those of the Church of England.

1665
The Great Plague starts in London.

1666
The Great Fire of London.

2 September 1666
Charles II orders that whole houses be blown up with gunpowder to stop the fire spreading.

1676
London starts to be rebuilt by architects such as Christopher Wren.

1680
The first insurance company is set up to help those people whose homes catch fire.

5.4 London: a city reborn

This lesson focuses on the role of the individual with Christopher Wren and Robert Hooke. Remember that while students already know the causes of London's regeneration, they won't be familiar with all the consequences of the new town planning, including the start of insurance companies. A focus on consequences will allow them to realise the significance of the fire and the individuals involved in rebuilding London. This lesson is open for lots of cultural capital, with the different buildings and the people associated with them throughout time.

Further reading and links

For teachers:

- In 2017, historian Kate Williams 'live tweeted' the events of the Great Fire. This could be a great sequencing task or an interesting way to find out precise facts from different parts of the day. Search Twitter using '#GreatFire @katewilliamsme' to find the tweets.
- Find out about the plague beyond London by researching its impact on the Derbyshire village of Eyam. www.eyam-museum.org.uk has statistics, records and an interesting narrative about the plague. Look under 'Education'.

For students:

- Pepys's diary is free to read at www.pepysdiary.com. Students can read through it to develop contextual understanding of the period. Other than the plague and fire can they find any other features of the period that they have learned about?
- Horrible Histories' 'King of Bling' song is a fun way for students to test their knowledge of the Restoration. Search on YouTube or BBC iPlayer.
- The novel *All Fall Down* by Sally Nicholls (Marion Lloyd Books, 2012) is about the plague in the 1300s. Although a different period, it is still the same social group that is largely affected. Students could read it and pick out themes applicable to the Restoration period.

Beyond the classroom

- Students could carry out an extension project on the life and achievements of Christopher Wren and his landmark buildings.
- Have a cross-curricular day with the Science department for students to learn about developments in science and how we understand disease now. At the end of the day the students should dramatise a conversation between a seventeenth-century plague doctor and a modern-day GP. How would the plague doctor explain cures for the plague? The GP should explain what we know about disease now.
- Take your class on a walking tour of London to see the impacts of the plague and fire – remember consequences can be positive!
- Songs and rhymes help students retain and recall information, so give them a chance to write a short song, rap or rhyme about Charles II and his reputation for being the Merry Monarch.

Chapter 5 Answers guidance

Answers guidance

The answers provided here are examples, based on the information provided in the Student Book. There may be other factors which are relevant to each question, and students may draw on as much of their own knowledge as possible to give detailed and precise answers. There are also many ways of answering questions, including exam-style questions (for example, of structuring an essay). However, these exemplar answers should provide a good starting point.

5.1 Who was the Merry Monarch?
STUDENT BOOK PAGES 92–93

Over to You

1 Charles brought back all the sports and entertainment that had been banned – and enjoyed them himself.
2 'Restore' means to return something to the state it was in before, so in returning to a monarchy, it was restoring it.
3 Charles had many children but none with his wife. To inherit the throne, the child would have to be from Charles's marriage to his wife. As a result the throne passed to the nearest 'official' blood relative – his brother.
4 Students will see many games and entertainments, including bear-baiting, a man at a table with cards, horse and carriage rides, ball sports and skittles.

Change and Continuity

1 Answers may include: People were unhappy with Cromwell's England, pleased to have a monarch again, Royalists would be happy, fed up with the Major-Generals.
2 Answers will reflect differences such as the fact that under Cromwell England was a republic, with Charles II it is a monarchy; also the limits on sports and entertainments during the Interregnum, while under Charles II sports and entertainments that had been banned were brought back, and Christmas, May Day and harvest time were celebrated again.

5.2A How deadly was the Great Plague?
PAGES 94–95

Over to You

1 Answers should include: boils under armpits, groin and neck, sweating, vomiting, coughing up blood, dark blotches/rash, dizziness and hallucinations.
2a There was a plague victim inside.
2b He thought it would keep away poisonous air that people believed carried plague.
2c There are several answers students might give – for example, people leaving the towns to flee the disease.
3 Diaries give insight into thoughts, feelings, actions at the time, first-hand account of someone who was there.

5.2B How deadly was the Great Plague?
PAGES 96–97

Over to You

1 Via a ship from the Netherlands.
2a Any from: Houses boarded up and marked with a large cross, no one to leave or enter the house for a month after the last victim has died or recovered and the house to be guarded; the dead only buried at night in special plague cemeteries; victims' clothing burned; pubs and theatres closed, homeowners to sweep the streets outside their homes; dogs and cats to be killed and all animals banned from the city.
2b Answers will vary, but should be a reasoned judgement. For example, if they have written one of the measures was that the houses were boarded up, marked with a large cross and guarded, then they would probably argue that this was effective to stop the spread because it might mean that the victim would not be allowed out (or anyone in) and the fleas that may have been on their clothing or in the house would not be able to bite visitors. However, they may argue that this was not particularly effective because the rats and fleas could still 'travel'!
3 The perfumes and spices in the beak are to avoid bad air, the leather is to avoid contact with victims and the stick is to protect from attacks by desperate people.
4 The list could include: Most of London's richer people (including the king) moved away from London. Parliament was postponed and court cases were moved to Oxford. By the end of the summer of 1665, mainly the poor were left. London changed from a busy, crowded centre of trade to a deserted city. Some people were forced to beg for food because the plague had affected trade and business in London so badly. Up to 100,000 Londoners died – possibly 500,000 across the country.

Source Analysis

1 A weekly list of the causes of death in a particular place.
2a 7165
2b 8297
2c 86 per cent.
2d Answers will vary, and the point is that at the time

Chapter 5 Answers guidance

people did not have sufficient medical knowledge, so they put reasons that seemed logical, but weren't based in science. Students may write: death from 'old age', dying of a broken heart, dying suddenly with no real explanation and some sort of tooth infection.

3 Answers may include insight into impact of the plague, also helps historians get a view of other common diseases and the fact that people did not really know what caused many deaths so they put reasons such as 'suddenly' and 'aged' instead of scientific reasons. Also tells us that they were trying to keep detailed records of what they must have regarded as a key event in history.

5.3 Was the Great Fire of London an accident – or arson?
PAGES 98–99

Over to You

1 Hubert was foreign, people wanted a scapegoat.
2 Student exhibitions will vary, but some good ideas might be to find a map of London before the fire, and a map of the devastation to show the impact; some first-hand accounts of the fire (Pepys was not the only famous diarist – John Evelyn also wrote about it); also fire hooks and buckets are on display in some museums.

Knowledge and Understanding

1 2 September 1666 and historians think it started in the bakery of Thomas Farriner in Pudding Lane.
2 Fire started in a bakery in Pudding Lane, near London Bridge on Sunday 2 September. As the day went on, the fire got worse and worse – London's dry, wooden buildings were packed close together, so the fire spread quickly. Attempts to fight the fire with water failed. By evening, Charles II ordered houses in the path of the fire to be pulled down to make 'fire breaks' – but people didn't want to lose their homes so they only allowed their houses to be pulled down at the last moment. And by then it was too late – the piles of wood and plaster just caught fire too. Strong winds fanned the fire for the next few days. Thousands of Londoners fled the city. On Wednesday, the king ordered whole rows of houses to be blown up with gunpowder. The gaps created by the explosions stopped the fire spreading so quickly and by Thursday the fire was dying down.

5.4 London: a city reborn
PAGES 100–101

Over to You

1a Five-sixths.
1b A city with broad, straight streets, wide-open spaces and magnificent new brick or stone churches and homes.
1c Answers might include: To show off the city, to prevent the spread of fire again (so wider spaces between houses and no new wooden ones).
1d People whose homes had been destroyed wanted them built quickly and in exactly the same places as their old ones. Few people wanted to – or could afford to – give up their land to make London a nicer place to live.
1e Students will probably agree, because Wren is buried in a building he designed in a city with many buildings he designed.

2 That the fire destroyed London to such an extent that designers/architects had to start again (blank canvas). Also that the fire was the biggest influence on the great changes that have taken place in London's history – and that London is always changing.
3 Student responses may include: Houses of the wealthy were symmetrical; lots of glass to reflect wealth; French, Dutch, Japanese, Indian, Chinese influences; Charles II himself was interested in science so ordered the building of the Royal Observatory at Greenwich, London.

Consequences

1 A house owner could pay small sums of money to 'insure' their property. If a fire started, the employees of the insurance company would put out the fire using their own fire engine. In 1680, the first insurance company (the 'Fire Office') was set up.
2 Answers will vary but students may write that insurance began, buildings were made of stone, no new wooden ones, all new streets were wide, houses over 9m wide were only allowed on main streets, 100 streets were widened, new common sewers were built.

Revolution, Industry and Empire: Britain 1558–1901 103

Chapter 5 Have you been learning?

Answers guidance

Chapter 5 Have you been learning?

Quick Knowledge Quiz

PAGE 102

1. **b** 1660
2. **c** the Merry Monarch
3. **b** 1665
4. **a** Samuel Pepys
5. **c** Bills of Mortality
6. **b** Sunday 2 September 1666
7. **b** baker
8. **b** to create 'fire breaks' to stop the fire spreading to more houses
9. **c** 13,000
10. **a** Christopher Wren

Literacy Focus

PAGE 103

Writing detailed answers

1. Answers will vary, but could include: Another consequence of the Great Fire was the destruction of the city and the new London that emerged afterwards. The fire spread through London very quickly and destroyed many houses. The fire spread more than it should have because the king's orders were not followed when he instructed houses to be pulled down to stop the spread. This resulted in around 100,000 people being made homeless. In the long term London became a new city with several architects writing up plans to share with Charles II. Among them was Christopher Wren whose plans for St Paul's Cathedral were used to replace the one that burned down. Furthermore, the rules put in place for new housing meant that houses were the same height, streets were cleaner, and as houses were made out of stone there was less chance of fire. This meant that London was like a new city with safer homes that were better for the population. Most importantly, there was never a Great Fire that spread through the city again.

Chapter 5 Assessment: Source analysis (historic environment)

Assessment summary

The assessments in this textbook have been carefully designed and tested with History teachers to support student progression throughout the course. This specific assessment is written to support Year 8 or Year 9 students in tackling questions relating to source analysis (historic environment).

> 1 Describe two features of the streets and buildings in the centre of London in 1666.
>
> 2 How useful are **Sources A** and **B** for an enquiry into the impact of the Great Fire of London in 1666? Explain your answer, using both sources and your knowledge of the historical context.
>
> 3 How could you find out more about the impact of the Great Fire? Name two sources (other than Sources A and B) you could use, and explain your reasons. (20)

▼ **SOURCE A** Adapted from the diary of Londoner John Evelyn (1620-1706), who kept a diary from 1640 to 1706. Evelyn did not write as regularly as the other well-known diarist of the time, Samuel Pepys, but his diary covers a much longer period of history.

> **3rd September 1666**
>
> The fire continued because of the wind after a very dry season. I saw the whole south part of the city burning and it was now taking hold of St. Paul's church. People were not even trying to save their goods. It burned the churches, public halls, hospitals and monuments, leaping from house to house and street to street devouring houses, furniture, and everything. Here we saw the Thames covered with barges and boats laden with what some had time and courage to save. In the fields people had set up tents to shelter both people and what goods they could get away.
>
> The fire could be seen from 40 miles away. I saw 10,000 houses all in one flame; the fall of towers, houses, and churches, was like an hideous storm, and the air so hot and inflamed that you could not go near it. London was, but is no more!

Chapter 5 Assessment: Source analysis (historic environment)

▼ **SOURCE B** A map of the City of London by surveyors John Leake, William Leybourne and four others, to show the extent of the area devastated by the Great Fire of 1666. The white areas near to the river show the parts of London destroyed by the fire. This map was produced in 1667.

106 Chapter 5 The Restoration: the Merry Monarch

Chapter 5 Assessment: Source analysis (historic environment)

Students will start by describing features of streets and buildings in London (Question 1). This will then lead to an analysis of two sources to show utility (Question 2) and then show source limitations by naming other sources that could provide more information about the Great Fire (Question 3). For the mark scheme, see page 109.

A note about the end-of-chapter assessments

There is an assessment for each Student Book chapter. Each is structured like a GCSE exam-style question, with scaffolding steps to support KS3 students. Each assessment has a total of 20 marks, and is designed to be completed in a typical lesson – each has been written with a time allowance of about 30 minutes.

There is a mark scheme for each assessment. You can choose how to give student outcomes: a mark out of 20; a percentage; a performance indicator (we use a three-stage indicator – 'Developing', 'Secure', 'Extending' – but you could adapt to match any performance indicators used in your school); or a GCSE grade indicator. To convert raw marks to a performance or GCSE grade indicator, use this table:

Raw marks			
0	1–6	7–13	14–20
GCSE grade (9–1) indicators*			
U	1–3	4–6	7–9
Performance indicator			
Ungraded	Developing	Secure	Extending

*Please appreciate that these are approximate grades based on grade boundaries from recent GCSE exam papers. If a student achieves a Grade 7 in one of these assessments, it is not the equivalent of a Grade 7 at GCSE. Instead it is an indicator of the grade the student could expect to get if they continue on their flight path through KS3 and GCSE. Please note:
- the raw-mark boundaries are based on but do not match precisely those for recent GCSE exam papers: this is because our assessments are focused around one exam-style question, likely to be done at the end of a chapter (topic) rather than at the end of the course. Secondly, we provide carefully considered scaffolded steps to allow KS3 students to tackle high level questions and gain confidence through the deliberate practice of building up detailed answers.
- the assessments for Student Book 3 are progressively more demanding in that they use higher-order command words and provide less scaffolded support – if you set one of them for Year 8 students, please take that into account when awarding GCSE grade indicators.

Entering student outcomes into the Kerboodle Markbook

The Kerboodle Markbook records scores and percentages to allow for quick comparison of performance. If you want to use the Markbook to record student outcomes, you will need to enter the appropriate values given in the raw marks row of the table above.

Chapter 5 Assessment: Source analysis (historic environment)

Links to GCSE

By the end of KS3, students should be familiar with the History skill of analysing sources. At GCSE, the exam boards specifically ask students to analyse sources. In some cases, the sources can relate to a specific place (historic environment). For example:

> **Edexcel:**
>
> How useful are Sources A and B for an enquiry into…? Explain your answer, using Sources A and B and your knowledge of the historic context. (8)
>
> How could you follow up Source A to find out more about…? In your answer, you must give the question you would ask and the type of source you could use. (4)
>
> Study Sources A and B. Which of these sources is more useful to a historian studying…? (10)

> **OCR A:**
>
> Study Sources D and E. Which of these sources is more useful to a historian studying…? (10)

> **OCR B:**
>
> How useful are Sources B and Interpretations C and D for a historian studying…? In your answer, refer to the source and the two interpretations as well as your own knowledge. (15)

Links to KS3 History resources

Student Book

This assessment question links to these lessons:

5.2A/B *How deadly was the Great Plague?*
5.3 *Was the Great Fire of London an accident – or arson?*
5.4 *London: a city reborn*

Kerboodle

Support for this assessment question on Kerboodle:

RIE 5 Assessment presentation: Source analysis (historic environment)
RIE 5 Assessment worksheet (Core): Source analysis (historic environment)
RIE 5 Assessment worksheet (Foundation): Source analysis (historic environment)

Curriculum and Assessment Planning Guide

Support for this assessment question in this guide:

5 Assessment mark scheme – page 109
5 Assessment sample student answers – pages 110–111

Chapter 5 Assessment: Source analysis (historic environment)

Student name: _____   Date: _____

Mark scheme

Assessment bands	Marks	GCSE grade indicators*	I have…
	0	Ungraded	
Developing	1–6	1–3	☐ identified one feature of London housing in 1666, without describing it in detail. ☐ completed one thing learned for each source from these categories: content, caption and context. ☐ given a basic description of the usefulness of each source. ☐ identified one new source to follow up, without providing reasons.
Secure	7–13	4–6	☐ described one feature of London housing in 1666 in some detail, or identified two features without describing them. ☐ completed some (perhaps two of the three – but not all) of the boxes for each source relating to content, caption and context. ☐ concluded about the usefulness of each source, with some relevant supporting knowledge. ☐ identified two new sources to follow up, with basic explanations of why they're useful.
Extending	14–20	7–9	☐ described two features of London housing in 1666 with precise, detailed supporting knowledge. ☐ described two things learned from each source from *each* of these categories: content and caption, *and* explained one thing I already know about the Great Fire (context) that relates to each source. ☐ concluded about the usefulness of each source with detailed accurate, relevant supporting knowledge. ☐ identified two new sources to follow up, with clear, detailed explanation of why they are useful.

* IMPORTANT: These are approximate indicators devised using publicly available information on the new GCSE grades. They are designed to assist in the process of tracking and monitoring. They cannot and should not be used to replace teachers' professional judgement. Teachers should use their own discretion in applying them, taking into account the cumulative test scores of an individual student (rather than just one assessment point), and should refer to their institution's assessment policy.

Mark: _____

Comment:

Chapter 5 Assessment: Source analysis (historic environment)

Sample student answers

Assessment: Source analysis (historic environment)

STUDENT BOOK PAGES 106–107

> 1 Describe two features of the streets and buildings in the centre of London in 1666.
> 2 How useful are **Sources A** and **B** for an enquiry into the impact of the Great Fire of London in 1666? Explain your answer, using both sources and your knowledge of the historical context.
> 3 How could you find out more about the impact of the Great Fire? Name two sources (other than **Sources A** and **B**) you could use, and explain your reasons. (20)

Sample Developing band answer

1 Houses in the centre of London in 1666 were made of wood.

2 Source A is useful for an enquiry into the impact of the Great Fire of London as it shows the different types of buildings that were ruined by the fire. Source B is useful as it shows the areas damaged by the fire.

3 I would find out more about the impact of the Great Fire with Samuel Pepys's diary.

Sample Secure band answer

1 Houses in the centre of London were made of wood. It had been a long, hot summer so the wood had dried out.

2 Source A is a diary entry by John Evelyn who was in London at the time of the Great Fire. The source provides information about the buildings the fire destroyed. From the content I learned that people tried to rescue their belongings on barges. This is useful because it shows how the people reacted to the fire. The caption tells me that Evelyn had been writing his diary about London since 1640. This is useful because it proves that he knew London well, so would be able to give accurate descriptions of the impact of the fire.

Source B is a map of the area destroyed by the Great Fire of London. The source provides information on the types of buildings destroyed – for example, it tells us which buildings were businesses or churches, like St Paul's. From the content I learned that the fire spread around the Tower of London. This is useful because it shows it was not just poorer people's housing that was destroyed. One thing I already knew about the Great Fire was that it destroyed many churches. This matches with what the source says about what the fire destroyed.

3 I would find out more about the impact of the Great Fire of London with Samuel Pepys's diary. I would use this source because it would help me find out more about how the fire spread. Another source I would also use is the plans for new buildings after the Great Fire.

Chapter 5 Assessment: Source analysis (historic environment)

⭐ **Sample Extending band answer**

1   Houses in the centre of London in 1666 were built very close together. They were built on top of each other so there was very little space between the houses.

   Another feature of housing in the centre of London in 1666 was that the houses were made of wood. There had been a hot summer so the wood had dried out, this made it easier for fires to spread.

2   Source A is a detailed account by John Evelyn, who had written a diary about London since 1640. The source describes the moment the flames took St Paul's and lists the different types of buildings that were destroyed. From the content I learned that people set up makeshift homes in fields and tried to save belongings by putting them on barges in the Thames. This is useful because it shows us how normal people responded to the fire. Furthermore, the source shows that it was not just poorer people's homes which were built cramped together that were destroyed by the fire – churches, hospitals and monuments were also destroyed. This is useful because it shows people's lives were probably greatly affected as they lost businesses and services. The caption tells me that Evelyn had been writing his diary for a long time, showing that he knew London well. One thing I already know about the impact of the fire is that St Paul's Cathedral was ruined. This matches what the source says about the impact of the fire as Evelyn talks about the flames 'taking hold' of St Paul's. In conclusion Source A is very useful to a study of the impact of the Great Fire as it shows the services that people lost and the impact on not just the landscape but on the lives of people who had lost their homes.

   Source B is a map detailing the impact of the Great Fire of London. It shows the scale of the destruction. This is useful because it shows that the fire was far-reaching. One thing I already knew about the impact of the Great Fire is that the king commissioned architects, such as Christopher Wren, to rebuild the city. Source B does not show how the city will be rebuilt after the fire – it just shows what had been destroyed. In conclusion, Source B is useful in some ways, as it shows the physical destruction of London after the fire, but does not show the positive impacts of the city being rebuilt.

3   I would find out more about the impact of the Great Fire with the diary of Samuel Pepys. I would use this source as he wrote more often in his diary than John Evelyn, and he gives several accounts that show the progress of the fire. This would give us more insight of the impact, because it would show the different stages of the fire.

   Another source I would use would be information from the insurance companies set up after the Great Fire. This would tell us about the way houses had to be built after the fire to try to stop such a big fire happening again, and would tell us a bit about the rules brought in by Charles I on how houses should be built.

Chapter 6 Exit the Stuarts, enter the Georgians

Links to KS3 History National Curriculum

This chapter covers plenty of the example content from the latest KS3 History National Curriculum – the 'Glorious Revolution' and power of Parliament; and the Act of Union of 1707, the Hanoverian succession and the Jacobite Rebellions of 1715 and 1745.

Each lesson encourages students to understand these pivotal moments in British history. Students will also have the opportunity to put events in chronological order, recognise and describe change and continuity, identify causes and rank them in order of importance, and assess the short- and long-term significance of the Glorious Revolution and the Bill of Rights.

The impact of new ideas, discoveries and inventions – in Britain and the wider world – are covered. Significant events (such as the founding of the Royal Society) and key ideas (such as Francis Bacon's 'Scientific Method') are examined, extending cultural capital and giving events more of a sense of period. Students will discover how people's lives (including their own) have been shaped by some of these developments. They will be required to recognise that some events, people and changes might be judged as more important than others. They will be asked to make use of appropriate historical terminology to produce structured work.

Skills and processes covered in this chapter

		Lesson/activity in the Student Book
History Skills	Knowledge and understanding	6.1A Over to You: 1
		6.1B Over to You: 1, 3
		6.2 Over to You: 1, 2a, 2b, 2c, 2d, 3; Causation: 1a, 1b
		6.3 Over to You: 1
		6.4A Over to You: 1c; Change and Continuity: 1, 2
		6.4B Over to You: 1, 2; Change and Continuity: 1
		Have you been learning? Quick Knowledge Quiz: 1, 2, 3, 4, 5, 6, 7, 8, 9, 10
	Interpretations	6.1B Significance: 3
		6.3 Interpretation Analysis: 1, 2
	Sources	
	Significance	6.1B Significance: 1, 2, 3, 4
	Cause and consequence	6.1A Over to You: 2a, 2b; Causation: 1, 2
		6.1B Over to You: 2a, 2b, 2c
		6.2 Over to You: 4; Causation: 2
		6.3 Over to You: 3
	Diversity/Similarity and difference	
	Change and continuity	6.3 Over to You: 2
		6.4A Over to You: 1a, 1b; Change and Continuity: 3
		6.4B Change and Continuity: 2
		6 Assessment: Change and continuity: 1, 2, 3, 4
Literacy and Numeracy	Literacy	Have you been learning? Literacy Focus: 1

Chapter 6 Exit the Stuarts, enter the Georgians

Lesson sequence

Lesson title	Student Book pages	Objectives
6.1A The Glorious Revolution	pp 108–109	• Discover why Charles II's brother became king.
6.1B The Glorious Revolution	pp 110–111	• Recall the changes that new Catholic King James II made. • Examine how the monarchy changed back from Catholic to Protestant.
6.2 From Stuarts to Georgians	pp 112–113	• Describe the consequences of the Glorious Revolution. • Explain the official establishment of the 'United Kingdom'.
6.3 The Battle of Culloden, 1746	pp 114–115	• Define the word 'Jacobite'. • Examine the Jacobite Rebellions of 1715 and 1745. • Explain why 'Bonnie Prince Charlie' was a threat to the Georgians.
6.4A From Tudor to Georgian times: what changed?	pp 116–117	• Examine the difference between the Age of Faith and the Age of Reason.
6.4B From Tudor to Georgian times: what changed?	pp 118–119	• Discover some of the key discoveries and inventions of the sixteenth to early eighteenth centuries.
Chapter 6 Have you been learning?	pp 120–121	• Choose the correct answer from the given options for a quick recap. • Define and use key terms relating to the later Stuart period.
Chapter 6 History skill: Change and continuity	p 122	• Understand how to assess change and continuity.
Chapter 6 Assessment: Change and continuity	p 123	• Assess change and continuity between the late Tudor period and the beginning of the Georgian period.

Revolution, Industry and Empire: Britain 1558–1901

Chapter 6 Exit the Stuarts, enter the Georgians

Links to the GCSE curriculum

This chapter provides some historical context to the following:

AQA: Health and the People c1000–Present

AQA: Restoration England 1660–1685

AQA: Britain: Migration, Empires and the People: c790–Present

Edexcel: Medicine in Britain c1250–Present

OCR A: Monarchy and Democracy in Britain c1000–2014

OCR A: War and British Society c790–2010

Eduqas: Changes in Health and Medicine in Britain c500–Present

Exam-style questions covered in this chapter

Exam board	Lesson/activity question location	Command words	History skills/concepts
AQA	6.1A Causation: 2	How far do you agree…	Cause and consequence
	6.1B Significance: 4	Explain the significance…	Significance
	6.4A Change and Continuity: 3	Explain two ways… different	Change and continuity
	6.4B Change and Continuity: 2	Explain two ways… similar	Change and continuity
Edexcel	6.1A Causation: 2	How far do you agree…	Cause and consequence
	6.2 Causation: 2	Explain why…	Cause and consequence
OCR A	6.1A Causation: 2	How far do you agree…	Cause and consequence
	6.2 Causation: 2	Explain why…	Cause and consequence
	6.3 Interpretation Analysis: 2	Do you think…	Interpretation analysis
OCR B	6.1A Causation: 2	How far do you agree…	Cause and consequence
Eduqas	6.2 Causation: 2	Explain why…	Cause and consequence
WJEC	6.2 Causation: 2	Explain why…	Cause and consequence
	6.2 Over to You: 2a, 2b, 2c, 2d	Complete the sentences…	Knowledge and understanding

A brief history

6.1A/B The Glorious Revolution

The chapter begins with a profile of James II as a Catholic monarch – this is a great opportunity to revisit and test students' recall on the Acts of Parliament during Charles II's reign as well as the problems Charles I created for himself with Catholic reforms. Students will get a chance at the end of this lesson to explain the most important reason for Parliament being worried about James. At all times students should be encouraged to link back to previous monarchs; this is especially the case for the causation question. The Glorious Revolution and the Bill of Rights provide excellent focus for the impact and significance questions. Do ensure students have grasped this content before moving on as you will certainly revisit it when building on the concept of power and government.

6.2 From Stuarts to Georgians

King William acts fast to secure Ireland and Scotland by squashing rebellions. Take this lesson further by getting students to compare the ways William the Conqueror and William and Mary secured power. Students' understanding of the Acts of Settlement and Union should be secured by the causation tasks. Then you could hold a class discussion about whether it was right to pass the Act of Settlement 1701 and the Act of Union 1707, and then to pass the crown to the house of Hanover. The activities are excellent for chronology and family links to ensure students understand who's who.

Timeline

1658
Charles II dies leaving no heir so his brother James takes the throne. He becomes King James II.

1687
King James states that both Catholics and Protestants can worship as they wish. He also shuts down Parliament.

1688
William and Mary land in Devon following the request of Parliament.

1689
William and Mary sign the Bill of Rights.

1690
William beats James's forces in Ireland at the Battle of the Boyne.

1692
At the Massacre of Glencoe, 38 members of the MacDonald clan are killed.

1701
The Act of Settlement states that Catholics cannot become king or queen.

1702
Queen Anne takes the throne.

1707
The Act of Union is passed joining the Parliaments of England and Scotland.

1714
The House of Hanover takes the throne and the Georgian period begins.

1745
The Battle of Culloden ends the Jacobite Rebellion to put Bonnie Prince Charlie on the throne.

Revolution, Industry and Empire: Britain 1558–1901

Chapter 6 Exit the Stuarts, enter the Georgians

A brief history continued

6.3 The Battle of Culloden, 1746

The Jacobite Rebellions of 1715 and 1745 are a great narrative with folklore and song to support learning. The character of Bonnie Prince Charlie who ran away to France may divide the loyalty of your class – take advantage of this by using the evidence provided in the lesson and get them to make a judgement about the different royal households. There is also the opportunity to develop GCSE skills by looking at similarities and differences of the two rebellions and to summarise the events of Culloden (supporting the demands of all exam boards).

6.4A/B From Tudor to Georgian times: what changed?

This lesson is an opportunity to revisit and test students on every chapter studied through to Georgian Britain. Students are given a timeline of key inventions across two centuries linked to science and technology, philosophy, and food and medicine. They will be asked to look at life in Elizabethan England and compare what life was like by 1750. The second order concepts of change and continuity, and similarity and difference have featured throughout the chapter, so this comparison exercise is a valuable way for students to consolidate both skills and knowledge. Building on the concepts and themes we have looked at throughout the series – power, wealth and culture – will also develop cultural capital and give students an insight into modern Britain.

Further reading and links

For teachers:

- *Restoration Scotland, 1660–1690: Royalist Politics, Religion and Ideas* by Clare Jackson (Boydell Press, 2003) offers a great insight into the relationship between Charles II, James, William and Mary with Scotland.
- Historian Dr Edward Vallance's 2014 article 'The Glorious Revolution' on www.bbc.co.uk will introduce you to new key terms for sharing with students. It categorises the causes of the Glorious Revolution. Search on 'History Glorious Revolution'.
- Watch the film *The Favourite* (2018) about Queen Anne and then read different historians' critiques of it. Do you defend or attack the film? You won't be able to show the film to your students as it is certificate 15, but you can share your insights.

For students:

- The National Trust for Scotland website has a page with key details about Culloden. Search for 'schools and learning guide to Culloden'.
- To help students focus on the change to government they could look at the fantastic BBC Bitesize revision page which goes all the way back to Magna Carta and tests their knowledge of power and government. Search for 'UK government through time'.

Beyond the classroom

- Students could research the Scottish Independence Referendum of 2014 and how the 1707 Union was discussed during it.
- Students could read Lord Belhaven's Mother Caledonia speech. What is he saying is going to happen to Scotland because of the Union? Students could rewrite the speech into today's language, perhaps using slang, or even make a rap.
- Read newspaper articles from 2013 when the law was changed to give female members of the royal family equality with men in the rules of succession. Students could consider how British people reacted and what it tells us about how women are viewed as rulers.
- Create a balloon debate for three to five of the inventions or developments from the Elizabethan period onwards. Students should be ready to justify their choices for those that stay in the balloon and those that get pushed out. Think about use at the time, impact and significance.

Chapter 6 Answers guidance

Answers guidance

The answers provided here are examples, based on the information provided in the Student Book. There may be other factors which are relevant to each question, and students may draw on as much of their own knowledge as possible to give detailed and precise answers. There are also many ways of answering questions, including exam-style questions (for example, of structuring an essay). However, these exemplar answers should provide a good starting point.

6.1A The Glorious Revolution
STUDENT BOOK PAGES 108–109

Over to You

1. None of them were the children of his wife, so the law prevented them from becoming monarch.
2a Some people worried that James might make major religious changes that could lead to some sort of religious war.
2b James was quite old and his only children, Mary and Anne, were Protestants. Some thought that King James might die soon and then his eldest daughter, Mary, would take over and everything would carry on as before.

Causation

1. Students' orders will vary, but they should argue that they all concerned Parliament – not consulting them was similar to the situation in the build-up to the Civil War, which was concerning; giving all the top jobs to Catholics made some worry that England would become a Catholic nation once more, and religious turmoil would follow (because most of the country were Protestant); creating his own army made some feel he might be planning to use it against Parliament, just like his father (Charles I) had done in the Civil War; when his wife gave birth to a son – with a Catholic father and mother – it was clear that the baby would be brought up as Catholic too, so Parliament feared that the country would have Catholic kings for ever more. And Parliament, made up mostly of Protestants, didn't want this.
2. Answers will vary, but should include why each of James's actions caused them concern – and whether they think the creation of a new army was the most concerning.

6.1B The Glorious Revolution
PAGES 110–111

Over to You

1.
   - James's wife has a son
   - Important Protestants invite William to invade
   - William lands in Devon with 12,000 soldiers
   - The leader of James's army joins William and Mary
   - James flees to France
2a Answers will vary, but students may write that it was a chance for power, or as a result of her strong Protestant beliefs that she did not want England to be Catholic.
2b This would cause William the problem of what to do with James – perhaps he wanted to avoid bloodshed, or a trial, or turning James into a martyr.
2c 5 November was a date known for rebellion or revolution (Gunpowder Plot) but this time it was Protestants removing Catholics, rather than the failed attempt in 1605 when Catholics tried to remove Protestants.
3. Because there are often wars and lots of fighting/bloodshed in revolutions, but this one was relatively peaceful.

Significance

1. The agreement between William and Mary and Parliament that states that the country has a monarch, who is the 'head of state', but their powers are clearly defined by Parliament and limited by laws and rules.
2. It changed the balance of power officially towards Parliament – for example, Parliament was to make all the laws, decide on taxes, share control of the army etc.
3. It had a long-lasting impact on the role of government in England – and it influenced laws, documents and ideas in the United States, Canada, Australia, Ireland, New Zealand and other countries. Also that it changed how the monarchy worked in England.
4. Answers will vary, but students should reference and explain that the Bill of Rights was important at the time and continued to be important and influential for many years to come.

6.2 From Stuarts to Georgians
PAGES 112–113

Over to You

1. 1689 – William and Mary become joint king and queen
   1690 – Battle of the Boyne, where James II's forces are crushed
   1692 – Massacre of Glencoe, where the MacDonalds of Glencoe are killed after failing to swear loyalty to William and Mary
   1694 – Mary dies of smallpox, leaving William to rule alone
   1701 – New law passed (the Act of Settlement) stating that the king or queen should always be a Protestant

Revolution, Industry and Empire: Britain 1558–1901 **117**

Chapter 6 Answers guidance

1702 – William dies, and Mary's sister (Anne) becomes queen
1707 – Act of Union – England, Wales, and now Scotland were united, with one Parliament based in London
1714 – Queen Anne dies and her closest Protestant relative (George Louis from Hanover) becomes king

2a Brother.
2b and c Father.
2d Sister.
3 Answers may include: In Ireland, William took away lots of land from Irish Catholics and gave it to English Protestants. Strict laws were introduced, banning Irish Catholics from teaching, voting or carrying a sword. In Scotland, William asked all the important Scottish families (clans) to swear an oath of loyalty to him. The MacDonalds of Glencoe were killed when they didn't. Later, in 1707, the Act of Union meant England, Wales and Scotland were united, with one Parliament based in London.
4 Queen Anne gave birth to 17 children, but they all died before she became queen. The law said that the throne should pass to her nearest Protestant relative after her death, who was George Louis from Hanover.

Causation

1a An Act passed by Parliament stating that after Queen Anne's death the throne would pass to the nearest Protestant heir.
1b An Act passed by Parliament to unite England, Scotland and Wales under the control of one Parliament, based in London.
2 To ensure that the monarchy would remain in Protestant hands, a new law was passed in 1701 (the Act of Settlement) that stated that the king or queen should always be a Protestant – and this is still the case today.

6.3 The Battle of Culloden, 1746
PAGES 114–115

Over to You

1 Someone who supported James Francis (the Latin for James is Jacobus).
2 Similarities: Catholic rebellion by a relative of James II, army gathered, ended in failure after defeat by English army. Differences: happened later, invaded England (as far south as Derby), but pushed back into Scotland, defeat at Culloden marked end of any serious attempt by the Jacobites, rebelling against a different king.
3 Answers will vary, but a summary could be: April 1746, King George II defeated Charlie and the Jacobites at Culloden, near Inverness. Jacobites were trying to restore a Catholic relative of King James II to the British throne. Jacobites were outnumbered two to one, poorly armed and half-starving. Soon beaten by George's forces. Charlie escaped, but hunted all over Scotland. Escaped to France dressed as a woman, and never returned to Britain. The defeat marked the end of any serious attempt by the Jacobites to restore the Stuart family to the British throne. The era of the Georgians was now firmly established.

Interpretation Analysis

1 The song commemorates Charlie being rowed in a small boat to the Isle of Skye by a woman called Flora MacDonald, after he had been hunted around Scotland after his defeat at Culloden.
2 Supporter of Charlie, because the language is supportive of him. For example, it says he's born to be king and that he will come again, it's not critical of him or says he was in the wrong or a rebel.

6.4A From Tudor to Georgian times: what changed?
PAGES 116–117

Over to You

1a Some choices may be: 1575: French army surgeon, Ambroise Paré, used bandages and soothing ointments (rather than boiling oil) to treat wounds and prevent infection. 1628: English doctor, William Harvey, proved that the heart is a pump and circulates blood around the body. Medical treatments like blood transfusions and heart surgery would not work without this understanding. 1717: Lady Mary Wortley Montagu experimented with smallpox inoculations (a way of preventing a person getting the disease). After the success of her experiments, King George I even had his own grandchildren inoculated!
1b Some choices may be: 1609: An Italian, Galileo Galilei, made the first practical telescope and saw planets such as Mars and Venus for the first time. 1661: Robert Boyle proved that air is essential for both breathing and burning. He showed that all substances are made up of elements – and not a mixture of earth, air, fire and water, which is what people had believed since ancient times. 1686: Isaac Newton discovered that a force (which we call gravity) pulls an object towards the ground. He realised that gravity is what keeps the moon moving around the Earth.
1c Answers will vary but they may mention things that remain

Chapter 6 Answers guidance

unknown (perhaps about the planets, or aliens, or about cures for disease).

Change and Continuity

1 Answers will vary but might say: God has answers to everything, not sure about the role of the heart, cannot explain why things drop down, sun moves around the Earth.
2 Answers will vary but might say: God has answers to everything – science is beginning to explain things; not sure about the role of the heart – Harvey proves it's a pump; cannot explain why things drop down – Newton writes about gravity; sun moves around the Earth – Galileo Galilei could prove the Earth moves around the sun.
3 Answers will vary but will focus on knowledge of inoculation, the planets, scientific experiments, astronomy, the heart etc.

6.4B From Tudor to Georgian times: what changed?
PAGES 118–119

Over to You

1 The fact file will reflect the information on these lesson pages.
2 Answers should reflect that one of the key reasons why the British wanted to control land in other parts of the world was related to trade – Britain imported goods from abroad for people to buy, and also exported goods to other customers abroad. Also, the goods made in Britain, like cloth, pottery and iron, were sold abroad in huge numbers. All this trade made a lot of money for British companies and provided plenty of jobs for British workers.

Change and Continuity

1 The information will reflect the information on these lesson pages.
2 Answers will vary, but examples of similarity may include: people still mainly communicate through word of mouth; hunting still popular for the rich; England still has largest population; monarch and the ruling classes such as landowners still very powerful; punishments still savage/execution still a punishment; people still don't know that germs cause disease.

Chapter 6 Have you been learning?

Answers guidance

Chapter 6 Have you been learning?

Quick Knowledge Quiz
PAGE 120

1 c 1685
2 b They were brothers
3 c The Glorious Revolution
4 c Only Catholics can be the king or queen
5 a constitutional monarchy
6 c Battle of the Boyne
7 b Act of Settlement
8 b Hanover, in modern-day Germany
9 a 1715
10 c Bonnie Prince Charlie

Literacy Focus
PAGE 121

Applying key words

Answers may vary, but could be:

1b The period from the execution of Charles I in 1649 to when Charles II became king. England had no monarchy between 1649 and 1660 – this was the time when Oliver Cromwell ruled as Lord Protector.
1c A complete change in the way a country is ruled. The Glorious Revolution of 1688–1689 replaced the Catholic James II with the joint monarchy of his Protestant daughter Mary and her Dutch husband, William III of Orange.
1d The return of a monarch to the throne of England when Charles II became king in 1660. After the Interregnum, Charles II (also known as the Merry Monarch) returned to the throne in May 1660.
1e A form of monarchy in which the king or queen rules in accordance with a set of rules and laws. The Bill of Rights established the type of monarchy that we still have today – a country with a monarch, who is the 'head of state', but their powers are clearly defined by Parliament and limited by laws and rules, known as a constitutional monarchy.

Revolution, Industry and Empire: Britain 1558–1901   119

Chapter 6 Assessment: Change and continuity

Assessment summary

The assessments in this textbook have been carefully designed and tested with History teachers to support student progression throughout the course. This specific assessment is written to support Year 8 or Year 9 students in tackling questions relating to change and continuity.

> ⭐ In what ways did the lives of British people change, and in what ways did it stay the same between the late Tudor period and the beginning of the Georgian period (c1550s–c1700s)? (20)

Students will be expected to identify different examples of change over the time period (Question 1) and then do the same for continuity (Question 2). Using these examples, students will make a judgement on the question about how far things changed and how far things stayed the same (Question 3) and write up their response (Question 4).

To support Year 8 and Year 9 students with this question sentence starters and key areas of change and continuity that they could focus on are provided.

For the mark scheme, see page 122.

A note about the end-of-chapter assessments

There is an assessment for each Student Book chapter. Each is structured like a GCSE exam-style question, with scaffolding steps to support KS3 students. Each assessment has a total of 20 marks, and is designed to be completed in a typical lesson – each has been written with a time allowance of about 30 minutes.

There is a mark scheme for each assessment. You can choose how to give student outcomes: a mark out of 20; a percentage; a performance indicator (we use a three-stage indicator – 'Developing', 'Secure', 'Extending' – but you could adapt to match any performance indicators used in your school); or a GCSE grade indicator. To convert raw marks to a performance or GCSE grade indicator, use this table:

Raw marks				
0	1–6	7–13	14–20	
GCSE grade (9–1) indicators*				
U	1–3	4–6	7–9	
Performance indicator				
Ungraded	Developing	Secure	Extending	

* Please appreciate that these are approximate grades based on grade boundaries from recent GCSE exam papers. If a student achieves a Grade 7 in one of these assessments, it is not the equivalent of a Grade 7 at GCSE. Instead it is an indicator of the grade the student could expect to get if they continue on their flight path through KS3 and GCSE. Please note:
 • the raw-mark boundaries are based on but do not match precisely those for recent GCSE exam papers: this is because our assessments are focused around one exam-style question, likely to be done at the end of a chapter (topic) rather than at the end of the course. Secondly, we provide carefully considered scaffolded steps to allow KS3 students to tackle high level questions and gain confidence through the deliberate practice of building up detailed answers.
 • the assessments for Student Book 3 are progressively more demanding in that they use higher-order command words and provide less scaffolded support – if you set one of them for Year 8 students, please take that into account when awarding GCSE grade indicators.

Entering student outcomes into the Kerboodle Markbook

The Kerboodle Markbook records scores and percentages to allow for quick comparison of performance. If you want to use the Markbook to record student outcomes, you will need to enter the appropriate values given in the raw marks row of the table above.

Chapter 6 Assessment: Change and continuity

Links to GCSE

By the end of KS3, students should be familiar with the History skill of identifying change and continuity. At GCSE, most exam boards specifically ask students to identify change and continuity. For example:

AQA:
- Explain two ways in which... and... were similar/different. (8)

Edexcel:
- Explain one way in which... was different from/similar to... (4)

OCR B:
- How far do you agree that...? Give reasons for your answer. (18)

Eduqas:
- Outline how... changed from... to... In your answer you should provide a written narrative discussing the... across three historical eras. (16) (SPaG 4)

Links to KS3 History resources

Student Book

This assessment question links to these lessons:

1.1 What was Britain like in 1558?
6.4A/B From Tudor to Georgian times: what changed?

Kerboodle

Support for this assessment question on Kerboodle:

RIE 6 Assessment presentation: Change and continuity
RIE 6 Assessment worksheet (Core): Change and continuity
RIE 6 Assessment worksheet (Foundation): Change and continuity

Curriculum and Assessment Planning Guide

Support for this assessment question in this guide:

6 Assessment mark scheme – page 122
6 Assessment sample student answers – pages 123–124

Chapter 6 Assessment: Change and continuity

Student name: _____   Date: _____

Mark scheme

Assessment bands	Marks	GCSE grade indicators*	I have...
	0	Ungraded	
Developing	1–6	1–3	☐ written about some of the features and characteristics of the lives of British people in the c1550s and c1700s and shown some understanding of them. ☐ shown limited understanding of the changes and continuities that have taken place. ☐ followed the basic essay structure and presented a summary of what changed and what didn't.
Secure	7–13	4–6	☐ shown knowledge and understanding of key features and characteristics of the lives of British people in the c1550s and c1700s. ☐ shown detailed understanding of the changes and continuities that have taken place. ☐ followed an organised essay structure and presented a well-developed summary of what changed and what didn't.
Extending	14–20	7–9	☐ shown strong, wide-ranging knowledge of key features and characteristics of the lives of British people in the c1550s and c1700s in ways that show a well-developed understanding of them. ☐ shown an excellent understanding of the changes and continuities that have taken place and set out a consistently focused and very well-supported answer. ☐ written a well-organised, structured answer and presented a full summary of the nature of both changes and continuities.

* IMPORTANT: These are approximate indicators devised using publicly available information on the new GCSE grades. They are designed to assist in the process of tracking and monitoring. They cannot and should not be used to replace teachers' professional judgement. Teachers should use their own discretion in applying them, taking into account the cumulative test scores of an individual student (rather than just one assessment point), and should refer to their institution's assessment policy.

Mark: _____

Comment:

Chapter 6 Assessment: Change and continuity

Sample student answers

Assessment: Change and continuity

STUDENT BOOK PAGE 123

> In what ways did the lives of British people change, and in what ways did it stay the same between the late Tudor period and the beginning of the Georgian period (c1550s–c1700s)? (20)

⭐ Sample Developing band answer

There were several areas where the lives of British people changed between the Tudor and Georgian periods. For example, the relationship between the king or queen and Parliament changed, because Parliament gained more power. The king or queen still had a say over some things, but by the Georgian period this was much less than in the Tudor period because of the Bill of Rights.

Some areas of life stayed the same, for example the different classes. Society was still divided into rich and poor. If you were a poor labourer, life would have stayed largely the same from the Tudor to the Georgian period.

⭐ Sample Secure band answer

There were several areas where the lives of British people changed between the Tudor and Georgian periods. For example, who controlled the country changed, because Parliament was given more power. This is different from the Tudor period as Elizabeth had controlled laws. Another key area of change was the food people ate – there were much more exotic foods that came from the voyages of discovery during the Tudor period, such as bananas and spices. However, there is continuity with this area of life and that is the diet of the different classes. The upper class would still eat more meat and have the new exotic foods. However, the poorer people would be unlikely to afford the new foods from other countries and still ate mostly seasonal vegetables.

There were several areas where the lives of British people stayed the same between the Tudor and Georgian periods. For example, entertainment stayed the same for the different classes. The poorer people went to ale houses and gambled on bear-baiting, as they had done in the Tudor period. The rich still hunted on their grounds. However, there was change in entertainment too – as the popularity of the theatre continued to grow, the rich spent their time watching plays and enjoying concerts instead of watching the blood sports they had attended in the Tudor period.

In conclusion life changed from the mid-1500s to the mid-1700s because who had control of the country changed, and new foods from around the world changed diets. However, for the poorer people in society, life mainly stayed the same over the 200 years.

Chapter 6 Assessment: Change and continuity

⭐ Sample Extending band answer

There were several areas where life in Britain changed from the mid-1500s to the early 1700s; one area is the development of science and medicine. In the Tudor and Stuart periods, people started to understand the human body better, such as Ambroise Paré, who used bandages with soothing ointment instead of boiling oil to treat wounds, and William Harvey, who discovered that the heart is a pump. However, it was in the Georgian period that more understanding of disease meant people's lives were improved. For example, in 1717, Lady Montagu experimented with smallpox inoculations to prevent people getting the disease. The medical advancements had a big impact on people's lives. However, there was some continuity in this area as there was still a limited understanding of how germs cause disease. Many people still died from basic operations because there were no painkillers or germ-free operating rooms.

One area of change that happened rapidly was who had power in Britain. In the early 1500s the monarch still had a lot of say over Parliament. However, by the early 1700s, the power of Parliament had surpassed the monarch, and the country had become a constitutional monarchy. This was because of the Glorious Revolution, which resulted in the Bill of Rights of 1689. This meant that the monarch could not dictate laws or raise taxes without consulting Parliament. However, for ordinary people, there was very little change as it was the rich in society who became members of Parliament. This continuity of life for the poor can be seen in travel, communication and where people lived. By the Georgian period, towns with ports that had opened up the world were still places that were mainly lived in by the rich. The poor still mainly lived in the countryside and had to walk everywhere, just like they had in the Elizabethan period. Although literacy levels had increased in the Elizabethan period it was still mainly the rich who read and had libraries. Poorer people still relied on word of mouth in the Georgian period.

Overall, people's lives were changed by the early 1700s in lots of ways, but the divisions of society were still clear between the rich and the poor. It is fair to say that the rich experienced greater change than the poor.

Chapter 7 The Industrial Revolution: from farming to factories

Links to KS3 History National Curriculum

'Britain as the first industrial nation – the impact on society' is defined as a possible area of study in the latest KS3 History National Curriculum. This chapter outlines the seismic changes that took place in Britain during the eighteenth and nineteenth centuries as the country changed from a mainly agrarian economy to the industrial powerhouse of the world. A great many second order concepts are explored here, including change, causation, and significance. The tasks in the work sections provide many opportunities for students to select and combine information from sources to answer questions, write a clear and organised summary, identify connections between different events, and show how one event led to another.

There is no doubt that the new machines, the working conditions in factories and mines, and the changing landscape of Britain will enthuse students. They will be engaged by the first-hand accounts and the focus on the many key pioneering individuals of the Industrial Revolution. Moreover, the chapter gives students a chance to develop and build on the first order concepts of government and empire.

Skills and processes covered in this chapter

		Lesson/activity in the Student Book
History Skills	Knowledge and understanding	7.1 Over to You: 1a, 1b, 2, 3
		7.2A Knowledge and Understanding: 1a, 1b, 1c, 1d
		7.2B Over to You: 1a, 2
		7.3 Over to You: 1a, 1c; Knowledge and Understanding: 1
		7.5 Over to You: 1
		7.6 Over to You: 1a, 1b, 1c
		7.7A Over to You: 1a, 1b, 1c, 1d, 1e, 1f
		7.8 Over to You: 1
		Have you been learning? Quick Knowledge Quiz: 1, 2, 3, 4, 5, 6, 7, 8, 9, 10
	Interpretations	
	Sources	7.2B Over to You: 1a, 1b, 3, 4a, 4b
		7.4 Source Analysis: 1, 2, 3
	Significance	7.5 Significance: 1
		7.7A Over to You: 2
		7.7B Over to You: 1; Significance: 1
	Cause and consequence	7.1 Over to You: 4
		7.2A Over to You: 1, 2b, 3
		7.2B Over to You: 1b, 4b; Causation: 1
		7.3 Over to You: 1b
		7.4 Over to You: 1a, 1b
		7.5 Over to You: 2, 3b, 4
		7.6 Over to You: 2
		7.8 Over to You: 2a, 2b, 2c; Causation: 1
		7 Assessment: Causation: 1, 2, 3, 4
	Diversity/Similarity and difference	
	Change and continuity	7.2A Over to You: 2b, 3
		7.3 Over to You: 2a, 2b

Revolution, Industry and Empire: Britain 1558–1901 125

Chapter 7 The Industrial Revolution: from farming to factories

		Lesson/activity in the Student Book
		7.4 Over to You: 2a, 2b
		7.5 Over to You: 3a
		7.6 Change: 1, 2
		7.7A Over to You: 2
		7.7B Over to You: 1
		7.8 Over to You: 2a, 2b, 2c
Literacy and Numeracy	Literacy	7.1 Over to You: 4
		Have you been learning? Literacy Focus: 1a, 1b, 1c
	Numeracy	7.2A Over to You: 2a
		7.5 Over to You: 3a

Lesson sequence

Lesson title	Student Book pages	Objectives
7.1 From homeworkers to factory workers	pp 124–125	• Explain how products were manufactured in Britain before the mid-1700s. • Examine how and why machines changed the way goods were made in Britain.
7.2A How did factories create towns?	pp 126–127	• Explain how factories caused the population of towns to increase. • Evaluate the impact of steam power on factories and towns.
7.2B How did factories create towns?	pp 128–129	
7.3 Peggy the pauper	pp 130–131	• Examine why so many children worked in factories. • Describe working conditions in some factories.
7.4 How were factory working conditions improved?	pp 132–133	• Identify why some factory owners were unwilling to improve working conditions. • Examine key reforms that eventually improved life for Britain's workers.
7.5 'Black gold' and the new 'Age of Iron'	pp 134–135	• Examine why there was an increase in the demand for coal. • Outline how iron was produced. • Describe how iron-making became such an important business.
7.6 From roads to canals to railways	pp 136–137	• Outline how changes in industry led to changes in Britain's transport networks. • Describe what these changes were and how they came about.
7.7A An age of invention	pp 138–139	• Identify some of the achievements of Britain's great inventors, designers and scientists. • Judge who you think deserves the title 'Greatest Inventor and/or Designer'.
7.7B An age of invention	pp 140–141	
7.8 So what was the Industrial Revolution?	pp 142–143	• Explain what is meant by the term 'Industrial Revolution'. • Analyse the causes of the Industrial Revolution.
Chapter 7 Have you been learning?	pp 144–145	• Choose the correct answer from the given options for a quick recap. • Compare and contrast two visual sources.
Chapter 7 History skill: Causation	p 146	• Explore how to respond to a statement about causation.
Chapter 7 Assessment: Causation	p 147	• Assess a variety of causes relating to the Industrial Revolution.

Chapter 7 The Industrial Revolution: from farming to factories

Links to the GCSE curriculum

This chapter provides some historical context to the following:

AQA: Power and the People c1170–Present

Edexcel: Medicine in Britain c1250–Present

Eduqas: Changes in Health and Medicine in Britain c500–Present

OCR B: The People's Health c1250–Present

WJEC: Radicalism and Protest 1810–1848

Exam-style questions covered in this chapter

Exam board	Lesson/activity question location	Command words	History skills/concepts
AQA	7.3 Knowledge and Understanding: 1	Describe…	Knowledge and understanding
	7.7B Significance: 1	Explain the significance…	Significance
	7.8 Causation: 1	How far do you agree…	Cause and consequence
Edexcel	7.2B Causation: 1	Explain why…	Cause and consequence
	7.3 Knowledge and Understanding: 1	Describe…	Knowledge and understanding
	7.4 Source Analysis: 3	How could you follow up…	Source analysis
	7.5 Over to You: 2	Explain why…	Cause and consequence
	7.8 Causation: 1	How far do you agree…	Cause and consequence
OCR A	7.2A Over to You: 1	Explain how…	Cause and consequence
	7.2B Causation: 1	Explain why…	Cause and consequence
	7.3 Knowledge and Understanding: 1	Describe…	Knowledge and understanding
	7.5 Over to You: 2	Explain why…	Cause and consequence
	7.5 Significance: 1	How significant was…	Significance
	7.7B Significance: 1	How significant was…	Significance
OCR B	7.6 Change: 2	Write a clear and organised summary…	Change and continuity
	7.8 Causation: 1	How far do you agree…	Cause and consequence
Eduqas	7.2B Causation: 1	Explain why…	Cause and consequence
	7.5 Over to You: 2	Explain why…	Cause and consequence
	7.7B Significance: 1	Why was… significant…	Significance
WJEC	7.2A Knowledge and Understanding: 1	Complete the sentences…	Knowledge and understanding
	7.2B Causation: 1	Explain why…	Cause and consequence
	7.5 Over to You: 2	Explain why…	Cause and consequence
	7.7A Over to You: 1	Complete the sentences…	Knowledge and understanding
	7.7B Significance: 1	Why was… significant…	Significance

Revolution, Industry and Empire: Britain 1558–1901

Chapter 7 The Industrial Revolution: from farming to factories

A brief history

7.1 From homeworkers to factory workers

This lesson sets the scene for what work was like for the – new to be – working class. We move from the domestic system to the factory system by tracking the inventions made in the early to mid-1700s and focusing on Arkwright. Students will be able to compare the domestic and factory systems and explain disadvantages and advantages, giving them an idea of what changed for the workers of the new industrial Britain. A good hook for future lessons would be for students to use their studies of earlier periods to predict how society and power might change with the new factories.

7.2A/B How did factories create towns?

Population increase has been a feature of earlier chapters so its causes and consequences will be familiar to students. The lesson has numeracy as a key focus as students will compare dates and look for trends in the figures they are shown. One activity asks them to make a bar chart – find out from your Maths and Science departments what language they use for teaching this skill. These cross-curricular links will help produce better graphs! The invention of steam is a real turning point in industrialisation and is important for future lessons. There is the opportunity for developing inference skills while using first-hand accounts.

7.3 Peggy the pauper

Nothing engages KS3 students quite like the conditions of factories and mines and the ages of the children who worked in them. This lesson explores the conditions and their effects on children through the eyes of a female pauper apprentice. The details of punishments used will make students appreciate their school conduct policy! This leads nicely to the activity exploring the change in children's routines then and now. The lesson is balanced with the introduction of new model villages such as New Lanark. Students will use all of the content to describe factory conditions.

7.4 How were factory working conditions improved?

There are lots of opportunities here to develop understanding of the role of government – even linking back to Elizabethan Poor Law. Although the term 'laissez-faire' is not mentioned you could share this with students to give them an idea of how politicians viewed the poor. The use of source accounts builds the picture towards reform, which would be a good time to develop the role of the individual, e.g. Michael Sadler. Students are asked to explain the importance of key acts in reforming working conditions, and will evaluate the utility of a personal account.

Timeline

1733
Flying Shuttle is invented, allowing weavers to make cloth much quicker.

1750s
Most people still live in the countryside.

1764
Spinning Jenny is invented, producing thread much quicker.

1768
James Watt invents the steam engine.

1769
Richard Arkwright invents the Spinning Frame, enabling production to move from the home to the factory.

1771
Arkwright opens his first factory in Cromford, Derbyshire.

1781
The iron bridge at Coalbrookdale is opened, the first major bridge made entirely of cast iron.

1825
The Stockton and Darlington Railway becomes the first public transport system to use steam locomotives.

1833
Factory Act stops children under nine working in factories and reduces the hours of older children.

1842
Mines Act states that no women or children under ten can work in the mines.

1850s
Britain's factories produce two-thirds of the world's cotton cloth.

A brief history

7.5 'Black gold' and the new 'Age of Iron'

Now that students understand why and how Britain first industrialised, they can look at the development of this industrialisation through the role of coal. This lesson links back to the importance of steam power, before moving on to the role of Coalbrookdale in the production of iron. It would be useful to speak with your Science or Design and Technology departments to see how they teach iron production. The lesson will culminate in students explaining the significance of coal mining for Britain.

7.6 From roads to canals to railways

At first glance, changes to Britain's transport network in the 1700s and 1800s may not sound the most enthralling topic. However, you should find that this section really captures students' imaginations and causes them to re-evaluate the world around them. The lesson starts with a fantastic fact about journey times and how they changed over the period, which links back again to steam power. The expectations are that students will write definitions of the different transport developments, use key dates, and summarise the developments. A good way to push students would be for them to link back to previous content about the period.

7.7A/B An age of invention

Most students will own, or have access to, a phone that is also a camera and a music player, and some may be shocked that none of these items existed before the nineteenth century. Indeed, the thought of only ever hearing live music, never seeing a photo of themselves, not using a computer or being able to switch on a light will leave many aghast! This lesson examines the origins of some of today's best-known inventions and the people behind them. Students must choose their favourite inventor/designer and write a persuasive speech to convince others – a great way to develop significance.

7.8 So what was the Industrial Revolution?

This lesson offers a chance for students to tie together all the changes they have covered so far about the Industrial Revolution. It requires students to take a more strategic view of their History studies. With the exception of the role played by the British Empire, all of the factors that contributed to the Industrial Revolution should already be familiar to students. Now they need to establish links between the factors through the use of a diagram, illustrating (as is so often the case in History) that the factors are interdependent and that their importance cannot be judged in isolation.

Further reading and links

For teachers:

- There are many novels about this period of British history. Elizabeth Gaskell's *North and South* (1854) has vivid descriptions of life in industrial Britain. This could be used for developing your own understanding of the period but can also be shared with students to improve contextual understanding, cultural capital and literacy.

- Research what Marx and Engels wrote about the Industrial Revolution and how this informed the idea of the working class in Britain. The British Library website has some documents to get you started: search for 'Condition of the Working Class in England'.

For students:

- Jacqueline Wilson's *Hetty Feather* novels (Doubleday, 2009–13) offer a great insight into industrial Britain and the dangers working-class children faced. Students could develop their understanding by reading some of them.

- Increase cultural capital by watching *Oliver!* (1968) and get students to make notes of what is and is not accurate about the Industrial Revolution.

- 'The Original Women in Tech' is a TedX talk about Ada Lovelace. After watching it, students should consider how women have been overlooked in history (discussed at the start of the talk) and research other women from the industrial period who have been left out of mainstream history. Search on 'Zoe Philpott Ada Lovelace TedX'.

Beyond the classroom

- Visit your nearest New Model village to see how they transformed the lives and working conditions for the working class during the Industrial Revolution.

- www.spartacus-educational.com has excellent first-hand accounts of this period. Go to 'British History' and then 'Child Labour in Britain'.

- Look at paintings of the industrial Black Country by Edwin Butler Bayliss (1874–1950). Ask students to describe them using their knowledge from the chapter.

- Students could research the Quakers, how they link to nineteenth-century reforms, and why they were so concerned with the lives of the working class.

Revolution, Industry and Empire: Britain 1558–1901

Chapter 7 Answers guidance

Answers guidance

The answers provided here are examples, based on the information provided in the Student Book. There may be other factors which are relevant to each question, and students may draw on as much of their own knowledge as possible to give detailed and precise answers. There are also many ways of answering questions, including exam-style questions (for example, of structuring an essay). However, these exemplar answers should provide a good starting point.

7.1 From homeworkers to factory workers
STUDENT BOOK PAGES 124–125

Over to You

1a Domestic system: people worked in their homes or small workshops.
1b Factory system: people worked in factories to produce goods in large numbers; replaced the domestic system.
2 Advantages: family worked together for the hours they wanted. Disadvantages: the vast profits were made by the merchant, rather than the family, long hours, boring.
3 Answers will vary, but will probably agree because he was the first to put his huge spinning machines in specially created buildings ('factories' or 'mills') – in 1771 at Cromford in Derbyshire.
4 Student reports will vary but should mention: A factory is a large building containing spinning machines that are too big for people's homes. The machines are powered by a waterwheel – and as the wheel turned all day and night it meant that the machines (and workers) could work 24 hours a day. Machine operators – these could be men, women and children – can produce over 60 times more cloth than a whole family working at home, for a fraction of the wages. This means the cloth can be sold for a much lower price but still make a big profit. It's possible for factory owners to make huge profits.

7.2A How did factories create towns?
PAGES 126–127

Over to You

1 The new factories pulled people into towns from the countryside looking for work, so the factory owners built houses for their workers to rent, and people began to set up shops and inns so the workers could buy food and drink. Soon, roads were being built, along with churches, schools and places of entertainment. This continued and, before long, places that were previously tiny villages had grown into large towns, and small towns became huge, overcrowded cities.
2a Bar charts will reflect the growth of the towns.
2b It tells us that population increased in all towns, and the growth was rapid.
3 Student descriptions will vary, but should mention that Bradford was a small town in 1800, but linked to the transport system by the Leeds and Liverpool Canal. From 1800, Bradford began to increase in size until the outlying areas became part of Bradford as a whole. By 1873, Bradford was a large town/city, that included many areas that were previously isolated – and had improved transport links as the railways arrived.

Knowledge and Understanding

1a Countryside.
1b 105,000.
1c Leeds and Liverpool.
1d Railways.

7.2B How did factories create towns?
PAGES 128–129

Over to You

1a Water power.
1b Dry weather caused the water levels to be too low, so the wheel wouldn't turn. Too much rain made water levels too high so the wheel stopped working properly.
2
- Coal: burned to turn the water in the boiler into steam.
- Piston: pushed up and down by steam, driving the beam.
- Sun-and-planet gears: change the vertical motion into a circular one, which turns the wheel.
- Beam: moves up and down, driving the wheel.
- Boiler: contains the water that is turned into steam.
- Wheel: is attached to belts that drive factory machines.

3 After – many houses (a feature of an industrialised town), 'flames, hissing and rattling' as a result of the coal being burned, windows shaking (the steam engines), dark clouds (smoke).
4a Powered by coal-fired steam engines, the dirty smoke is a by-product of this.
4b Answers will vary, but might reference pollution of the environment because of the smoke, lung/breathing difficulties.

Causation

1 Steam power was faster and more reliable than water power; it also meant that factories no longer had to be built next to fast-flowing rivers – they could be built anywhere.

7.3 Peggy the pauper
PAGES 130–131

Over to You

1a Answers might include: Long hours, work that is too hard for them at their ages (not strong enough to lift heavy things and it damages their bodies), workers beaten, silly fines.

1b Answers might include: No strict government guidelines or laws to control what went on in the early factories, local authorities themselves were sending children to work in the factories, most factory owners only cared about making a profit, not wasting money on providing a safe place to work.

1c Owen built good quality houses, schools, shops and parks for his workers in New Lanark, Scotland. He also reduced working hours.

2a Student timelines will vary.

2b Answers will vary but might include: Today, children go to school, rather than work; don't get beaten for doing something wrong – punishments exist (at school, for example), but not so severe; if children do work (Saturday job/paper round) there are limits on what hours can be worked, whereas children in the early 1800s worked a 12–15-hour day; more breaks today, whereas children had fewer in early 1800s; no expectation to work, or go to school for six days – time for hobbies/socialising today, no time for this in early 1800s.

Knowledge and Understanding

1 Answers will vary but include: Long hours, brutal punishments, poor safety measures.

7.4 How were factory conditions improved?
PAGES 132–133

Over to You

1a Some were motivated by religious beliefs, others thought that people might work harder if they were treated better.

1b Some felt politicians had no right to interfere in their business; they believed that it was up to the owners to decide how to run their factories and mines and that introducing laws that forced owners to spend money on improvements could harm profits. They also argued that reducing the hours that children and women worked might cause money problems for the family.

2a Answers will vary.

2b Answers will vary, but, for example, if they chose the 1833 Factory Act, they might write that it was a positive move that finally children were getting some protection – and some schooling.

Source Analysis

1 Answers will vary, but words might include: pity, horror, anger, shock, surprise.

2 Answers might vary, but generally it will be 'no' because they might point out that it might not be exaggerated – but if it was, there may be some truth in it anyway. Also, if he did exaggerate, it tells historians of the motives and tactics of reformers and the lengths they were willing to go to to bring about change.

3 Students may suggest consulting a wide variety of sources – from factory owners, as well as reformers, witnesses, factory workers, images etc. Also looking at the work of academics who have made it their job to study these things.

7.5 'Black gold' and the new 'Age of Iron'
PAGES 134–135

Over to You

1 Answers may include: Iron ore is dug from the ground, melted together with limestone and charcoal to such a temperature that it melts and pours out of the bottom of the furnace. This red-hot, liquid iron is poured into casts to make cast iron. If cast iron is reheated and hammered, the pockets of air are removed and it becomes wrought iron, which is purer and stronger.

2 Reasons include: Coal burns for a long time – much longer than wood – so was used to cook with and heat homes. As the population increased, more coal was needed. It was also needed to power steam engines in the new factories. Coal was used in the making of bricks, pottery, glass, beer, sugar, soap and iron as well.

3a Student bar charts will reflect the chart.

3b Answers will reflect that the production of iron, coal and steel dramatically increased in a short period of time.

4 Students may say it was the first in the world, new ideas and applications cause sensation, and it showed the possibilities of iron.

Significance

1 Answers will vary, but students may say that the coal mining industry was significant at the time because the increased population needed fuel to heat their homes and cook food, so it was vital that more was produced. Also, coal was vital in the production of iron, and iron was increasingly used in all areas of life. The army used it for cannons, the navy for 'iron-clad' ships, and the new factories were held up with iron beams, and used iron machines that were powered by iron steam engines. Iron was used to make tools, trains and railway tracks, and at home people had fireplaces with iron grates and cooked on iron

Revolution, Industry and Empire: Britain 1558–1901

Chapter 7 Answers guidance

stoves using iron pans. The coal industry was a vital part of the iron industry at this time – as well as being needed in its own right.

7.6 From roads to canals to railways
PAGES 136–137

Over to You

1a Turnpike trust: a group of businesspeople who promised to improve and maintain a section of road. In return, they were allowed to charge a toll to every person that used their section of road.
1b Canal: a long, narrow, man-made channel of water.
1c Locomotive: a steam engine that moved wheels along a set of rails or track – often called 'trains'.
2 • 1706: first turnpike trust – meant roads could be improved, travel became faster.
 • 1761: first canal (11km long) built by the Duke of Bridgewater from his mines in Worsley to the city of Manchester – ideal for moving heavy and fragile goods, began an era of 'canal mania'.
 • 1804: Richard Trevithick built a locomotive that pulled ten tons of iron and 70 passengers for 14.5km in Merthyr Tydfil, South Wales – showed the possibilities of steam power being used in transport.
 • 1825: Stockton and Darlington Railway became the first public transport system in the world to use steam locomotives – showed the possibilities of using steam locomotives to move large numbers of people, not just goods.
 • 1830: Liverpool and Manchester Railway built, linking two major industrial cities for the first time.

Change

1 Students should recall that if you travelled from one city to the other in the early 1700s, it would have taken you a week by boat or about two weeks by road. By 1900, you could make the same journey in just nine hours by train.
2 Answers will vary, but fuller, more developed answers will explain why changes in transport were needed and then summarise the advances and changes relating to roads, canals and railways, with examples of the developments in these transport systems (for example, 'By 1900, there were over 32,000 km of train track that carried millions of passengers every year'). Students should also mention the decrease in travel time.

7.7A An age of invention
PAGES 138–139

Over to You

1a James Watt.
1b Birmingham.
1c Liverpool and Manchester.
1d Miners.
1e 1831.
1f Power stations.
2 Notes may include:
 • James Watt: Made steam engines faster and more reliable, more efficient. Designed a new steam engine (rotary motion). Now steam power could be used to drive machinery. Produced some of the finest steam engines in the world. Changed the source of power – steam power replaced horse, water, wind and muscle power. Some scientists argue that his designs should serve as the starting point of a new era in the Earth's history, in which human activity began to alter Earth's surface, atmosphere and oceans.
 • George Stephenson: Produced a safety lamp for miners. Designed Britain's first passenger railway – the Stockton and Darlington Railway. Designed and made locomotives for the first city-to-city line – Liverpool to Manchester. Some say he created the British railway system – designed most of the railway that connects the major cities.
 • Michael Faraday: Discovered how to generate electricity. Same basic principle that electric power stations work on today. His research into the relationship between electricity and magnetism led to the invention of the electric motor and many other technological advances.

7.7B An age of invention
PAGES 140–141

Over to You

1 Notes may include:
 • Ada Lovelace: Added lots of detail to Babbage's report. Worked out how the machine could be programmed with a code to calculate numbers. Some consider Lovelace's plans for a machine to carry out an instruction to be the world's first ever computer programme. Was such a brilliant mathematician and programmer that her notes, all written in the early to mid-1800s, were actually used by codebreakers in the Second World War and in future computer design.
 • Isambard Kingdom Brunel: Designed the Clifton Suspension Bridge and designed and built the Great Western Railway. He also

132   Chapter 7 The Industrial Revolution: from farming to factories

Chapter 7 Answers guidance

built two grand stations – Paddington (London) and Temple Meads (Bristol). Designed three huge record-breaking iron ships – one of which laid the first underwater communications cable between America and Britain. Lasting engineering legacy, visible in the bridges, tunnels, viaducts, buildings and rail routes he left behind.
- Henry Bessemer: Invented a 'converter', a machine for turning iron into steel. Laid the foundations for global mass production of steel, which is so widely used in the modern world.
- Alexander Graham Bell: Worked all his life on making electrical hearing aids for deaf people. Invented his telephone in 1876 (but lots of people were trying to make telephones at this time and he was accused of copying other inventors' designs). Invented other things too – medical, aeronautical.

Significance

1 Student speeches will vary, but should include details about their contribution at the time and over time.

7.8 So what was the Industrial Revolution?
PAGES 142–143

Over to You

1 Answers may include: A dramatic change in the way things were made; a time when factories replaced farming as the main form of business in Britain; sometimes used to describe the changes in population, transport, cities and so on in the period between c1750 and 1901.
2 Student connections will vary but examples include:
- Britain had a large and growing population that supplied labour to the new factories and could purchase the new goods.
- The large empire could provide the raw materials for the factories and the vast number of workers who worked in them.
- Britain's vast stores of coal and iron meant the country had the raw materials to make iron and steel and the products associated with it.

Causation

1 Answers will vary, but the answer should explain how the named factor (in this case, the British Empire) contributed to the Industrial Revolution, but students should also focus on other factors (at least two, perhaps) and explain how they also contributed. They should conclude with their thoughts on whether the growth of the British Empire was the main reason or not.

Chapter 7 Have you been learning?

Answers guidance

Chapter 7 Have you been learning?

Quick Knowledge Quiz
PAGE 144

1 **a** domestic system
2 **c** Richard Arkwright
3 **b** Lunar Society
4 **c** pauper apprentice
5 **b** Sadler Report
6 **a** reformer
7 **c** Darby
8 **c** Stockton and Darlington Railway
9 **b** Ada Lovelace
10 **b** Birmingham

Literacy Focus
PAGE 145

Writing about historical change

1a Student answers will vary but adjectives might include: Source A: unspoilt, rural, peaceful, charming, picturesque; Source B: polluted, crowded, dirty, noisy, lively.
1b Students reasons may include: Source A is the earlier image of Manchester before the onset of the changes that took place in the Industrial Revolution. Source A shows a more rural, peaceful scene that was typical of towns before the factories and houses of the Industrial Revolution arrived in the 1800s and towns became more crowded and polluted, as shown in Source B.
1c Student answers will vary but might include: Factories were built; workers were attracted to the year-round work in the factories; houses were built for the workers, so Manchester became more crowded; more factories were built because the people were there to work in them; mentions of Industrial Revolution.

Revolution, Industry and Empire: Britain 1558–1901 133

Chapter 7 Assessment: Causation

Assessment summary

The assessments in this textbook have been carefully designed and tested with History teachers to support student progression throughout the course. This specific assessment is written to support Year 8 or Year 9 students in tackling questions relating to causation.

> ⭐ 'Britain's entrepreneurs were the main cause of the Industrial Revolution.' How far do you agree with this statement? Explain your answer. (20)

The first stage of the assessment is to identify the different causes of the Industrial Revolution (Question 1). Then students must make a judgement on the most important cause (Question 2). Using this judgement, students will directly answer the exam question (Question 3) and respond to the given statement. Finally, students will provide details to explain their response (Question 4) and write a conclusion.

Key event prompts, starter sentences and connectives are provided to support students in this assessment.

For the mark scheme, see page 136.

A note about the end-of-chapter assessments

There is an assessment for each Student Book chapter. Each is structured like a GCSE exam-style question, with scaffolding steps to support KS3 students. Each assessment has a total of 20 marks, and is designed to be completed in a typical lesson – each has been written with a time allowance of about 30 minutes.

There is a mark scheme for each assessment. You can choose how to give student outcomes: a mark out of 20; a percentage; a performance indicator (we use a three-stage indicator – 'Developing', 'Secure', 'Extending' – but you could adapt to match any performance indicators used in your school); or a GCSE grade indicator. To convert raw marks to a performance or GCSE grade indicator, use this table:

Raw marks				
0	1–6	7–13	14–20	
GCSE grade (9–1) indicators*				
U	1–3	4–6	7–9	
Performance indicator				
Ungraded	Developing	Secure	Extending	

*Please appreciate that these are approximate grades based on grade boundaries from recent GCSE exam papers. If a student achieves a Grade 7 in one of these assessments, it is not the equivalent of a Grade 7 at GCSE. Instead it is an indicator of the grade the student could expect to get if they continue on their flight path through KS3 and GCSE. Please note:
- the raw-mark boundaries are based on but do not match precisely those for recent GCSE exam papers: this is because our assessments are focused around one exam-style question, likely to be done at the end of a chapter (topic) rather than at the end of the course. Secondly, we provide carefully considered scaffolded steps to allow KS3 students to tackle high level questions and gain confidence through the deliberate practice of building up detailed answers.
- the assessments for Student Book 3 are progressively more demanding in that they use higher-order command words and provide less scaffolded support – if you set one of them for Year 8 students, please take that into account when awarding GCSE grade indicators.

Entering student outcomes into the Kerboodle Markbook

The Kerboodle Markbook records scores and percentages to allow for quick comparison of performance. If you want to use the Markbook to record student outcomes, you will need to enter the appropriate values given in the raw marks row of the table above.

Chapter 7 Assessment: Causation

Links to GCSE

By the end of KS3, students should be familiar with the History skill of causation. At GCSE, most exam boards specifically ask students to identify causes. For example:

AQA:

- Has… been the main factor/main way in…? Explain your answer with reference to… and other factors/ways. (16) (SPaG 4)
- Which of the following was the more important reason…
  - …
  - …?

  Explain your answer with reference to both reasons. (12)
- '…' How far do you agree with this statement? Explain your answer. (16) (SPaG 4)

Edexcel:

- Explain why…/what was important about… (12)
- 'The most significant reason/consequence/cause… was…' How far do you agree? Explain your answer. (16)

OCR A:

- Explain why… (10)
- '…' How far do you agree? (24)

OCR B:

- How far do you agree that…? Give reasons for your answer. (18)
- '…' How far do you agree with this view? (18)

Eduqas:

- Why was…? (12)
- Explain why… (9)
- Outline how… changed… In your answer you should provide a written narrative discussing the main causes… across three historical eras. (16) (SPaG 4)

WJEC:

- Explain why… (12)
- This question is about the causes of… To what extent has… been the main/most effective… over time? (16) (SPaG 4)
- How far did/Was… the main cause/reason…? Use your own knowledge and understanding of the issue to support your answer. (16) (SPaG 3)

Links to KS3 History resources

Student Book

This assessment question links to these lessons:

7.1 From homeworkers to factory workers
7.2A/B How did factories create towns?
7.5 'Black Gold' and the new 'Age of Iron'
7.6 From roads to canals to railways
7.7A/B An age of invention
7.8 So what was the Industrial Revolution?

Kerboodle

Support for this assessment question on Kerboodle:

RIE 7 Assessment presentation: Causation
RIE 7 Assessment worksheet (Core): Causation
RIE 7 Assessment worksheet (Foundation): Causation

Curriculum and Assessment Planning Guide

Support for this assessment question in this guide:

7 Assessment mark scheme – page 136
7 Assessment sample student answers – pages 137–138

Revolution, Industry and Empire: Britain 1558–1901

Chapter 7 Assessment: Causation

Student name: _____   Date: _____

Mark scheme

Assessment bands	Marks	GCSE grade indicators*	I have...
	0	Ungraded	
Developing	1–6	1–3	☐ given a basic explanation of one or two of the causes of the Industrial Revolution. ☐ written an answer that shows limited knowledge and understanding relating to the Industrial Revolution.
Secure	7–13	4–6	☐ written a detailed explanation of several causes relating to the Industrial Revolution, suggesting that one cause is more important than the others. I have reached a judgement that answers the question. ☐ written an answer that shows a range of accurate knowledge and understanding that relates to the question.
Extending	14–20	7–9	☐ written a well-developed explanation of several causes relating to the Industrial Revolution, leading to a judgement that is backed up by reasons, and answers the question. ☐ included a wide range of accurate and detailed knowledge and understanding that is relevant to the question.

* IMPORTANT: These are approximate indicators devised using publicly available information on the new GCSE grades. They are designed to assist in the process of tracking and monitoring. They cannot and should not be used to replace teachers' professional judgement. Teachers should use their own discretion in applying them, taking into account the cumulative test scores of an individual student (rather than just one assessment point), and should refer to their institution's assessment policy.

Mark: _____

Comment:

Chapter 7 Assessment: Causation

Sample student answers

Assessment: Causation

STUDENT BOOK PAGE 147

> 'Britain's entrepreneurs were the main cause of the Industrial Revolution.' How far do you agree with this statement? Explain your answer. (20)

Sample Developing band answer

The Industrial Revolution was a period in history when people moved from working in their homes to working in factories. Britain produced many goods that were sold all over the world. The Industrial Revolution had several causes. One cause was the entrepreneurs. Entrepreneurs were an important cause because they built new machines. This made Britain more productive.

Another cause was Britain's empire. This meant that there was access to lots of materials around the world which could then be used in the new machines being invented.

Sample Secure band answer

I agree with the statement that Britain's entrepreneurs were the main cause of the Industrial Revolution. The Industrial Revolution was a time when making things moved from people's homes into factories. The Industrial Revolution had several causes. The main cause was entrepreneurs. This was an important cause because without the entrepreneurs who helped to create the factory system, by supporting inventors like Richard Arkwright, we would not have had the Industrial Revolution on such a scale. Britain became a world power in industry because of inventors like James Watt and his steam engine, which could be used to drive machinery.

Another important cause was the British Empire. As Britain controlled huge countries like Canada and India, they could get hold of cheap goods like cotton, which they could make huge profits on. Also the colonies had to import lots of British goods which meant there was more demand, this helped to cause the Industrial Revolution. This cause is not as important as entrepreneurs, because without the people who invested money into the factory system, people would still be working in their homes and not in factories.

Other causes of the Industrial Revolution were less important. For example, the increase in population meant the number of people living in towns increased very quickly, such as in Liverpool and Birmingham. However, the increase in population of these towns was down to the new factories, which would not have existed without the entrepreneurs and inventors. Overall, I agree that the Industrial Revolution was caused by entrepreneurs who used the new population and the goods from the empire to work in their factories.

Chapter 7 Assessment: Causation

⭐ Sample Extending band answer

I strongly agree with the statement that 'entrepreneurs were the main cause of the Industrial Revolution'. These were people who were willing to take risks to buy raw materials and make them into goods, for a profit. They invested in new inventions that would build the factory system that created the Industrial Revolution. Josiah Wedgewood was one of these people. He was from Stoke-on-Trent, and he started a pottery business that used the latest machinery, pottery techniques and business ideas. Banks were willing to lend money to these entrepreneurs to invest in the new factories and support inventors like Arkwright and Watt. Both of these inventors had a massive impact on the factory system and the production of goods that could be sold around the world. This is what created the Industrial Revolution, because without business owners and their money, the goods could not be produced on a large scale.

Although this was the most important cause, there were also other causes, such as the increase in the population. Without people moving from the countryside to industrial towns, there would not have been enough people to work the new machines and produce what was needed. Towns such as Liverpool, Birmingham and Manchester saw their populations increase by at least 200,000 in the hundred years from the 1750s, and it was these factory workers who helped make Britain the leading world power in industry. However, the population increase was mainly a reaction to the Industrial Revolution, not a main cause of it. It is true that workers would be needed for the factories to be successful, but the factories encouraged people to move to towns.

Another cause of the Industrial Revolution was the empire. Britain, by the late 1800s, ruled over about 450 million people living in 56 colonies all over the world. From these colonies Britain could take goods like cotton to bring back to Britain to turn into cloth in the new factories. As the goods were taken from colonies such as America, Canada and India, there was a lot of profit. However, without the entrepreneurs, there would not have been the demand for these raw materials, and so there would have been no factories or workers to make use of them.

Chapter 8 Terrible towns

Links to KS3 History National Curriculum

Britain's emergence as the first industrial nation saw increasing numbers of people move to the towns and cities to find work. Chapter 8 assesses the impact of this change and relates it to public health, crime, punishment and class division. This focus helps students work towards an understanding of 'ideas, political power, industry and empire: Britain, 1745–1901', as required by the latest KS3 History National Curriculum. The chapter has two excellent enquiries about the role of Elizabeth Fry in prison reform, and then the Jack the Ripper murders. These enquiries develop the second order concepts of cause and consequence and source analysis, supporting the teaching of knowledge and independent, critical thought. A focus on the role of the individual will bring reform to life by exploring some fascinating characters such as John Snow and Florence Nightingale.

Through sources, storyboards, narrative text and cartoons students will be required to think critically, make judgements, weigh evidence, and develop their own opinions. They will begin to compare and contrast why events and changes happened and use historical terms and concepts in increasingly sophisticated ways.

Skills and processes covered in this chapter

		Lesson/activity in the Student Book
History Skills	Knowledge and understanding	8.1A Over to You: 1b
		8.1B Consequences: 1a, 1b, 1c
		8.2A Over to You: 1a, 1b, 2a
		8.2B Over to You: 1a, 1b
		8.3 Over to You: 1, 3b
		8.4 Over to You: 1a, 1b; Knowledge and Understanding: 1, 2
		8.5 Over to You: 1, 2a, 3; Causation: 1
		8.6 Over to You: 1a, 1b
		8.7B Over to You: 1
		Have you been learning? Quick Knowledge Quiz: 1, 2, 3, 4, 5, 6, 7, 8, 9, 10
	Interpretations	8.1A Over to You: 2a, 2b
	Sources	8.1A Source Analysis: 1, 2a, 2b, 3
		8.4 Over to You: 2, 3a, 3b, 4
		8.5 Over to You: 3, 4a, 4b
		8.7A Over to You: 1a, 1b
		8.7B Source Analysis: 1, 2
	Significance	8.2B Significance: 1
		8 Assessment: Significance: 1, 2, 3, 4, 5
	Cause and consequence	8.1B Over to You: 1a, 2; Consequences: 2
		8.2A Over to You: 2b, 2c, 3
		8.2B Over to You: 2, 3
		8.3 Over to You: 3a, 3c
		8.4 Over to You: 1c, 1d
		8.5 Over to You: 2b, 2c; Causation: 2
		8.6 Cause and Consequence: 1a, 1b, 2
		8.7B Over to You: 2, 3
	Diversity/Similarity and difference	8.3 Over to You: 3a, 3c, 4; Similarity and Difference: 1

Revolution, Industry and Empire: Britain 1558–1901

Chapter 8 Terrible towns

		Lesson/activity in the Student Book
Literacy and Numeracy	Change and continuity	8.1A Over to You: 1a
		8.1B Over to You: 1b, 2
		8.2B Over to You: 4
		8.6 Over to You: 2; Cause and Consequence: 1a, 1b
	Literacy	8.1B Over to You: 2
		8.3 Over to You: 4
		8.5 Over to You: 3
		Have you been learning? Literacy Focus: 1, 2, 3a, 3b, 3c, 4a, 4b, 4c
	Numeracy	8.5 Over to You: 4a

Lesson sequence

Lesson title	Student Book pages	Objectives
8.1A What made towns and cities stink?	pp 148–149	• Investigate what life was like for ordinary people in newly expanded industrial towns and cities of the nineteenth century. • Discover why disease was so common at the time.
8.1B What made towns and cities stink?	pp 150–151	
8.2A Heroes of public health: Chadwick, Snow, Bazalgette and Nightingale	pp 152–153	• Explain why the government was slow to improve public health. • Evaluate the contribution of Chadwick, Snow, Bazalgette and Nightingale to improving public health.
8.2B Heroes of public health: Chadwick, Snow, Bazalgette and Nightingale	pp 154–155	
8.3 How divided was society?	pp 156–157	• Examine class divisions in eighteenth- and nineteenth-century society. • Compare life for the different classes at this time.
8.4 Crime and punishment	pp 158–159	• Identify whose role it was to catch criminals in 1800. • Explain the terms 'capital crime' and 'transportation'.
8.5 How did the first police force begin?	pp 160–161	• Explain the difference between a Bow Street Runner and one of Robert Peel's 'Bobbies'. • Assess why Peel established Britain's first police force.
8.6 Why was Elizabeth Fry on a £5 note?	pp 162–163	• Describe conditions in prisons in the 1800s. • Outline the efforts made by Elizabeth Fry and John Howard to improve conditions.
8.7A History Mystery: Why did the police fail to catch Jack the Ripper?	pp 164–165	• Examine the 'Jack the Ripper' series of murders. • Analyse the area in London in which the murders took place, and the police investigation.
8.7B History Mystery: Why did the police fail to catch Jack the Ripper?	pp 166–167	
Chapter 8 Have you been learning?	pp 168–169	• Choose the correct answer from the given options for a quick recap. • Examine and answer questions relating to an academic text in detail.
Chapter 8 History skill: Significance	p 170	• Define historical significance.
Chapter 8 Assessment: Significance	p 171	• Assess the significance of Florence Nightingale in the development of nursing. • Consider the short-term and long-term impact of Florence Nightingale on the development of nursing.

Chapter 8 Terrible towns

Links to the GCSE curriculum

This chapter provides some historical context to the following:

AQA: Health and the People c1000–Present

Edexcel: Crime and Punishment in Britain c1000–Present

Edexcel: Whitechapel c1870–c1900: Crime, Policing and the Inner City

Edexcel: Medicine in Britain c1250–Present

Eduqas: Changes in Health and Medicine in Britain c500–Present

Eduqas: Changes in Crime and Punishment in Britain c500–Present

WJEC: Changes in Crime and Punishment c1500–Present

WJEC: Changes in Health and Medicine c1340–Present

OCR B: The People's Health c1250–Present

OCR B: Crime and Punishment c1250–Present

Exam-style questions covered in this chapter

Exam board	Lesson/activity question location	Command words	History skills/concepts
AQA	8.1A Source Analysis: 3	How useful…	Source analysis
	8.2B Significance: 1	Explain the significance…	Significance
	8.3 Similarity and Difference: 1	Explain two ways… different	Similarity and difference
	8.4 Over to You: 4	How useful…	Source analysis
	8.6 Cause and Consequence: 2	Describe…	Cause and consequence
	8.7B Source Analysis: 2	How useful…	Source analysis
Edexcel	8.1A Source Analysis: 3	How useful…	Source analysis
	8.1B Over to You: 2	Explain why…	Cause and consequence
	8.1B Consequences: 2	Explain two consequences…	Cause and consequence
	8.4 Over to You: 4	How useful…	Source analysis
	8.5 Causation: 2	Explain why…	Cause and consequence
	8.6 Cause and Consequence: 2	Describe…	Cause and consequence
	8.7B Source Analysis: 2	How useful…	Source analysis
OCR A	8.1A Source Analysis: 3	How useful…	Source analysis
	8.1B Over to You: 2	Explain why…	Cause and consequence
	8.4 Over to You: 4	How useful…	Source analysis
	8.5 Causation: 2	Explain why…	Cause and consequence
	8.6 Cause and Consequence: 2	Describe…	Cause and consequence
	8.7B Source Analysis: 2	How useful…	Source analysis
OCR B	8.1A Source Analysis: 3	How useful…	Source analysis
	8.4 Over to You: 4	How useful…	Source analysis
	8.7B Source Analysis: 2	How useful…	Source analysis
Eduqas	8.1B Over to You: 2	Explain why…	Cause and consequence
	8.4 Knowledge and Understanding: 2	Describe…	Knowledge and understanding
	8.5 Causation: 2	Explain why…	Cause and consequence
WJEC	8.1B Over to You: 2	Explain why…	Cause and consequence
	8.4 Knowledge and Understanding: 2	Describe…	Knowledge and understanding
	8.5 Causation: 2	Explain why…	Cause and consequence

Revolution, Industry and Empire: Britain 1558–1901

Chapter 8 Terrible towns

A brief history

8.1A/B What made towns and cities stink?

This chapter starts with an enquiry question about why industrial towns stank, focusing on Sheffield. However, this could be easily supplemented with examples from your local area. Students will study migration, house building and design, overcrowding, and other features of industrial towns to explain why they did in fact stink! Of course, the causes are then linked with the consequences of poor health – students really do get a solid understanding of the problems with industrial towns and cities. There is also a chance for a literacy focus along with considering interpretations, sources and change over time.

8.2A/B Heroes of public health: Chadwick, Snow, Bazalgette and Nightingale

What a lesson! Cholera: its spread, symptoms and government reactions always generate a buzz in the classroom. This lesson delivers this, along with a focus on key people – an increasingly important element for History teachers. It begins by looking at the impact of people and their findings and/or achievements, for example the work of Chadwick who identified that something should be done about cholera but blamed the spread on miasma. We then journey with John Snow while he investigates where residents get their water to make the correlation between water-borne contagion and the spread of the disease. They should be encouraged to link their work on cholera to living conditions, overcrowding and poverty. By the end of the lesson students will be able to explain the significance of different people on public health by focusing on their short- and long-term impact.

8.3 How divided was society?

By this point in their History studies students will be able to express social divisions from the medieval through to the Stuart periods; this lesson builds on that understanding by exploring class divisions in more modern society. By using first-hand accounts of housing, the areas different social classes lived in, and typical diets, students will be able to explain who was in each part of the 'social pyramid' and explain differences between the classes. It would be useful to get students to look at accounts from politicians of the time showing their attitudes to the poor and discuss the concept of 'laissez-faire' (which you may have raised in *7.4 How were factory working conditions improved?*) to give students more context to social class and government intervention.

Timeline

1749
Henry Fielding creates the Bow Street Runners to help police the area around his London office.

1829
Robert Peel sets up the Metropolitan Police. They become known as 'Peelers' or 'Bobbies'.

1831
Cholera breaks out in Britain for the first time.

1842
The Chadwick Report is published about the filthy state of towns and cities. People are shocked by the findings. Chadwick blames miasma for the spread of the disease.

1848
The Public Health Act is passed giving councils money to clean up the streets, but not every town and city does it.

1854
Another outbreak of cholera. John Snow plots the deaths and finds everyone dying is drinking from the same pump. He proves the disease spreads through water.

1854
Florence Nightingale goes to Crimea to help nurse soldiers.

1858
The Great Stink leads to the government giving Bazalgette £3 million to create a sewerage system.

1868
Public executions end, as does transportation.

1888
The Jack the Ripper murders take place in Whitechapel.

A brief history continued

8.4 Crime and punishment

Students will enjoy exploring the different types of policing, but even more so the punishments that people were given – often the same for petty theft and murder! The activities develop literacy by defining different terms and then describing how criminals were executed – a useful exercise for practising using only relevant information (the note-taking literacy activity from Chapter 4 would be a useful tool for focusing students). Transportation is explored, and there are lots of interesting case studies available from GCSE courses you could draw on to show the human aspect of a harsh punishment. Students will then look at sources and make a judgement on utility.

8.5 How did the first police force begin?

Moving on from what felt like the lawless Victorian city, we see the creation of the Bow Street Runners and then the Metropolitan Police. Students will find out what it was like to be in the Met by looking at the expectations for all recruits. Then they explore how attitudes towards the Met changed over time and how this model was adapted by towns around the country. The timeline activity will enable you to push students to gather context of the period, recalling what they know was happening throughout this time from previous lessons and adding it to the development of the police force. This builds to a causation question on the creation of the Metropolitan Police.

8.6 Why was Elizabeth Fry on a £5 note?

This lesson takes students on a journey through the harsh and frightening world of prisons in the nineteenth century, using the example of a teenage boy to help them visualise conditions. The enquiry focuses on Elizabeth Fry, the great reformer, with students discovering why she appeared on a £5 note – this is a great hook! They will also explore the role of John Howard and his book *The State of Prisons*. Once the causes of their activism have been explored students will then look at the consequences of their work: government reform.

8.7A/B History Mystery: Why did the police fail to catch Jack the Ripper?

The final lesson never fails to engage and outrage students! They hate that we don't know who Jack the Ripper was. Nevertheless, this enquiry will grip them from the start. Students will get a chance to bring in their contextual understanding of industrial towns and cities and the development of the police force, along with the opportunity to evaluate the role of science and technology in solving murders. All of this culminates in them writing an account of the murders, focusing on the difficulties in catching the Ripper. One way to take the lesson further would be to explore the role of the media and compare that today with the problem of 'fake news'.

Further reading and links

For teachers:

- Research the life and work of Josephine Butler, who made a significant impact on Victorian society. She worked with women and girls who were being sex-trafficked and were contracting STIs. Learning about her will enrich your teaching of the industrial age.

- Fern Ridell is a historian who writes on the Victorian period. She rejects the view that the Victorians were all buttoned up and prudish. Her BBC4 documentary *A Victorian Scandal: The Rudest Book in Britain* (2019) is a great insight into the lives of those who lived in industrial Britain.

For students:

- BBC Bitesize has many useful clips to help students consolidate and extend their understanding of the period. Navigate to 'Secondary' and then the KS3 History section of the site. Select 'Industrial Revolution' to find interesting clips on topics such as nineteenth century reform and crime and punishment.

- *Jane Eyre* by Charlotte Brontë (1847) is a wonderful novel for students to test their understanding of the industrial period. It offers more insight into how children were viewed within and across the class divide.

Beyond the classroom

- Find examples of a Penny Dreadful from the time of the Ripper murders. Once they have been studied and their features identified, students could create their own. This would also work well as a cross-curricular task with your English or Media departments.

- Organise a visit to your local police station or arrange for a community police officer to come in. Students could interview them and ask questions that allow them to compare Victorian prisons and policing with today.

Chapter 8 Answers guidance

Answers guidance

The answers provided here are examples, based on the information provided in the Student Book. There may be other factors which are relevant to each question, and students may draw on as much of their own knowledge as possible to give detailed and precise answers. There are also many ways of answering questions, including exam-style questions (for example, of structuring an essay). However, these exemplar answers should provide a good starting point.

8.1A What made towns and cities stink?
STUDENT BOOK PAGES 148–149

Over to You

1a Student answers will vary, but answers may include: gardens, open spaces around them, inside toilets.
1b Student answers will vary, but they will probably mark houses near the pub (noise, drunken behaviour), near an alleyway (noise) or near the toilets (filth, smell).
2a Villages grew and their streams and rivers became polluted. Fields disappeared and old cart tracks became roads. Town centres became poor areas full of factories and mills and richer people moved out of the centre of towns into the outskirts (suburbs).
2b As a historian, he will have done his job: looked at interviews with people who lived at the time, carried out research, looked at maps of town growth.

Source Analysis

1 Answers will focus on the dirty streets, houses crowded together, lack of open space (gardens, etc). Some students might mention poverty, lower classes, etc.
2a Seven – widow woman, two daughters, two sons and two 'younger children'.
2b The author seems disgusted with the conditions (he describes the 'slushing noise') and the fact that the widow is paying so much for such an unsanitary place. He also says that these conditions will continue if people ignore them.
3 Student answers will vary, but it is important that they understand that both are useful. Source B shows us vividly what conditions were like in this particular place. The image does not show us living conditions in all places around Britain, but based on students' contextual knowledge, this scene is typical of an industrial city at this time. Source C again gives us insight into what is behind the doors of houses like those in Source B. Source C tells us about the sanitation issues as well as overcrowding and population growth. It also gives us insight into what people were thinking at the time about living conditions.

8.1B What made towns and cities stink?
PAGES 150–151

Over to You

1a Student answers could include: overcrowding – disease spread easily. Washing in, cleaning in and drinking river water, as well as using shared street toilets – water-borne diseases (e.g. cholera) could spread.
1b Answers might include: more toilets – better sanitary conditions, so less disease; improved sewage systems – people would not have to get all their water from the river; limits on number of people sharing a house – less overcrowding might mean fewer epidemics.
2 Student letters will vary but will cover each of the bullet points. Students should ensure that they mention why towns expanded so quickly as well as mentioning how this expansion led to problems such as overcrowding, poor sanitation and disease.

Consequences

1a Rows of houses built very close together without room for a garden.
1b Something that has been made impure by infecting it with an unclean or dangerous substance.
1c The rapid spread of a disease.
2 Student answers will vary but examples might include: overcrowding as a result of the influx of workers from the countryside looking for jobs in the new factories of the industrial towns; the growth of towns, in particular poor quality back-to back housing in the centre of towns near to factories; poor sanitation as a result of the lack of care in construction and speed at which the new housing was built and the use of rivers for washing, cleaning, drinking water.

8.2A Heroes of public health: Chadwick, Snow, Bazalgette and Nightingale
PAGES 152–153

Over to You

1a The general health and well-being of ordinary people.
1b Most town and city centre homes lacked basics such as toilets and running water. No street cleaners, no sewers to take away the waste, so rubbish and sewage piled up in the streets and floated in the rivers. This led to outbreaks of disease and low average age of death.
2a Government official asked to investigate the state of towns in the 1830s, report published in 1842.
2b Chadwick believed in miasma theory – that disease was caused by bad air.

Chapter 8 Answers

2c Because of his report – it highlighted the state of towns and spurred the 1848 Public Health Act.

3 Still no real understanding that germs caused disease; the Public Health Act allowed councils to spend money cleaning up only if they wanted to, so many towns didn't do it. As a result, the filth continued!

8.2B Heroes of public health: Chadwick, Snow, Bazalgette and Nightingale
PAGES 154–155

Over to You

1a They would think that disease is carried through the air like a poisonous gas or an infected mist.

1b They would think that disease is caused by having personal contact with a sick person, or their clothes or bedding, for example. The sick person is 'contagious' and passes on the disease to someone else.

2 Students will recall the details of the cartoon – Snow marked on a map where all the victims lived during an 1854 cholera outbreak. He noticed all the victims got their water from the same water pump in Broad Street – and those who didn't catch cholera were getting their water from other places. Snow concluded that there must be something wrong with the water and had the pump handle removed.

3 Florence Nightingale: led a team of 38 nurses in Turkey, caring for British soldiers; when she arrived she found horrific, unhygienic conditions; with her nurses, she set up a kitchen to feed the soldiers properly, cleaned the hospital, and got vital supplies for patients.

Mary Seacole: set up a 'British Hotel' in Crimea that provided hot food and clean beds for sick soldiers; visited battlefields to nurse the wounded.

4 Nightingale wrote several books on nursing, raised money to set up a nurse training school, and advised the government on hospital design. By the time of her death in 1910, there were around 60,000 properly trained nurses in Britain and nursing had become a highly skilled and well-respected medical profession.

Significance

1 Student answers will vary, but they should focus on the basic details of their selected person's life, and outline their achievements in their lifetime and how they changed/improved public health (this is one of the criteria for 'significance'). They should also explain their contribution in the long-term (another criteria of 'significance').

8.3 How divided was society?
PAGES 156–157

Over to You

1 A group of people with the same economic or social status.

2 A name given to the structure of society; the richest people are at the very top of the pyramid, with the working class at the very bottom.

3a Close to their work/factories; they didn't have the transport links we have today.

3b An area of a town or city away from the centre; usually on the edge of the town near the countryside.

3c Away from the factories; more peaceful; also away from the smell of the city centre, which is why their houses were built upwind.

4 Student answers will vary but the diary entries will reflect the different diets that the classes had (using Source D) as well as the type of home (using diagram C) and elements of the education plan (to reflect the type of schooling the families might have had).

Similarity and Difference

1 Student answers will vary, but examples might include that they lived in different areas of town, for example, the working classes often lived in the centre, near to the factories where they worked. However, the upper classes would live away from the centre, in the countryside on large family estates (if upper class landowners) or in large detached houses with big gardens (if upper middle class). Also, the type of education they received would be different (students will use diagram B to help them).

8.4 Crime and punishment
PAGES 158–159

Over to You

1a • Capital crime: a crime for which a guilty person could be executed.
 • Transportation: a punishment; guilty criminals could be sent to a faraway land for a number of years.

1b Students could choose any from the ones listed – for example, murder, arson, being a pirate.

1c Answers may include: As a deterrent/warning to others; to rid the country of the criminals.

1d Courts took pity on young children or desperate people, for example.

Revolution, Industry and Empire: Britain 1558–1901

...art, priest ...onlooker, ...information ...oldiers there to ... ...er. 4: gallows. 5: grandstand. 6: people selling to the crowd.

3a Answers will reflect the source: Prisoners placed on carts; rope around the necks, end fastened to the gallows; priest prays with them; friends and relations tug at the feet so they die quicker; bodies and clothes of dead belong to the executioner; relatives buy them from him; unclaimed bodies are sold to surgeons for them to experiment on.

3b So they die quicker – to put them out of their misery/stop the pain.

4 Students may answer that both are useful – contemporary, C is visual, gives an idea of what we know based on what the students have read, B is a witness. They each back the other up, making it more convincing.

Knowledge and Understanding

1 Constables and watchmen (or Charlies).

2 Magistrate (sometimes called a Justice of the Peace) would question suspects and witnesses in court. They could punish criminals however they wanted for minor crimes (such as fighting or drunken behaviour).

8.5 How did the first police force begin?
PAGES 160–161

Over to You

1 1749 – London magistrate Henry Fielding sets up Bow Street Runners
1763 – Henry's brother, John, sets up a patrol on horseback
1792 – Seven other areas in London had their own versions of the Bow Street Runners
1829 – Robert Peel sets up the Metropolitan Police
1830 – There were 18,000 convictions for major crimes
1842 – Non-uniformed detectives, based at Scotland Yard, appear
1856 – Every large town had its own policemen
1900 – There were 48,000 policemen and 25,000 convictions

2a Truncheon: to protect themselves from the criminals, to use as weapon to threaten criminals. Rattle: to summon help, attract attention. Iron-lined top hat: protection.

2b Henry Peel was responsible for law and order as Home Secretary, and crime levels were rising, despite the Bow Street Runners.

2c Some felt the police were a waste of money or spied for the government.

3 Student letters will vary, but should be based on the information on pages 160–161, focusing on the fact that they want the job to reduce crime/ respectable job; and that they possess some of the qualities required (friendly and good humoured, for example).

4a Prostitution, thieving/robbery, fighting, disturbing the peace.

4b Answers may vary but inferences might include: most crime was low-level, rather than serious crimes such as murders; prostitution and theft were very common in London.

Causation

1 Home Secretary, responsible for law and order, set up the first government, official police force.

2 Despite the fact that there were local police forces – for example, by 1792, several areas in London had their own versions of the Bow Street Runners. But this was not a national, official police force and crime levels were on the increase so it became clear that the country needed a proper police force. The job was given to a politician named Robert Peel, who set up the Metropolitan Police in 1829. By 1856, every large town had its own policemen.

8.6 Why was Elizabeth Fry on a £5 note?
PAGES 162–163

Over to You

1a Because conditions were so bad, there were lots of fleas/ mice etc. – and some diseases are spread by these, such as typhus.

1b To make money – they weren't paid.

2 Whipping of women ended, jailers paid wages (so prisoners were not charged for everything), female prisoners kept separate from male prisoners, prison doctors, priests and teachers employed, prison inspectors appointed, government took control of all prisons.

Cause and Consequence

1a Howard visited several hundred prisons across Britain to assess conditions. After, he advised Parliament about how to improve conditions in prisons, and later wrote an important book called *The State of Prisons*.

1b After being appalled by what she saw on a visit to a prison in 1813, Fry spent the rest of her life trying to help prisoners. She read to the inmates, taught them to read and write, and helped them tidy up their cells. Many of her ideas influenced prison reforms, such as teaching prisoners to read and write and keeping female

Chapter 8 Terrible towns

Chapter 8 Answers guidance

prisoners separate from male prisoners.

2 Student answers may include: Whipping of women ended, jailers paid wages, female prisoners kept separate from male prisoners, prison doctors, priests and teachers employed, prisoners taught to read and write, prison inspectors appointed, government took control of all prisons.

8.7A History mystery: Why did the police fail to catch Jack the Ripper?
PAGES 164–165

Over to You

1a A basic description would outline that the cover shows the discovery by police of the third and fourth victims of Jack the Ripper – Elizabeth Stride and Catherine Eddowes.

1b Answers will vary but students may say that newspapers such as this might be more concerned with sensational stories than the truth – so might exaggerate certain details and leave others out, making it more dramatic to generate sales.

8.7B History mystery: Why did the police fail to catch Jack the Ripper?
PAGES 166–167

Over to You

1 Answers may include: Whitechapel, in the East End of London, was near Spitalfields and Aldgate and was collectively known as the 'evil square mile' because it was the ideal environment for crime. Smoke and stinking gases from factories and housing choked the narrow city streets so badly that, at times, it was impossible to see more than a metre in front of your face. It was occupied by lower/working class people and the maze-like streets were full of pubs, houses for rent and cheap 'lodging houses' where a bed in a room cost a few pennies per week.

2a It meant that the police could never get an accurate description upon which to base their investigation.

2b No handwriting to compare with that of suspects; disposing of evidence meant it was lost to future investigations.

2c Meant they could not use DNA technology or fingerprinting – so harder to convict.

2d Witnesses may refuse to cooperate, making investigation harder.

2e Police had no real scientific knowledge, which made investigation harder.

2f Hard to get reliable witnesses; easy for attacker to slip away.

2g Seen by police as 'just another crime'; not taken seriously because of the class of the victims.

3 Answers will vary but the focus might include: forensic techniques were not as developed as they are today (e.g. fingerprinting), mistakes were made by the police (washing away potential evidence), lack of police attention to the people who were killed, difficult investigative conditions.

Source Analysis

1 That the police are blind to what's going on in Whitechapel, that they are being 'taken for fools' by the criminals and are unable to see/work effectively or investigate properly.

2 Shows opinion of the police at the time. Shows what people believed about the police force, despite the fact that there had been a police force for many years, it was still unable to conduct a proper investigation.

Revolution, Industry and Empire: Britain 1558–1901 **147**

Chapter 8 Have you been learning?

Answers guidance

Chapter 8 Have you been learning?

Quick Knowledge Quiz

PAGE 168

1 **a** back-to-back
2 **c** cholera
3 **b** Boards of Health
4 **b** 1848
5 **a** that disease is carried through the air like a poisonous gas or an infected mist
6 **c** John Snow
7 **b** a crime for which a guilty person could be executed
8 **c** Robert Peel
9 **a** Elizabeth Fry
10 **a** the Whitechapel area of London's East End

Literacy Focus

PAGE 169

Understanding academic texts

1 The general health and well-being of the population.
2 The authors make the point that, in the 1800s and early 1900s, many of the major diseases people caught and the illnesses they died from were caused by dirty and dangerous living conditions such as poor quality water supply and sewage facilities, overcrowding, poor quality food and nutrition, poor working conditions and a poor health service. The lawmakers then tried to deal with these things, and it led to major improvements.
3a Answers may vary, but they should point to the fact that, when towns began to expand, none of the houses had indoor toilets, and some streets had a pump that provided water, but often people collected water from the local river, and this would usually be filthy. There were no rubbish collections, litter bins, street cleaners, sewers or fresh running water.
3b Answers will vary, but they should point to, for example, the fact that many of the new factories were not concerned with health and safety practices – machines were not fitted with safety covers or guards and workers were not provided with goggles to protect their eyes. Factories were so noisy that people often went deaf and the dust made people sick.
3c Answers may vary, but they should point to the fact that there was little understanding of the cause of disease (many doctors thought disease was caused by miasma) and nurses (and the nursing profession) had a bad reputation. Hospital conditions were often terrible, and there was no proper training.
4a Answers will vary, but reforms/individuals that could be mentioned include: Edwin Chadwick's report (1842) about the filthy state of towns and cities shocked people; the 1848 Public Health Act – allowing councils to spend money cleaning up if they wanted to – led to some cities, like Liverpool, making huge improvements; the work of John Snow and his identification of cholera as a water-borne disease; Bazalgette's sewage system to remove sewage from London – soon other cities began building sewer systems; Parliament introduced all sorts of laws to improve the nation's health. For example, it gave councils the power to pull down poor quality housing and insisted pavements be clean and well lit.
4b Answers will vary, but reforms/individuals that could be mentioned include: Reformers like Lord Shaftesbury, Richard Oastler, John Fielden and Michael Sadler began to campaign for laws to protect factory and mine workers. Examples of new acts include 1833 Factory Act (no children under nine to work in factories, nine hours of work per day for children aged nine to 13, two hours of school per day, factory inspectors appointed), 1842 Mines Act (no women or children under ten to work down a mine, mine inspectors appointed).
4c Answers will vary, but reforms/individuals that could be mentioned include: the work of John Snow, work of Florence Nightingale – influence during Crimean War, wrote several books on nursing after war, raised money to set up a nurse training school, and advised the government on hospital design. By the time of her death in 1910, there were around 60,000 properly trained nurses in Britain and nursing had become a highly skilled and well-respected medical profession.

Chapter 8 Assessment: Significance

Assessment summary

The assessments in this textbook have been carefully designed and tested with History teachers to support student progression throughout the course. This specific assessment is written to support Year 8 or 9 students in tackling questions about significance.

> Explain the significance of Florence Nightingale in the development of nursing. (20)

Students will build a picture of historical significance by identifying who Florence Nightingale is and what the key features of nursing were before she had an impact (Question 1), and then linking this to the impact her work had at the time (Question 2) by looking at how she changed things. Then the focus will turn to the long-term impact of Nightingale's work (Question 3). This will then lead students to consider her significance today (Question 4) with the knowledge we have about nursing now and the influence she had on the wider world. This will lead to a conclusion giving an overall judgement on significance (Question 5).

Sentence starters, prompt questions and key areas of significance are all provided to support students with this assessment. For the mark scheme, see page 151.

Note: In the Book 1 assessment on significance, to get students started on the concept of historical significance, they are rewarded more for their initial work on understanding the topic. In Book 2, as students develop their historical skills, they are expected to tackle the main focus of the question (which is about the impact of a person, Florence Nightingale) and therefore, the students are rewarded with more marks in the scaffolded support when writing about her impact.

A note about the end-of-chapter assessments

There is an assessment for each Student Book chapter. Each is structured like a GCSE exam-style question, with scaffolding steps to support KS3 students. Each assessment has a total of 20 marks, and is designed to be completed in a typical lesson – each has been written with a time allowance of about 30 minutes.

There is a mark scheme for each assessment. You can choose how to give student outcomes: a mark out of 20; a percentage; a performance indicator (we use a three-stage indicator – 'Developing', 'Secure', 'Extending' – but you could adapt to match any performance indicators used in your school); or a GCSE grade indicator. To convert raw marks to a performance or GCSE grade indicator, use this table:

Raw marks			
0	1–6	7–13	14–20
GCSE grade (9–1) indicators*			
U	1–3	4–6	7–9
Performance indicator			
Ungraded	Developing	Secure	Extending

* Please appreciate that these are approximate grades based on grade boundaries from recent GCSE exam papers. If a student achieves a Grade 7 in one of these assessments, it is not the equivalent of a Grade 7 at GCSE. Instead it is an indicator of the grade the student could expect to get if they continue on their flight path through KS3 and GCSE. Please note:
  - the raw-mark boundaries are based on but do not match precisely those for recent GCSE exam papers: this is because our assessments are focused around one exam-style question, likely to be done at the end of a chapter (topic) rather than at the end of the course. Secondly, we provide carefully considered scaffolded steps to allow KS3 students to tackle high level questions and gain confidence through the deliberate practice of building up detailed answers.
  - the assessments for Student Book 3 are progressively more demanding in that they use higher-order command words and provide less scaffolded support – if you set one of them for Year 8 students, please take that into account when awarding GCSE grade indicators.

Entering student outcomes into the Kerboodle Markbook

The Kerboodle Markbook records scores and percentages to allow for quick comparison of performance. If you want to use the Markbook to record student outcomes, you will need to enter the appropriate values given in the raw marks row of the table above.

Chapter 8 Assessment: Significance

Links to GCSE

By the end of KS3, students should be familiar with the History skill of considering significance. At GCSE, most exam boards specifically ask students to consider the significance of an event, person or movement. For example:

AQA:
- Explain the significance of… in/for… (8)

Edexcel:
- How far do you agree with Interpretation 2 about the significance of…? (20)

OCR A:
- How significant was…? (14)

Eduqas:
- Arrange the [bullet points] in order of their significance in… Explain your choices. (9)

Links to KS3 History resources

Student Book

This assessment question links to these lessons:

8.2A/B Heroes of public health: Chadwick, Snow, Bazalgette and Nightingale
8.6 Why was Elizabeth Fry on a £5 note?

Kerboodle

Support for this assessment question on Kerboodle:

RIE 8 Assessment presentation: Significance
RIE 8 Assessment worksheet (Core): Significance
RIE 8 Assessment worksheet (Foundation): Significance

Curriculum and Assessment Planning Guide

Support for this assessment question in this guide:

8 Assessment mark scheme – page 151
8 Assessment sample student answers – pages 152–153

Chapter 8 Assessment: Significance

Student name: _____   Date: _____

Mark scheme

Assessment bands	Marks	GCSE grade indicators*	I have…
	0	Ungraded	
Developing	1–6	1–3	☐ given some basic information on Florence Nightingale. ☐ supported my answer with examples of limited knowledge of Florence Nightingale.
Secure	7–13	4–6	☐ given a detailed description of the work of Florence Nightingale and attempted to explain one aspect of significance (short term, long term, or relevance today). ☐ supported my answer with accurate knowledge and understanding that is mostly relevant to the question.
Extending	14–20	7–9	☐ given a well-developed explanation and analysis of the significance of the work of Florence Nightingale at the time, her long-term impact, and relevance in today's world. ☐ supported my answer with a range of accurate knowledge and understanding that is fully relevant to the question. ☐ concluded my answer with a judgement that gives my opinion about the significance of Florence Nightingale.

*IMPORTANT: These are approximate indicators devised using publicly available information on the new GCSE grades. They are designed to assist in the process of tracking and monitoring. They cannot and should not be used to replace teachers' professional judgement. Teachers should use their own discretion in applying them, taking into account the cumulative test scores of an individual student (rather than just one assessment point), and should refer to their institution's assessment policy.

Mark: _____

Comment:

Chapter 8 Assessment: Significance

Sample student answers

Assessment: Significance

STUDENT BOOK PAGE 171

> Explain the significance of Florence Nightingale in the development of nursing. (20)

☆ Sample Developing band answer

Florence Nightingale was born in the 1800s. She was a nurse who helped make hospitals safer by training nurses properly. She went to help nurse British soldiers in the war and made sure the hospital conditions were cleaner. She changed nursing in Britain.

☆ Sample Secure band answer

Florence Nightingale was born in the 1800s. She was a nurse who changed nursing. In the early 1800s, hospital conditions were dreadful, with many people dying of diseases. This was the case in a hospital in Turkey that Nightingale worked in. At the time, there were outbreaks of diseases like cholera and typhus, when there was not enough medical understanding to explain why they spread so easily. Nightingale set up a kitchen to feed the soldiers properly, she cleaned the hospital and she improved the water supply. All of this meant that the hospitals were cleaner, and the death rate dropped dramatically. This shows the impact that Florence Nightingale had at the time.

⭐ Sample Extending band answer

Florence Nightingale was a nurse who was born in 1820. At the time Britain's cities were growing and this caused the spread of diseases such as cholera and typhus, and nursing had a bad reputation because of the conditions in hospitals. There was also no proper training for nurses, so they did not always make people better. Florence Nightingale became a significant person at the time due to her work during the Crimean War. In 1854 she was sent with a team of nurses to care for wounded British soldiers. Even worse than in Britain, the hospitals were filthy, the wounded were not fed well, and many patients died from diseases they caught in hospital rather than from war wounds. Nightingale and her nurses changed this by setting up kitchens to feed the soldiers and cleaning the hospital. All of this made hospital care much better.

In the longer term, Nightingale was also significant because she changed nursing in Britain – she wrote several books on nursing and set up training schools for nurses. She encouraged the setting up of the British Red Cross, which is an organisation that still helps people who are caught up in wars. She also advised the government on hospital design. It is clear this worked as people started to live by up to 20 years longer by 1900. By the time Nightingale died in 1910, the nursing profession had become highly skilled and respected.

Today, Nightingale and her work are significant as many of the changes she encouraged can still be seen in hospitals today. International Nurses Day is still observed around the world each year, on Nightingale's birthday, to mark the contributions that nurses make.

In conclusion, Florence Nightingale is significant as she changed how nursing was viewed in Britain in the short term, and in the longer term, she helped lead the changes in public health in Britain, which led to fewer diseases and people living longer. However, she was not the only one who contributed to nursing developments – for example, Mary Seacole was another nurse who helped improve conditions for soldiers in the Crimean War.

Chapter 9 The slave trade

Links to KS3 History National Curriculum

'Britain's transatlantic slave trade: its effects and its eventual abolition' is listed as one of the potential areas of study in the latest KS3 History National Curriculum. This dark chapter in Britain's history is covered in great detail and should help students gain a sense of Britain's pivotal role in the slave trade and its efforts – along with those of slaves themselves – to abolish it in the early nineteenth century. The lessons in this chapter will challenge students to think like historians and evaluate the facts while dealing with controversial content. It is vital when teaching this content that students are offered time and space to express how they feel about what they are learning. Students will be required to focus on key individuals, such as Olaudah Equiano, and key events, such as the Saint-Domingue rebellion, and judge their impact.

Throughout the chapter, students are required to interrogate sources accurately in order to find answers to support their ideas and writing, and to make use of and deploy historical terminology accurately. The transatlantic slave trade is useful context for understanding the British Empire but will also offer insight for most GCSE specifications, regardless of topics covered.

Skills and processes covered in this chapter

		Lesson/activity in the Student Book
History Skills	Knowledge and understanding	9.1A Over to You: 1a, 1b, 1c, 3
		9.1B Over to You: 1; Interpretation Analysis: 1, 2
		9.2B Over to You: 1a, 1b, 2
		9.3A Over to You: 1, 3a
		9.3B Over to You: 2
		Have you been learning? Quick Knowledge Quiz: 1, 2, 3, 4, 5, 6, 7, 8, 9, 10
	Interpretations	9.1B Over to You: 2a, 2b, 3; Interpretation Analysis: 3
	Sources	9.2A Source Analysis: 1, 2, 3
		9.2B Over to You: 2, 4; Source Analysis: 1, 2, 3
		9.3A Over to You: 3b, 3c, 3d
		9.3B Over to You: 1
	Significance	
	Cause and consequence	9.1A Over to You: 2; Causation: 1, 2
		9.2A Over to You: 1, 2, 3
		9.2B Over to You: 3, 4, 5a, 5b
		9.3A Over to You: 2
		9.3B Causation: 1, 2
		9 Assessment: Causation: 1, 2, 3, 4
	Diversity/Similarity and difference	9.2A Over to You: 4
		9.3A Over to You: 2
	Change and continuity	
Literacy and Numeracy	Literacy	Have you been learning? Literacy Focus: 1a, 1b, 1c
	Numeracy	

Chapter 9 The slave trade

Lesson sequence

Lesson title	Student Book pages	Objectives
9.1A What was the slave trade?	pp 172–173	• Examine how the slave trade was organised. • Assess Britain's role in the slave trade.
9.1B What was the slave trade?	pp 174–175	
9.2A A life of slavery	pp 176–177	• Examine conditions on a slave ship. • Compare two ways in which slaves were sold. • Describe life on a plantation.
9.2B A life of slavery	pp 178–179	
9.3A Why was slavery abolished?	pp 180–181	• Discover when both slave trading and slave ownership ended in Britain. • Outline the different factors that contributed to the abolition of slavery. • Assess the different factors that led to the abolition of slavery.
9.3B Why was slavery abolished?	pp 182–183	
Chapter 9 Have you been learning?	pp 184–185	• Choose the correct answer from the given options for a quick recap. • Write down the important words from sentences to practise note-taking.
Chapter 9 History skill: Causation	p 186	• Compare different causes relating to the abolition of slavery.
Chapter 9 Assessment: Causation	p 187	• Construct an answer that judges which was the most important reason for the abolition of slavery.

Links to the GCSE curriculum

This chapter provides some historical context to the following:

AQA: Power and the People c1170–Present

AQA: Migration, Empires and the People c790–Present

Edexcel: British America 1713–83: Empire and Revolution

OCR A: The Impact of Empire on Britain 1688–c1730

Exam-style questions covered in this chapter

Exam board	Lesson/activity question location	Command words	History skills/concepts
AQA	9.2A Source Analysis: 3	How useful…	Source analysis
	9.3B Causation: 2	How far do you agree…	Cause and consequence
Edexcel	9.2A Source Analysis: 3	How useful…	Source analysis
	9.2B Source Analysis: 3	Give two things… infer	Source analysis
	9.3B Causation: 2	How far do you agree…	Cause and consequence
OCR A	9.1B Interpretation Analysis: 3	Explain why…	Interpretation analysis
	9.2A Source Analysis: 3	How useful…	Source analysis
	9.3B Causation: 2	How far do you agree…	Cause and consequence
OCR B	9.1A Causation: 2	Write a clear and organised summary…	Cause and consequence
	9.2A Source Analysis: 3	How useful…	Source analysis
	9.3B Causation: 2	How far do you agree…	Cause and consequence

Revolution, Industry and Empire: Britain 1558–1901

Chapter 9 The slave trade

A brief history

9.1A/B What was the slave trade?

The lesson starts by clearly defining what trade is. This might seem obvious, but any misconception will make it difficult for students to comprehend the slave trade, the profit it made, and the impact it had on different cities around Britain. To test understanding students will need to define and describe the slave trade and the emerging 'triangle'. Using clear and organised summaries they must explain how slavery was profitable and the impact this profit had on Britain. Building on *4.7 Why does Cromwell divide opinion?*, students must decide whether the statue of slave trader Edward Colston in Bristol is still appropriate. Prepare for strong opinions!

9.2A/B A life of slavery

Students will feel mixed emotions when exploring the conditions of a slave ship and how the enslaved African people dealt with their floating prisons. To consolidate this they will be expected to explain why slave ships were packed in tightly – this links back to *9.1A/B What was the slave trade?* where they looked at profit. Then the lesson describes the horror of the scramble and the auction. Key questions such as why slaves were cleaned up before they were sold will challenge students' understanding of humanity so be sure to offer them the chance to express their feelings about what they have read. All this content builds towards a GCSE-style question on utility using a source that is an emotive account of an auction – can we still trust it? The lesson ends with plantation life, punishments and slave rebellions, both passive and violent. Students will see the role that slaves played in liberating themselves and challenging slavery – not seeing these people as totally passive will serve them well in the next lesson.

Timeline

1500s
Europeans settle in the newly discovered continents of North and South America.

1619
The first slaves to work on British-owned farms arrive in North America from Africa.

1701–1800
The Atlantic slave trade is at its height, with 6,090,000 slaves being taken from Africa.

1770s
The price of sugar begins to fall with less profit being made for plantation owners.

1787
The Society for the Abolition of the Slave Trade is set up by a group of Christians.

1789
Olaudah Equiano publishes his autobiography, which changes many people's attitude towards slavery.

1791
Led by Toussaint L'Ouverture, slaves in Saint-Domingue take control of their French-controlled island. They defeat British and French troops and become free.

1807
The British Parliament abolishes the slave trade in the British Empire.

1833
Parliament bans slave ownership with the Slavery Abolition Act.

9.3A/B Why was slavery abolished?

This lesson sets a challenging tone from the start with the great question: '[the] anti-slavery group was very important – but was slavery banned just because of this group, or were there other reasons why it ended?' Students are then expected to analyse other causes such as a lack of profit and slave rebellion – using slave actions from 9.2A/B *A life of slavery* and new incidents, such as the Saint-Domingue revolt. Within each factor there are key individuals to explore, such as Olaudah Equiano and William Wilberforce, whom students will need to reference and evaluate their contribution. Higher ability students may enjoy reading modern-day criticism of Wilberforce and other abolitionists for taking the 'glory' for the end of slavery. The skills of inference, change and continuity, and source analysis will all be developed, with a chance for students to show off everything they know with the main cause question, which builds to the demands of GCSE.

Further reading and links

For teachers:

- The 1977 TV drama series Roots – and its 2016 remake – offers a fantastic insight into the slave trade from capture to plantation. This will enrich your teaching of the topic.
- David Olusoga's *Black and British: A Forgotten History* (Pan, 2017) gives an insight into the long relationship between Britain and the people of Africa and the Caribbean. It will enrich your teaching of black history by showing different narratives; not just that of slaves and slave owners.

For students:

- BBC Bitesize has a clip called 'Interpretations of the abolition of slavery' that looks at the different reasons for the end of slavery. Students could use the video to extend their explanations for the causation question in *9.3B Why was slavery abolished?*
- Students should research the life of Harriet Tubman to look at another way that slaves challenged slavery. Focusing learning around an individual helps to humanise the topic.

Beyond the classroom

- Students could prepare an assembly on how their nearest town or city benefited from slavery. They should look at key buildings, institutions and people.
- Organise a trip to Liverpool's Slavery Museum to deepen students' understanding of the transatlantic slave trade and its impact on Britain.
- Read the poetry of Hannah More – a leading abolitionist – and get students to pick out features of the poems that could persuade people to end slavery. Collaborate with your English department to get students to write their own poetry to persuade staff and students to support a cause they are passionate about.
- Students could research modern-day slavery and how this links to the clothes they buy, the food they eat and the phones they use. They could then write to their local MP about the issue of slavery and explain how it links to what they have learned in this chapter.

Chapter 9 Answers guidance

Answers guidance

The answers provided here are examples, based on the information provided in the Student Book. There may be other factors which are relevant to each question, and students may draw on as much of their own knowledge as possible to give detailed and precise answers. There are also many ways of answering questions, including exam-style questions (for example, of structuring an essay). However, these exemplar answers should provide a good starting point.

9.1A What was the slave trade?
STUDENT BOOK PAGES 172–173

Over to You

1a The buying and selling of goods.
1b A person who is treated as someone's property and can be traded.
1c The capturing, selling and buying of slaves.
2 Answers may include: Many European settlers in North and South America and the West Indies were farmers who grew crops that were very popular in Europe (cotton, tobacco, sugar and coffee) and sold for high prices. To begin with, some farmers forced local tribespeople to do the farming for them, but some local tribes ran away, and others died out from disease or cruel treatment. So, when they ran out of local slaves, the European settlers went to Africa to find new ones.
3 There are three stages to the trade journey – goods to Africa, to be swapped for slaves that are taken to the Americas, and then goods back to Europe.

Causation

1 Answers will vary but may include: The first point of the journey, where the goods left Europe, was low on cost (the goods were cheap), they were then traded for people, which were sold for a lot of money (so a lot of profit). Then some money was used to buy goods that were cheap at source (cotton, sugar etc.) but were high cost in Europe – so again, high profit. In short, there were two high profit points at the end of Stage 2 and Stage 3.
2 Student answers will vary, but they should summarise how the slave triangle worked, highlighting what happened on each stage of the journey. They should also cover the reasons why slaves were traded, focusing on the high profits that could be made and the free labour that plantation owners wanted.

9.1B What was the slave trade?
PAGES 174–175

Over to You

1 Answers could include: Queen Elizabeth I was a business partner of John Hawkins, a slave trader; King Charles II was a partner in a slave trading company; Liverpool and Bristol were large slave trading ports; 20 of Liverpool's mayors between 1787 and 1807 are thought to have been slave traders; National Gallery in London received its first major donation from a slave dealer; several men who ran the Bank of England were involved in slavery; Britain's oldest insurance company (Lloyd's of London) insured slave ships; Barclays Bank was started by slave traders.
2a During the 1700s Liverpool was Britain's main port and formed part of the 'slave trade triangle'. Ships from Liverpool took at least 1.5 million Africans across the Atlantic. The slave trade made the city rich and powerful.
2b The city thrived doing ship repairs and importing goods. Approximately half of Liverpool's trade was linked to slavery.
3 Student views will differ, but it might be worth getting them to think whether street names and statues of slave traders should be kept, so that people won't forget this part of British history. Or do they think the street names should be changed so that the traders are no longer celebrated?

Interpretation Analysis

1 A rich slave trader from Bristol.
2 Colston was a slave trader, but there is no mention of his slave connections on the statue – but that's how he made his money, so a statue in his honour appears to support his work.
3 Student answers should reflect that he was not just known for his charity work – but, in fact, made his money from the exploitation of people as slaves.

9.2A A life of slavery
PAGES 176–177

Over to You

1 More profit – and many would die on the journey.
2 Fear of rebellion, to show who was in control.
3 Slaves were washed down with water and given oil to rub into their skin to make them look shinier and healthier.
4 An auction was a public sale in which the slaves were sold to the person who offered the highest price. A scramble was where a price was agreed before the buyers rushed into a cage to grab the 'best' slave they could.

Source Analysis

1 An early 1800s plan of how slaves were loaded into the French slave ship *Vigilante*.
2 Answers will vary but may include: The writer witnessed a mother with seven children who were all auctioned to

Chapter 9 Answers guidance

a slave trader. The mother begged the trader to tell her where her children were going, but he refused. She thought he would sell them, one by one, wherever he could get the highest price. The writer met the mother who said, 'Gone, all gone! Why don't God kill me?'

3 Answers will vary but students should mention that both are useful because they are contemporary sources of two key components of the slave trade – the Middle Passage and the selling process.

9.2B A life of slavery
PAGES 178–179

Over to You

1a Three- and four-year-olds would work in 'trash gangs' (weeding) or as water-can carriers. As they got older, they would work longer hours out in the fields with the adults – as farm workers.

1b They would clean, cook and serve.

2 The new owner of a slave would burn his initials onto the slave using this branding tool.

3 To try to make the slaves forget their past and to demonstrate that they owned them outright, in all ways.

4 To show they were in charge of them, as a warning to others about rebellion and escape.

5a Answers will vary but the revolt probably sent shockwaves of fear through the slave-owning community – and the owners became more repressive.

5b Because the slave rebellion was successful and led to the establishment of a country that still exists today.

Source Analysis

1 It shows a sugar plantation in the West Indies. Slaves are harvesting the sugar cane, the plantation owner (or someone in charge) is talking to what appears to be a slave manager or overseer. The slaves are well dressed.

2 Students may answer that the painting would go on show in the plantation owner's house, so it is unlikely to show any of the negative sides of slavery, such as the punishments or harsh conditions, because the slave owner would not necessarily want visitors to see this.

3 Answers will vary but inferences may include that conditions were not cruel (because there are no whips being used, for example) and that slave owners would be involved in the day-to-day running of the plantation and would converse with the slaves (he is shown doing this).

9.3A Why was slavery abolished?
PAGES 180–181

Over to You

1 To bring an end to something.

2 The 1807 law made it illegal to trade in slaves (but you could still own slaves). The 1833 law also made ownership illegal.

3a A former slave who led a rebellion on the French colony Saint-Domingue (in the Caribbean) in 1791. He and the slaves kept control of the island despite attacks from both French and British soldiers and in 1804, the island was renamed Haiti.

3b Answers may vary but words might include: leader, strong, powerful.

3c Answers will vary but students may say, for example, 'in control' because of the way he is positioned and how dominating and powerful he appears.

3d They may be concerned to see him looking so powerful, determined etc., because it is not how they view slaves.

9.3B Why was slavery abolished?
PAGES 182–183

Over to You

1 Answers will vary but they should focus on the fact that the source and the interpretation do help explain the trade and the way slaves were treated because they help us understand views at the time and how something that is both illegal and wrong in today's world carried on for so long at that time.

2 Students' designs will vary but should have a slogan and an image.

Causation

1 Answers will vary, but if, for example, the student writes that one of the reasons why slavery ended was as a result of the slaves themselves, they might write about the actions of Toussaint L'Ouverture on the French colony Saint-Domingue in 1791; that this rebellion proved to many people that their argument about the slaves' inability to organise themselves and that they were only suitable for following orders was wrong. They might also point to the work of Ottobah Cugoano, Mary Prince and Olaudah Equiano, for example.

2 Answers will vary but the students should write about the reason mentioned in the question (that one of the reasons why slavery was abolished was because it wasn't making money anymore) and also write about other reasons why slavery was abolished – for example, the work of the anti-slavery movement and the work of the slaves themselves. Students should conclude with what they think – was the main reason for the abolition of slavery that slavery wasn't making money anymore?

Revolution, Industry and Empire: Britain 1558–1901   159

Chapter 9 Have you been learning?

Answers guidance

Chapter 9 Have you been learning?

Quick Knowledge Quiz

PAGE 184

1. a Middle Passage
2. b cotton, sugar and tobacco
3. a John Hawkins
4. a the Royal African Company
5. c Bristol and Liverpool
6. b A price was agreed before the buyers rushed into a cage to grab the slave they wanted
7. a plantations
8. c Haiti
9. b 1807
10. b Olaudah Equiano

Literacy Focus

PAGE 185

Note-taking

1a Traders → Britain and European ports → Africa with alcohol, guns and cloth where they are expensive (38 words down to 17).

1b Trade with African tribesmen, return prisoners, kidnap, loaded ships with slaves → Atlantic, slave triangle/Middle Passage (51 words down to 16).

1c Americas, slaves, sold to plantations, profits, buy sugar, cotton and tobacco, onto ships, sail → Britain or European ports, big profit (46 words down to 21).

Chapter 9 Assessment: Causation

Assessment summary

The assessments in this textbook have been carefully designed and tested with History teachers to support student progression throughout the course. This specific assessment is written to support Year 8 or Year 9 students in tackling questions relating to causation.

> Which of the following was the more important reason why the slave trade was abolished in the British Empire in 1807:
> - the efforts of the slaves themselves, and former slaves
> - the anti-slavery campaign in Britain?
>
> Explain your answer with reference to both reasons. (20)

The first stage of the assessment is to identify the two given causes of the abolition of the slave trade in 1807 (Question 1). Then students must make a judgement on the more important cause (Question 2). Using this judgement, students will directly answer the exam question (Question 3) and respond to the bullet points. Finally, students will provide details to explain their response (Question 4) and write a conclusion.

Starter sentences are provided to support students in this assessment.

For the mark scheme, see page 163.

A note about the end-of-chapter assessments

There is an assessment for each Student Book chapter. Each is structured like a GCSE exam-style question, with scaffolding steps to support KS3 students. Each assessment has a total of 20 marks, and is designed to be completed in a typical lesson – each has been written with a time allowance of about 30 minutes.

There is a mark scheme for each assessment. You can choose how to give student outcomes: a mark out of 20; a percentage; a performance indicator (we use a three-stage indicator – 'Developing', 'Secure', 'Extending' – but you could adapt to match any performance indicators used in your school); or a GCSE grade indicator. To convert raw marks to a performance or GCSE grade indicator, use this table:

Raw marks			
0	1–6	7–13	14–20
GCSE grade (9–1) indicators*			
U	1–3	4–6	7–9
Performance indicator			
Ungraded	Developing	Secure	Extending

* Please appreciate that these are approximate grades based on grade boundaries from recent GCSE exam papers. If a student achieves a Grade 7 in one of these assessments, it is not the equivalent of a Grade 7 at GCSE. Instead it is an indicator of the grade the student could expect to get if they continue on their flight path through KS3 and GCSE. Please note:
- the raw-mark boundaries are based on but do not match precisely those for recent GCSE exam papers: this is because our assessments are focused around one exam-style question, likely to be done at the end of a chapter (topic) rather than at the end of the course. Secondly, we provide carefully considered scaffolded steps to allow KS3 students to tackle high level questions and gain confidence through the deliberate practice of building up detailed answers.
- the assessments for Student Book 3 are progressively more demanding in that they use higher-order command words and provide less scaffolded support – if you set one of them for Year 8 students, please take that into account when awarding GCSE grade indicators.

Entering student outcomes into the Kerboodle Markbook

The Kerboodle Markbook records scores and percentages to allow for quick comparison of performance. If you want to use the Markbook to record student outcomes, you will need to enter the appropriate values given in the raw marks row of the table above.

Chapter 9 Assessment: Causation

Links to GCSE

By the end of KS3, students should be familiar with the History skill of causation. At GCSE, most exam boards specifically ask students to explain and analyse the causes of events and to make judgements on the most important cause. For example:

AQA:

- Has… been the main factor/main way in…? Explain your answer with reference to… and other factors/ways. (16) (SPaG 4)
- Which of the following was the more important reason…
  - …
  - …?

  Explain your answer with reference to both reasons. (12)
- '…' How far do you agree with this statement? Explain your answer. (16) (SPaG 4)

Edexcel:

- Explain why…/what was important about… (12)
- 'The most significant reason/consequence/cause… was…' How far do you agree? Explain your answer. (16)

OCR A:

- Explain why… (10)
- '…' How far do you agree? (24)

OCR B:

- How far do you agree that…? Give reasons for your answer. (18)
- '…' How far do you agree with this view? (18)

Eduqas:

- Why was…? (12)
- Explain why… (9)
- Outline how… changed… In your answer you should provide a written narrative discussing the main causes… across three historical eras. (16) (SPaG 4)

WJEC:

- Explain why… (12)
- This question is about the causes of… To what extent has… been the main/most effective… over time? (16) (SPaG 4)
- How far did/Was… the main cause/reason…? Use your own knowledge and understanding of the issue to support your answer. (16) (SPaG 3)

Links to KS3 History resources

Student Book

This assessment question links to these lessons:

9.1A/B *What was the slave trade?*
9.2A/B *A life of slavery*
9.3A/B *Why was slavery abolished?*

Kerboodle

Support for this assessment question on Kerboodle:

RIE 9 *Assessment presentation: Causation*
RIE 9 *Assessment worksheet (Core): Causation*
RIE 9 *Assessment worksheet (Foundation): Causation*

Curriculum and Assessment Planning Guide

Support for this assessment question in this guide:

9 Assessment mark scheme – page 163
9 Assessment sample student answers – pages 164–165

Chapter 9 Assessment: Causation

Student name: _____   Date: _____

Mark scheme

Assessment bands	Marks	GCSE grade indicators*	I have...
	0	Ungraded	
Developing	1–6	1–3	☐ given a basic explanation of one or two of the bullet points. ☐ written an answer that shows limited knowledge and understanding relating to why the slave trade was abolished.
Secure	7–13	4–6	☐ written a detailed explanation of each bullet point. I have reached a judgement that answers the question. ☐ written an answer that shows a range of accurate knowledge and understanding that relates to why the slave trade was abolished.
Extending	14–20	7–9	☐ written a well-developed explanation of each bullet point, leading to a judgement that is backed up by reasons, and answers the question. ☐ included a wide range of accurate and detailed knowledge and understanding that is relevant to why the slave trade was abolished.

* IMPORTANT: These are approximate indicators devised using publicly available information on the new GCSE grades. They are designed to assist in the process of tracking and monitoring. They cannot and should not be used to replace teachers' professional judgement. Teachers should use their own discretion in applying them, taking into account the cumulative test scores of an individual student (rather than just one assessment point), and should refer to their institution's assessment policy.

Mark: _____

Comment:

Chapter 9 Assessment: Causation

Sample student answers

Assessment: Causation

STUDENT BOOK PAGE 187

> ⭐ Which of the following was the more important reason why the slave trade was abolished in the British Empire in 1807:
> - the efforts of the slaves themselves, and former slaves
> - the anti-slavery campaign in Britain?
>
> Explain your answer with reference to both reasons. (20)

☆ Sample Developing band answer

The slave trade was abolished for several reasons. Many slaves and former slaves helped to end slavery. One example was the rebellion in 1791. The rebels set fire to crops and killed plantation owners. It inspired other slave rebellions.

The anti-slavery campaign in Britain also helped by campaigning and showing people how cruel slavery was. One of the leaders of the movement was William Wilberforce. He was an MP and gave many speeches in Parliament to persuade the government to abolish slavery.

☆ Sample Secure band answer

Slavery was abolished in 1807 in Britain after hundreds of years of profit from the trade. When looking at the reasons for the abolition of the slave trade in Britain, I think that the anti-slavery campaign was a more important reason than the role of slaves and former slaves. Throughout the history of slavery there were many slave rebellions. In 1791 the slaves on the Caribbean island of Saint-Dominique were led by Toussaint L'Ouverture in a rebellion against the French who controlled the island. They successfully fought French and British forces and showed that they were capable of running the island, which is something that was against popular opinion at the time. Many argue that the rebellions were not the right way to go about getting independence, but another way slaves made an impact on the abolition of slavery was to write. For example, the former slave Olaudah Equiano had a big impact in Britain when he wrote about his time as a slave. He detailed the cruel way that slaves were treated, and showed that slaves were intelligent. This showed people that slavery was wrong.

On the other hand, the anti-slavery campaign in Britain was another cause of the slave trade abolition. This was a group of people who believed it was wrong because of their Christian faith and campaigned for its abolition. The movement also had William Wilberforce, who was an MP who made many speeches in Parliament and campaigned for the end of slavery. To conclude, the anti-slavery campaign was the more important cause of the abolition of slavery, because without them, it would have been harder to get the law changed, as they were in Britain campaigning.

Chapter 9 Assessment: Causation

⭐ Sample Extending band answer

Slavery was abolished in 1807 after campaigning on both sides of the Atlantic. The most important cause of the abolition of slavery was from slaves themselves and former slaves. Slaves had led rebellions on many islands, such as in Barbados in 1816. The most successful was the rebellion led by Toussaint L'Ouverture in Saint-Dominique in 1791. Slaves took control of this French-controlled Caribbean island, set fire to sugar-cane crops, and killed plantation owners. They eventually defeated British and French troops. The rebellion was a success and in 1804 the free slaves renamed their island Haiti. This inspired many slaves to rebel, and it also showed that they were capable of being independent. In Britain, the former slave Olaudah Equiano had a big impact on the campaign for abolition, as he wrote a book detailing his time as a slave and the barbaric way he was treated. This made it harder for people to ignore what was happening in the colonies, and inspired many British people to campaign for abolition.

The anti-slavery movement was strong in Britain. It had the support of workers, such as factory workers in Manchester. Granville Sharp was part of this movement: he helped former slaves in court cases against their old masters. Many of those involved in the anti-slavery campaign were motivated by their Christian faith. One of those was Thomas Clarkson, who collected evidence of the terrible treatment of slaves. The politician William Wilberforce would then use this evidence when giving speeches in Parliament, where he called for a law to end the slave trade. Campaigners appealed to people to see slaves as humans and not property.

On the one hand, the efforts of the anti-slavery campaigners were a key reason for the abolition of the slave trade in the British Empire, as they convinced those who profited from slavery to change the law. On the other hand, the rebellion from slaves themselves and former slaves was the more important cause, because it was their stories that showed the horrors of slavery and that slaves were humans capable of organising and leading themselves. To conclude, slave rebellions inspired anti-slavery campaigns, so it was the more important cause for the abolition of the slave trade.

Chapter 10 Britain versus France

Links to KS3 History National Curriculum

Both 'the Seven Years War and the American War of Independence' and 'the French Revolutionary wars' are listed in the latest Key Stage 3 History National Curriculum as suggested areas of study. Despite being particularly complex topics, they are without doubt utterly absorbing and fascinating. Chapter 10 offers context for how Europe and Britain developed over the nineteenth and twentieth centuries regarding empire, workers and democracy – all of which are concepts that have been explored already and will be built on in subsequent chapters and even Book 3: *Technology, War and Independence 1901–Present Student Book*. The role of key individuals, such as Napoleon, Nelson and Wellington, help to make revolution and war real to students and therefore easier to digest and apply.

Throughout Chapter 10 there will be the chance for students to develop the second order concepts of inference, significance and causation, together with the added skills of reading sources and evaluating interpretations. This chapter offers students the opportunity to understand Britain and the wider world, setting the scene for the British Empire.

Skills and processes covered in this chapter

		Lesson/activity in the Student Book
History Skills	Knowledge and understanding	10.1A Over to You: 2, 3a
		10.1B Over to You: 1a, 1b, 1c, 2
		10.2 Over to You: 1a, 2a
		10.3 Over to You: 1a, 2a, 3a, 3b
		Have you been learning? Quick Knowledge Quiz: 1, 2, 3, 4, 5, 6, 7, 8, 9, 10
	Interpretations	10.1A Over to You: 3b, 3c
		10.1B Interpretation Analysis: 1, 2
	Sources	10.2 Over to You: 1a; Source Analysis: 1a, 1b, 2c, 1d, 2, 3
	Significance	10.2 Over to You: 2b
	Cause and consequence	10.1A Over to You: 1
		10.1B Over to You: 3
		10.2 Over to You: 1b, 3
		10.3 Over to You: 1b, 2b, 3c
		10.4 Over to You: 1a, 1b, 1c; Causation: 1
		10 Assessment: Consequences: 1, 2, 3
	Diversity/Similarity and difference	
	Change and continuity	
Literacy and Numeracy	Literacy	Have you been learning? Literacy Focus: 1

Chapter 10 Britain versus France

Lesson sequence

Lesson title	Student Book pages	Objectives
10.1A Britain versus France... in North America	pp 188–189	• Outline where European settlement occurred in North America. • Explain how Britain came to dominate the continent.
10.1B Britain versus France... in North America	pp 190–191	
10.2 In what way is the execution of a French king linked to Britain?	pp 192–193	• Recall why the French Revolution took place. • Discover how the war in North America between Britain and France was connected to the French Revolution.
10.3 Napoleon versus Nelson: Battle of Trafalgar	pp 194–195	• Examine Napoleon's career. • Explain how successful Nelson's tactics were. • Recognise the importance of the Battle of Trafalgar.
10.4 Waterloo: Napoleon's last stand	pp 196–197	• Discover why the Battle of Waterloo was so important in the Napoleonic wars. • Judge whether Wellington's brilliance or Napoleon's mistakes contributed to the outcome of the battle.
Chapter 10 Have you been learning?	pp 198–199	• Choose the correct answer from the given options for a quick recap. • Improve the quality of written responses.
Chapter 10 History skill: Consequence	p 200	• Explore how to answer questions relating to consequences.
Chapter 10 Assessment: Consequence	p 201	• Explain the importance of two events relating to the relationship between Britain and France, and the consequences of these events.

Links to the GCSE curriculum

This chapter provides some historical context to the following:

AQA: Power and the People c1170–Present

Edexcel: British America 1713–83: Empire and Revolution

OCR A: War and British Society c790–2010

Eduqas: The Development of Warfare in Britain c500–Present

WJEC: Radicalism and Protest 1810–1848

WJEC: The Development of Warfare c1250–Present

Exam-style questions covered in this chapter

Exam board	Lesson/activity question location	Command words	History skills/concepts
AQA	10.1B Over to You: 3	Write a narrative account...	Cause and consequence
	10.2 Source Analysis: 3	How useful...	Source analysis
Edexcel	10.1B Over to You: 3	Write a narrative account...	Cause and consequence
	10.2 Source Analysis: 3	How useful...	Source analysis
Eduqas	10.1B Interpretation Analysis: 2	How does the interpretation support the view...	Interpretation analysis
	10.4 Causation: 1	How important...	Cause and consequence
OCR A	10.2 Source Analysis: 3	How useful...	Source analysis
OCR B	10.2 Source Analysis: 3	How useful...	Source analysis

Revolution, Industry and Empire: Britain 1558–1901

Chapter 10 Britain versus France

A brief history

10.1A/B Britain versus France... in North America

The chapter starts with much-needed context not only for Britain and France's relationship but also for the importance of North America in shaping the relationship. These visual spreads use maps and cartoons to explain how territories were divided and how those divisions eventually led to the Seven Years War. Woven into this is the complex issue of the indigenous people of America who were pushed off their land to make way for the new settlers. Through these diverse histories students will have to answer the uncomfortable question: did the settlers have the right to settle? After Britain's victory in the Seven Years War we then move to the American Revolution and the French role in helping the American bid for independence. To consolidate, students will practise their narrative writing and analyse an interpretation of the Seven Years War, and consider the view that it was the 'first world war'.

10.2 In what way is the execution of a French king linked to Britain?

What a hook: someone has had their head chopped off, but why? Students will enjoy finding out about the French Revolution and the events that follow. Firstly, they continue to learn about how France assisted America's successful War of Independence. Then they will assess the impact of war on France and how this led to revolution. Students will test their understanding of this by 'reading' picture sources and using them to explain the causes of the French Revolution. They will then see how events turn and France finds itself in the Reign of Terror. Eventually they will have to connect the events in France to Britain and explain how the execution of the French king links to Britain.

Timeline

1600–1700s
North America is divided up between the French, the British and the Spanish.

1754
The French build Fort Duquesne, directly threatening British territory in America.

1756
The Seven Years War starts.

1763
The Treaty of Paris is signed, giving French land in North America to Britain.

4 July 1776
The British colonies in America issue a Declaration of Independence.

1783
The area that had been under British control in North America becomes officially known as the United States of America.

1789
The French Revolution starts.

September 1793–July 1794
The Reign of Terror begins in France.

21 October 1805
The Battle of Trafalgar takes place and Britain defeats Napoleon's navy.

18 June 1815
Britain defeats Napoleon's forces in the Battle of Waterloo and emerges as the most powerful nation in Europe.

1821
Napoleon dies in exile on the island of St Helena.

A brief history

10.3 Napoleon versus Nelson: Battle of Trafalgar

Some important historical figures are more fun to find out about than others – Napoleon Bonaparte is one of those people. Students will learn about him as the leader of France who eventually controlled most of Europe and then – with the help of defeated countries – turned his sights on Britain. Then they will meet Horatio Nelson, the Vice Admiral in charge of the British navy, and consider the concept of a 'national hero'. Through tactics and the key events of the Battle of Trafalgar students will develop the skill of significance by considering whether the victory was a key moment in British history.

10.4 Waterloo: Napoleon's last stand

Wellington's brilliance or Napoleon's mistakes? This lesson is built around this question; to answer it students will have to use evidence to collate the information and make a judgement on the outcome of Waterloo. They will also be expected to bring in any other relevant factors to explain the British victory. This all builds to a causation question that you will find – in some form – in all GCSE specifications. This would work well as a visual lesson – you could recreate the battle on a tabletop with a large piece of paper and a board pen, drawing farmhouses and soldiers, to give students an aerial view of the British victory as it unfolds.

Further reading and links

For teachers:

- Watch the film *Danton* (1983) to find out more about the Reign of Terror and the key people involved.
- Search for Professor Steven Conway's article '10 things you (probably) didn't know about the American War of Independence' (2018) on www.historyextra.com. It offers fascinating insight into the war.
- The Daughters of Liberty was the name of the women's association that opposed the Stamp Act, but then it became the name given to women who opposed the British during the American Revolution. Researching the key people associated with the group would enrich your teaching of the revolution.

For students:

- Read about the role of black people fighting with and against the British in North America. The National Archives have put some resources together: search for 'Black Presence exhibition', then 'enter' the exhibition and navigate to the section on 'Work and Community'.
- The BBC has a clip about the Reign of Terror that focuses on Robespierre and Danton. Students should think about why they disagreed and if the values of the Declaration of the Rights of Man were being upheld. Search for 'BBC Two Curriculum Bites France in Revolution and the Reign of Terror'.

Beyond the classroom

- Students could research the different American Indian tribes and how they lived. Understanding their ways of life will help them explain why there was so much conflict when European settlers arrived, especially around farming, hunting and land ownership.
- France celebrates Bastille Day on 14 July. Ask students to find out why this event is so important and still commemorated. Get them to imagine they are writing the Student Book with Aaron Wilkes. They have to design a double page spread about the Storming of the Bastille – they should include causes, key events and short- and long-term consequences.
- Making an explainer animation of Britain's history with France would be a fantastic way to summarise this chapter's content. www.commoncraft.com has lots of ideas for how the animations should look and some examples of cut-outs the students could make. They should keep the videos as simple as possible.

Chapter 10 Answers guidance

Answers guidance

The answers provided here are examples, based on the information provided in the Student Book. There may be other factors which are relevant to each question, and students may draw on as much of their own knowledge as possible to give detailed and precise answers. There are also many ways of answering questions, including exam-style questions (for example, of structuring an essay). However, these exemplar answers should provide a good starting point.

10.1A Britain versus France... in North America
STUDENT BOOK PAGES 188–189

Over to You

1 Answers may include a new life, business opportunities (to grow cotton and tobacco), religious freedom, opportunity to own land.
2 Answers will vary but students should note that the Spanish controlled land in the south, the British on the east coast and around Hudson Bay and the French around the Great Lakes and St Lawrence, Mississippi and Ohio rivers.
3a An indigenous person, which means they were the original settlers before European settlers arrived.
3b To Europeans, owning land meant wealth and power, and was something they didn't have the chance to do in Europe, but American Indians believed that no one could own land. They believed that anyone could use it, but after this they would move on.
3c Answers will vary, but in general the idea that American Indians believed that the settlers were not going to keep the land caused conflict. And the settlers not only kept the land that American Indians thought was for all, they took more land, cut down trees, fenced it off and prevented the American Indians from using it.

10.1B Britain versus France... in North America
PAGES 190–191

Over to You

1a George Washington led a defeated British army when trying to capture the French Fort Duquesne. He later became the first President of the United States.
1b British Prime Minister William Pitt sent lots of troops over to North America to defend British territory.
1c James Wolfe led 5000 men in rowing boats down the St Lawrence River, climbed the steep cliffs and launched a surprise and successful dawn raid on the French at Quebec.
2 The treaty gave French land in North America to Britain. The French lost New Orleans (to Spain) also. Britain also gained French territory in the Caribbean, and took Florida from the Spanish.
3 Student accounts will vary, but the successful ones will include: the reasons for the build-up in tension between Britain and France (the French wanted the rich farmland that the British had developed near the east coast and the British wanted to expand into French land so they could set up more farms). Also the trigger of the conflict (in 1754, the French built a new fort very close to British territory) and then the story of the conflict based on the cartoon story on page 190.

Interpretation Analysis

1 Because it was a conflict that occurred in different places around the world, involving several major countries.
2 Yes: it says it was a global conflict. The interpretation mentions how major powers were affected both negatively (France) and positively (Britain) and again confirms that the war was 'the first true world war'.

10.2 In what way is the execution of a French king linked to Britain?
PAGES 192–193

Over to You

1a Detail may include: large crowd, watching the execution by guillotine of the French king, Louis XVI, in 1793. Executioner is holding up the king's head to show the crowd.
1b The French were on the winning side in the American War of Independence, but the war cost the French a fortune. As a result, the French king increased taxes to pay for it, and the poor French people were furious because it left them unhappy, hungry and poor while the royals and their supporters lived in luxury.
2a A list of 'rights' that its authors believed people should have.
2b It has inspired other countries when writing similar documents for their nations – including the UN when writing its Universal Human Rights document.
3 Answers will vary, but they should write that between 1756 and 1763, Britain and France were at war over who should control North America. Britain won the Seven Years War, but the French wanted revenge and went on to support the Americans when they declared their independence from Britain in 1776. The French support of the Americans cost them a lot of money and the French king raised taxes to pay for it. As a result, the French people became poorer, until

170 Chapter 10 Britain versus France

Chapter 10 Answers guidance

they finally rebelled against the French king (the French Revolution) and this resulted in his execution.

Source Analysis

1. Teachers can direct students towards the details in the source.
2. Answers may include: negative view of the revolutionaries; they are shown as greedy and grotesque. They are shown as cannibals who eat babies and heads, which is a very negative view of the poor people. Lots of revolting details are shown. Students might mention the details to emphasise how the poor people are portrayed.
3. It is useful in showing the reaction of some British people to the actions of the revolutionaries. By showing them in such a negative way, a historian can understand the views of the cartoonist.

10.3 Napoleon versus Nelson: Battle of Trafalgar
PAGES 194–195

Over to You

1a Someone who is famous in the country and has done something positive for the nation. A modern example might be a current high-achieving Olympian, for example.
1b Because Nelson beat a brilliant French commander who was dominating Europe, saved Britain from invasion, used new tactics and died heroically.
2a Student diagrams will be based on the one on page 195. Description might be: break through enemy line at 90° angle, allowing ships to fire through length of enemy ships without them firing back.
2b Yes. The British ships attacked in two different places, and caused colossal damage. Of 27 British ships, none were sunk. Of 33 French and Spanish ships, 15 were sunk, blown up or run ashore, eight were captured and only ten got back to France. Around 1700 British and 7000 French and Spanish sailors were killed or wounded. With Napoleon's navy destroyed, he couldn't invade Britain.
3a Nelson was injured by French gunshot and died later that day.
3b In London with Trafalgar Square and Nelson's Column. Constructed in the 1840s, four bronze lions were made from captured French cannons and placed at the base of a column with a statue of Nelson on the top.
3c Answers will vary but may include: The victory stopped the immediate threat of French invasion. It also enabled Britain to become richer and more powerful. Having control of the seas meant that Britain could trade with countries such as India and China safely and without competition.

10.4 Waterloo: Napoleon's last stand
PAGES 196–197

Over to You

1a In the 'Wellington's brilliance' column, student answers may include: 'D: Wellington's order to move his troops and instruct them to lie down in long grass over a ridge was a clever move and showed his ability to "think on his feet" because it caused the French to think the British were retreating and allowed the British soldiers to wipe the French out as they came over the ridge.' In the 'Napoleon's mistakes' column, student answers may include: 'G: Napoleon's decision to put all his artillery in one place at the front of his army was a mistake because it meant that he could not shoot to all areas of the battlefield.'
1b Answers will vary, based on students' work in 1a.
1c Answers may vary, but students may point to B (the fact that it rained heavily the night before the battle) because Napoleon could do nothing about the weather.

Causation

1. Answers will vary but the better ones will begin with a short introduction to the battle (When? Where? Who? etc.) and then outline Napoleon's mistakes that led to his defeat. Students will also write how other factors (such as Wellington's brilliance) led to Napoleon's defeat before concluding by answering the question.

Chapter 10 Have you been learning?

Answers guidance

Chapter 10 Have you been learning?

Quick Knowledge Quiz

PAGE 198

1. **b** 1756
2. **c** James Wolfe
3. **c** Treaty of Paris
4. **a** the American War of Independence
5. **a** the guillotine
6. **a** Louis XVI
7. **a** Horatio Nelson
8. **b** 1805
9. **b** Russia
10. **a** Belgium

Literacy Focus

PAGE 199

Writing in detail: adding adjectives

1. Student descriptions will vary but they could write: In **late** June 1815, at Waterloo, Napoleon's forces were defeated by the **brilliant** Duke of Wellington, **heroic** leader of British, Prussian, Dutch and Belgian troops. Wellington used a variety of **military** tactics. For example, Wellington investigated the **farm** land around the battlefield before the battle. He realised it would be important to control the farmhouses in the middle of the battlefield and got **experienced** soldiers to defend them. These farmhouses were a **vital** line of defence that shielded the soldiers and provided **safe** cover. The **courageous** French attacked them many times but failed to occupy them. Also, when Wellington's infantry came under **heavy** fire from artillery, he **cunningly** ordered them to move behind a **small** ridge and lie down in **long** grass. This caused the French to think they were retreating and allowed the **British** soldiers to wipe out the **confused** French as they came over the ridge.

Chapter 10 Assessment: Consequences

Assessment summary

The assessments in this textbook have been carefully designed and tested with History teachers to support student progression throughout the course. This specific assessment is written to support Year 8 or Year 9 students in tackling questions relating to consequences.

> Explain the following:
> - the importance of the treaty, signed in Paris (1763), for Britain's position in North America
> - the importance of the Battle of Trafalgar for relations between Britain and France. (20)

The first step to success with this question is to identify what is known about the main topics (Question 1), then to consider their importance (consequences) in relation to the given question (Question 2). This will allow students to create a response that introduces both events and explains the consequences, before they conclude with their judgement and explain the importance of the topics (Question 3).

Sentence starters and prompt questions are provided to support students with this assessment.

For the mark scheme, see page 175.

A note about the end-of-chapter assessments

There is an assessment for each Student Book chapter. Each is structured like a GCSE exam-style question, with scaffolding steps to support KS3 students. Each assessment has a total of 20 marks, and is designed to be completed in a typical lesson – each has been written with a time allowance of about 30 minutes.

There is a mark scheme for each assessment. You can choose how to give student outcomes: a mark out of 20; a percentage; a performance indicator (we use a three-stage indicator – 'Developing', 'Secure', 'Extending' – but you could adapt to match any performance indicators used in your school); or a GCSE grade indicator. To convert raw marks to a performance or GCSE grade indicator, use this table:

Raw marks			
0	1–6	7–13	14–20
GCSE grade (9–1) indicators*			
U	1–3	4–6	7–9
Performance indicator			
Ungraded	Developing	Secure	Extending

* Please appreciate that these are approximate grades based on grade boundaries from recent GCSE exam papers. If a student achieves a Grade 7 in one of these assessments, it is not the equivalent of a Grade 7 at GCSE. Instead it is an indicator of the grade the student could expect to get if they continue on their flight path through KS3 and GCSE. Please note:
- the raw-mark boundaries are based on but do not match precisely those for recent GCSE exam papers: this is because our assessments are focused around one exam-style question, likely to be done at the end of a chapter (topic) rather than at the end of the course. Secondly, we provide carefully considered scaffolded steps to allow KS3 students to tackle high level questions and gain confidence through the deliberate practice of building up detailed answers.
- the assessments for Student Book 3 are progressively more demanding in that they use higher-order command words and provide less scaffolded support – if you set one of them for Year 8 students, please take that into account when awarding GCSE grade indicators.

Entering student outcomes into the Kerboodle Markbook

The Kerboodle Markbook records scores and percentages to allow for quick comparison of performance. If you want to use the Markbook to record student outcomes, you will need to enter the appropriate values given in the raw marks row of the table above.

Chapter 10 Assessment: Consequences

Links to GCSE

By the end of KS3, students should be familiar with the History skill of cause and consequence. They should be able to categorise causes and consequences, and make judgements. At GCSE, most exam boards specifically ask students to explain cause and consequence. For example:

AQA:

- Has... been the main factor/main way in...? Explain your answer with reference to... and other factors/ways. (16) (SPaG 4)
- Which of the following was the more important reason...
  - ...
  - ...?

  Explain your answer with reference to both reasons. (12)
- '...' How far do you agree with this statement? Explain your answer. (16) (SPaG 4)

Edexcel:

- Explain why... /what was important about... (12)
- 'The most significant reason/consequence/cause was...' How far do you agree? Explain your answer. (16)

OCR A:

- Explain why... (10)
- '...' How far do you agree? (24)

OCR B:

- How far do you agree that...? Give reasons for your answer. (18)
- '...' How far do you agree with this view? (18)

Eduqas:

- Why was...? (12)
- Explain why... (9)
- Outline how... changed... In your answer you should provide a written narrative discussing the main causes... across three historical eras. (16) (SPaG 4)

WJEC:

- Explain why... (12)
- This question is about the causes of... To what extent has... been the main/most effective... over time? (16) (SPaG 4)
- How far did/Was... the main cause/reason...? Use your own knowledge and understanding of the issue to support your answer. (16) (SPaG 3)

Links to KS3 History resources

Student Book

This assessment question links to these lessons:

10.1A/B Britain versus France... in North America
10.2 In what way is the execution of a French king linked to Britain?
10.3 Napoleon versus Nelson: Battle of Trafalgar
10.4 Waterloo: Napoleon's last stand

Kerboodle

Support for this assessment question on Kerboodle:

RIE 10 Assessment presentation: Consequences
RIE 10 Assessment worksheet (Core): Consequences
RIE 10 Assessment worksheet (Foundation): Consequences

Curriculum and Assessment Planning Guide

Support for this assessment question in this guide:

10 Assessment mark scheme – page 175
10 Assessment sample student answers – pages 176–177

Chapter 10 Assessment: Consequences

Student name: _____   Date: _____

Mark scheme

Assessment bands	Marks	GCSE grade indicators*	I have...
	0	Ungraded	
Developing	1–6	1–3	☐ written about the importance (consequence) of one of the topics/events mentioned in the bullet points. ☐ written a basic answer but have not organised it well or backed up my judgement with reasons. ☐ included limited knowledge and understanding of a topic/event.
Secure	7–13	4–6	☐ explained the consequences of each of the topics/events mentioned in the bullet points. ☐ made a judgement that focuses on each of the questions. ☐ included accurate and relevant information, showing some knowledge and understanding of each of the topics/events.
Extending	14–20	7–9	☐ analysed the consequences of each of the topics/events mentioned in the bullet points. ☐ directed my answer consistently to each of the questions, giving reasons that are coherent and logically structured to arrive at a judgement. ☐ included accurate and relevant information that is precisely selected to address the question directly, showing good knowledge and understanding of each of the topics/events.

*IMPORTANT: These are approximate indicators devised using publicly available information on the new GCSE grades. They are designed to assist in the process of tracking and monitoring. They cannot and should not be used to replace teachers' professional judgement. Teachers should use their own discretion in applying them, taking into account the cumulative test scores of an individual student (rather than just one assessment point), and should refer to their institution's assessment policy.

Mark: _____

Comment:

Chapter 10 Assessment: Consequences

Sample student answers

Assessment: Consequence

STUDENT BOOK PAGE 201

> Explain the following:
> - the importance of the treaty, signed in Paris (1763), for Britain's position in North America
> - the importance of the Battle of Trafalgar for relations between Britain and France. (20)

Sample Developing band answer

The Paris Peace Treaty was an important event – it was signed in 1763 and it meant that French and Spanish land was given to Britain. This meant that the French and Spanish were unhappy with the British, and this caused wars between them. This became the Seven Years War.

Sample Secure band answer

In 1763, a treaty was signed in Paris between Britain, France and Spain. It was signed to end the Seven Years War, which had seen the fight for land in North America. During the war, Britain had captured parts of North America controlled by the French. The Treaty of Paris gave Britain French land in North America, such as parts of the Caribbean. I think the treaty was important for Britain's position in North America because it gave Britain a lot of power and control in North America, but it also meant they had to deal with the threat of France.

In 1805 the French, led by Napoleon Bonaparte, and the British, led by Horatio Nelson, met at sea for the Battle of Trafalgar. After the French Revolution, there was a fear that the same thing might happen in other countries, which increased tensions across Europe. This resulted in the Revolutionary Wars. Napoleon wanted to invade Britain. Britain won the Battle of Trafalgar, which meant that the French could not invade Britain. This was important for British and French relations, because after the battle, Britain became more powerful than France as they had control of the seas.

Chapter 10 Assessment: Consequences

⭐ Sample Extending band answer

In 1763, a treaty was signed in Paris between France and Britain. It was signed after years of fighting over territory in North America, India and the Caribbean. This was known as the Seven Years War. Britain had defeated France and took Quebec in September 1759, which then resulted in the British capturing all French forts. The Treaty of Paris gave Britain French land in North America, along with the Caribbean. The treaty was very important for Britain's position in North America because it had secured more land, which would bring Britain power, but it also left Britain vulnerable as it faced the threat of French retaliation. This threat became a reality in the American Wars of Independence twelve years later, when the French supported the American 'rebels' by sending troops.

The Battle of Trafalgar was important, because after the French Revolution, many European leaders were worried that the ideas of the revolution would spread to their countries, so they joined forces against the French. However, France was being ruled by Napoleon Bonaparte, who had a successful army and had taken control of many European countries. He wanted to invade Britain, but it would be difficult to defeat Britain's superior navy. Joined by Spanish and Dutch forces, the French started their attack on the British (led by Nelson) at the Battle of Trafalgar in 1805. Even with fewer ships, the British forces were able to defeat the French. The Battle of Trafalgar gave Britain security from French invasion and made clear the power of Britain's navy. The battle was important for French and British relations as it showed that Britain was superior. After the battle, Britain became more powerful as it controlled the seas, which brought it wealth through trade in Asia.

Chapter 11 India: a British Empire case study

Links to KS3 History National Curriculum

There is a suggestion in the latest KS3 History National Curriculum Programme of Study that a depth study is used to exemplify the development of Britain's empire. India is suggested as an example depth study, and so this is the topic we have chosen. This depth study not only explores the development of the British Empire in general, it also looks at the history of the pre-imperial Indian subcontinent and analyses the impact of Britain's imperial ambitions as India gradually became Queen Victoria's 'jewel in the crown'. Students will consider key players such as the East India Company, and events such as the Battle of Plassey and the 'Indian Mutiny'.

Chapter 11 requires students to identify change, infer meaning and make connections. The chapter builds on what has been developed in Chapters 8, 9 and 10 to deepen understanding of 'ideas, political power, industry and empire: Britain, 1745–1901'. The spreads are visual and encourage discussion and debate to consolidate learning.

Skills and processes covered in this chapter

		Lesson/activity in the Student Book
History Skills	Knowledge and understanding	11.1 Over to You: 1; Knowledge and Understanding: 1
		11.2 Over to You: 1
		11.3 Over to You: 1a, 2a, 2b
		11.4 Over to You: 1, 5a
		11.5 Over to You: 1a, 1b; Interpretation Analysis: 1
		Have you been learning? Quick Knowledge Quiz: 1, 2, 3, 4, 5, 6, 7, 8, 9, 10
	Interpretations	11.1 Over to You: 3a, 3b
		11.4 Over to You: 3
		11.5 Interpretation Analysis: 2, 3
		11 Assessment: Interpretation analysis: 1, 2, 3
	Significance	11.4 Over to You: 5b
	Cause and consequence	11.1 Over to You: 3a, 3b
		11.3 Over to You: 1b
		11.4 Over to You: 2, 3, 4, 5a, 5b; Consequences: 1
		11.5 Over to You: 2, 3
	Diversity/Similarity and difference	
	Change and continuity	11.1 Over to You: 2
		11.3 Change: 1
Literacy and Numeracy	Literacy	Have you been learning? Literacy Focus: Writing in detail: 1; Defining key words and terms: 1a, 1b, 1c, 1d, 2a, 2b
	Numeracy	

Chapter 11 India: a British Empire case study

Lesson sequence

Lesson title	Student Book pages	Objectives
11.1 The development of the British Empire	pp 202–203	• Define the words 'empire' and 'colony'. • Explain how and why Britain gained an empire.
11.2 What was India like before the British arrived?	pp 204–205	• Describe what India was like before the British took over. • Examine why India was such a rich prize for a conquering nation.
11.3 Invasion of India	pp 206–207	• Examine how trading works. • Discover the importance of the Battle of Plassey.
11.4 Indian mutiny… or war of independence?	pp 208–209	• Examine the causes and consequences of events in India in 1857–1858. • Compare different interpretations of the events of 1857–1858.
11.5 The jewel in the crown	pp 210–211	• Identify a variety of viewpoints on the British takeover of India.
Chapter 11 Have you been learning?	pp 212–213	• Choose the correct answer from the given options for a quick recap. • Improve sentences by adding specific factual detail. • Define and use key terms correctly.
Chapter 11 History skill: Interpretation analysis	pp 214–215	• Define what is meant by the term 'interpretation'. • Compare and contrast two interpretations about the impact of British control on India.
Chapter 11 Assessment: Interpretation analysis	pp 216–217	• Identify differences in two interpretations about the impact of British control on the British Empire. • Consider why the two interpretations differ and explain whether you agree with one of them.

Links to the GCSE curriculum

This chapter provides some historical context to the following:

AQA: Migration, Empires and the People c790–Present

OCR B: Britain in Peace and War 1900–1918

Exam-style questions covered in this chapter

Exam board	Lesson/activity question location	Command words	History skills/concepts
AQA	11.1 Knowledge and Understanding: 1	Describe…	Knowledge and understanding
Edexcel	11.3 Change: 1	…turning point…	Change and continuity
	11.4 Consequences: 1	Explain two consequences…	Cause and consequence
	11.5 Interpretation Analysis: 3	Suggest one reason…	Interpretation analysis
OCR A	11.1 Knowledge and Understanding: 1	Describe…	Knowledge and understanding

Chapter 11 India: a British Empire case study

A brief history

11.1 The development of the British Empire

This lesson starts with the definition of an empire – one of the most important first order concepts. It then goes on to explain why Britain wanted an empire; at this point students should be able to link back to their previous learning on North America and slavery. Interpretation reading will form the activities to consolidate why Britain wanted an empire. Students will then explore the various means by which the British Empire was attained and the timescale of conquests, ending with a GCSE-style 'describe' question. This lesson provides the foundations that are needed to build the case study of India.

11.2 What was India like before the British arrived?

Why was India known as the 'jewel in the crown'? The lesson explains why so many powers tried to colonise India: it was rich in natural resources so offered power and wealth to whoever owned it. The long and diverse history of India, particularly the period under Mughal control, will fascinate students, and will provide much of the information to be included in the presentation they must produce to demonstrate their learning. It would be advantageous to encourage students to categorise the content: they could include religion, economy and government.

11.3 Invasion of India

This lesson describes the establishment of trading stations in India by various countries, the foundation of the East India Company, and the importance of the Battle of Plassey. Students will look at the financial profits to be made from colonising India; this is laid out in a cartoon to help them digest the difficult content. However, students will also see the human profit that can be made from colonies, with Indian men becoming soldiers in the Company army. Students should be encouraged to link back to Chapter 10 when evaluating how Britain finally took control of India. The activities focus on turning points – this requires a judgement.

Timeline

1497
Vasco da Gama discovers how to reach India from Europe by sea.

1500s
The Mughals invade India and take control. Akbar the Great unites many of the states and rules over the Hindu princes.

1600
The East India Company is founded.

1612
The East India Company establishes its first trading post, in Surat, India.

1632–1648
Emperor Shah Jahan builds the Taj Mahal in memory of his wife.

Early 1770s
The Mughals lose control of India.

1757
Victory in the Battle of Plassey makes the East India Company more powerful in India.

10 May 1857
An uprising by Sepoys begins in Meerut. It becomes known as both the Indian Mutiny and the Indian War of Independence.

1858
Indian rule moves from the East Indian Company to the India Office of the British government.

1947
India becomes an independent nation.

A brief history

11.4 Indian mutiny… or war of independence?

As with Chapter 9, it is all too easy to see those who have been colonised as passive victims. This lesson gives students the chance to study the events surrounding the uprising in the 1850s by the Indian people. They will then be expected to explain the consequences of the rebellion. Do remind students that consequences are not always negative – think about the change of British policy after 1858. Then, using the evidence provided, students explain why there are two different names for it: was this the start of the Indian people challenging British rule or was it simply a mutiny that Britain squashed?

11.5 The jewel in the crown

History is rarely clear cut, which this lesson shows. Students will be expected to work their way through interpretations of British rule in India to explain both the positives and negatives of British rule, building towards a discussion around the statement: 'It is not clear cut whether British rule in India was a good thing or a bad thing.' They will then use their context of British rule in India to infer meaning from an interpretation. This discussion could easily be given a literacy focus by each student writing down when their partner uses key terms, such as 'raj', 'viceroy' and 'empress'.

Further reading and links

For teachers:

- E. M. Forster's *A Passage to India* (1924) is a novel about British and Indian people co-existing and developing relationships under the Raj. It would be easy to use extracts to enrich your teaching.
- Historian David Olusoga accepted an OBE (Order of the British Empire) and explained in the *Guardian* (6 January 2019) why he did so despite how uncomfortable it made him. Although he is of Nigerian descent, this powerful piece adds context to the treatment of those in colonies like India. Academic Priyamvada Gopal responded to Olusoga's justification (8 January 2019), giving an equally powerful argument for why the British Empire is still a problem for black and Asian people. For both articles search 'David Olusoga OBE' on the *Guardian* website.

For students:

- Rudyard Kipling's *The Jungle Book* (1894) has been heavily criticised for how the people of India were viewed by the British. Create an information pack on Kipling and the book, provide students with extracts and let them decide if they find it acceptable or unacceptable.
- There are lots of clips online from Jeremy Paxman's BBC2 series *Empire* (2012). He explores different interpretations of the empire in India and talks with Indian people about their country's experience under British rule. Search 'BBC2 Empire Learning Zone'.

Beyond the classroom

- Artists The Singh Twins use their art to highlight issues with imperial rule in India. Their 2018 exhibition 'Slaves of Fashion' explored the history of Indian textiles and the British Empire, showing how far imperialism stretched into Indian culture and how things that are seen as 'British' are, in fact, Indian. Students can search 'past exhibitions Walker' on the National Museums Liverpool website and navigate to 'Slaves of Fashion' to find out more about their work.
- Look at the poetry of Benjamin Zephaniah about the British Empire. He famously turned down an OBE because of its links to empire. Students could create a whole-school assembly on the Empire and Britain's legacy using his poetry.
- Students could research the life of Sophia Duleep Singh, an Indian princess who moved to Britain and became a suffragette.
- We know that Britain got lots of raw materials and money from India but what about the role of the Empire troops in the world wars? Give students access to different textbooks and media on the Empire troops and get them to make a school display.

Chapter 11 Answers guidance

Answers guidance

The answers provided here are examples, based on the information provided in the Student Book. There may be other factors which are relevant to each question, and students may draw on as much of their own knowledge as possible to give detailed and precise answers. There are also many ways of answering questions, including exam-style questions (for example, of structuring an essay). However, these exemplar answers should provide a good starting point.

11.1 The development of the British Empire
STUDENT BOOK PAGES 202–203

Over To You

1. Empire: a collection of areas of land or even countries that are ruled over and controlled by one leading or 'mother' country. Mother country: the main or leading country that controls the empire. Colony: areas of land that form a country's empire.
2. The empire grew substantially. An area of empire on the east coast of America was lost (American War of Independence), but large gains in Canada, Africa, India, New Zealand and Australia.
3a.
   - to get valuable raw materials and riches: D
   - so Britain could sell goods to the people in the colonies and make money: B
   - to become a more powerful country: E
   - because Britain thought it was the right thing to do: C
3b. Answers will vary but students could write, to support the fact that Britain wanted an empire to get valuable raw materials and riches, that 'One of the reasons was to obtain valuable raw materials and riches from the conquered countries. This is supported by Paul Turner who gives example of "silk, calico, dyes, saltpetre, cotton, pepper, cardamom, other spices and tea" that the British could exploit.'

Knowledge and Understanding

1. Answers will vary, but students can choose any two of the four methods mentioned in this lesson. Whichever two are mentioned, better answers will be backed up by an example. For example: Sometimes British people would go to another part of the world to look for new business opportunities, a chance to own land or they could be running away from the ill-treatment they received in their home country as a result of their religion. This happened on the east coast of America in the 1600s and 1700s.

11.2 What was India like before the British arrived?
PAGES 204–205

Over To You

1. Student presentations or posters will vary, but they will cover the information required in the task – they must use details of India's eventful history and rich culture, and explain why European nations took an interest in it, in no more than 100 words.

11.3 Invasion of India
PAGES 206–207

Over To You

1a. Portugal, Britain, the Netherlands, France, Denmark.
1b. Resources/raw materials that could be easily obtained in India and sold for a high price back home. Also, the Indian population would buy goods made back home.
2a. A British trading company that set up trading posts in India from the 1600s. It had its own army and navy.
2b. The East India Company (EIC) used its own army and navy against the rulers of different regions of India. After a famous British victory at the Battle of Plassey in 1757, for example, the EIC expanded more and more into India and took over more trading posts and settlements.

Change

1. Student answers will vary but should include detail about the battle itself (date, who fought, outcome etc.) and then the legacy of the battle (it was an important one in the history of the EIC's role in India). After this victory, the EIC expanded more and more into India – increasing trade and military power and taking over French and Dutch trading posts.

11.4 Indian mutiny... or war of independence?
PAGES 208–209

Over To You

1. An Indian soldier working for the British in India.
2. Answers might include: Short-term: rumours that the grease for new cartridges was made from a mixture of pork and beef fat – the worst possible mixture for Hindus and Muslims; the Sepoys' objections to the new cartridges being largely ignored; 85 Sepoys refusing to use the cartridges; arrests and jail for ten years. Long-term: many Sepoys felt that they weren't treated very well, had little hope of promotion, and were often the first to be sent to the most dangerous places. Some Sepoys also felt that they were being pressured into converting to Christianity.
3. Answers might include: as a warning to others who might rebel; revenge; anger at the rebellion.

182 Chapter 11 India: a British Empire case study

Chapter 11 Answers guidance

4   After the mutiny, the British government took over complete responsibility for running India from the East India Company. A new government department (the India Office) was set up in 1858, and a viceroy was put in charge of India on behalf of Queen Victoria. After 1858, the British tried to interfere less with religious matters, and started to allow Indians more say in the running of India by allowing them jobs in local government. (However, by 1900, nine out of ten jobs running the country were still done by Britons.)

5a Answers might include: A mutiny is an act of refusing to follow the orders of a person in authority – and the British were in charge so believed it was mutiny.

5b Answers might include: because Indians resented the control of their country and wanted more control – more independence – so they regard it as one of several (the first, in fact) wars to gain control of their own nation.

Consequences

1   Answers could include: The British government took over complete responsibility for running India from the EIC; a new government department (the India Office) was set up in 1858; a viceroy was put in charge of India on behalf of Queen Victoria; the British tried to interfere less with religious matters; the British said they would allow Indians more say in the running of India by allowing them jobs in local government. (However, by 1900, nine out of ten jobs running the country were still done by Britons.)

11.5 The jewel in the crown
PAGES 210–211

Over To You

1a Queen Victoria was given the title when the British government took complete control of India in the 1850s.

1b Term used to describe the period of British rule in India between 1858 and 1947. The word 'raj' is Hindi for 'rule'.

2   Answers may include:
Positive: building of roads, railways, schools, hospitals (Interpretation C); building of transport infrastructure such as railway stations (Source B); a national irrigation system to help relieve famine, and rebuilding many old Indian buildings (Source D, Interpretation E); a new legal system and helped settle ancient feuds between rival areas and regions (main text).
Negative: Curzon divided up Hindu and Muslim areas and angered locals – and killed wildlife (Source D); did not do enough about famine (Source F); took Indian land and ruled it for their own benefit; kept important jobs for British people and took away money/resources (Source G); British customs were forced on the people and local traditions, culture and religions tended to be ignored. Indian workers were often exploited, India's raw materials were taken back to Britain and native lands were seized. The British Army usually came down very hard on any Indian resistance (main text).

2   Student discussions will vary, but the focus will be on the fact that there were benefits to British rule for India, but negatives too. Students might use words such as 'exploited', 'benefits' and 'controversial' when discussing this.

Interpretation Analysis

1   India's first Prime Minister.

2   Answers will vary but may include: Nehru did not think very highly of the viceroys other than Curzon, because he says they will be forgotten. Nehru thinks highly of Curzon because of his contribution to saving India's culture – he says he will be remembered, which implies that he did things that are worth remembering in a positive way.

3   Because he views Curzon's time in India in a positive way. He is remembered negatively by some in India, but not Nehru, who focuses on his achievements – building schools, setting up a national irrigation system to help relieve famine and rebuilding many old Indian buildings. It was Curzon who restored the Taj Mahal after it had started to decay.

Revolution, Industry and Empire: Britain 1558–1901   183

Chapter 11 Have you been learning?

Answers guidance

Chapter 11 Have you been learning?

Quick Knowledge Quiz

PAGE 212

1. **b** an empire
2. **a** Hinduism, Buddhism and Sikhism
3. **c** the Mughals
4. **b** the Taj Mahal
5. **a** Vasco da Gama
6. **a** East India Company
7. **c** Battle of Plassey
8. **a** Sepoy
9. **c** 1857
10. **a** British Raj

Literacy Focus

PAGE 213

Writing in detail

1. Answers will vary, but may include: India was a large country that was rich in natural resources such as iron ore, copper, gold, silver, gemstones, spices, tea and timber. This meant that many countries tried to make strong trade links with India in the hope that they might potentially become very rich and powerful. The people who lived there followed different religions. Three of the world's major religions – Hinduism, Buddhism and Sikhism – originated in India. Other religions arrived in India too, by the 1500s. India was divided into kingdoms. Most were run by Hindu princes – and occasionally the kingdoms would go to war against each other – but there were long peaceful periods too. In the early 1500s, the Mughals, who were Muslims, invaded India and took control. Within decades, the great Mughal emperor, Akbar, had managed to unite many of the Indian states and ruled over all the Hindu princes. However, Akbar's great-grandson, Aurangzeb, was a fanatical Muslim and picked on followers of India's other religions. As wars broke out all over India, the Mughals eventually lost control of the country.

Defining key words and terms

Please note: questions 2a–2d in the first printing of the Student Book were labelled 1a–1d and question 3 was labelled as question 2.

2a Cotton, silk, spices and tea.
2b East India Company.
2c Surat.
2d Plassey.
3
- colony: **a** A country that is part of an empire (8 words); **b** A country that is controlled by another country, usually taken over by force, for raw materials or people. India was a colony of Britain (24 words).
- Battle of Plassey: **a** 1757 battle giving East India Company more control in India (10 words); **b** Battle between British forces and those of Prince Sirajud-Daulah in 1757. France supported the prince against their enemy Britain. The East India Company won and gained more power in India (30 words).
- Indian Mutiny: **a** Uprising of Sepoys against the British army (7 words); **b** Sepoy uprising against the British as they were forced to put animal fat grease in their mouths. To Britain it was a mutiny; for Indians it began the fight for independence (32 words).
- Empress of India: **a** The title Queen Victoria gave herself (6 words); **b** When the British government took over the running of India from the East India Company, Queen Victoria's role grew and she saw herself as Empress of India (27 words).
- viceroy: **a** Person in charge of India on behalf of Queen Victoria (10 words); **b** When the British government took over running India from the East India Company in 1858 it set up a new government department, the India Office. A viceroy was put in charge of India on behalf of Queen Victoria (38 words).
- Sepoy: **a** An Indian soldier who worked for the British (8 words); **b** Indian Hindu and Muslim soldiers who fought for the British but led an uprising against discrimination and being forced to use animal fat to grease their guns, against their beliefs (30 words).
- Raj: **a** The name given to British rule in India (8 words); **b** The period of British rule in India between 1858 and 1947. The word 'raj' is Hindi for 'rule' (18 words).

Chapter 11 Assessment: Interpretation analysis

Assessment summary

The assessments in this textbook have been carefully designed and tested with History teachers to support student progression throughout the course. This specific assessment is written to support Year 8 or Year 9 students in tackling questions relating to historical interpretations.

1. Interpretations **C** and **D** give different views on the impact of British control of India. What is the main difference between the views?
2. Suggest one reason why Interpretations **C** and **D** give different views about the impact of British control of the British Empire.
3. How far do you agree with Interpretation **C** about the impact of British control of the British Empire? Explain your answer, using both interpretations and your own knowledge of the historical context. (20)

▼ **INTERPRETATION C** Clement Attlee, British Prime Minister at the time, in a speech in the House of Commons in relation to the independence of India (10 July 1947).

> The history of our connection in India begins with the East India Company. In the earlier days we were concerned mainly with trade providing opportunities for making fortunes. But, as time went on, there was an increasing appreciation of the responsibility which fell to the British. The British government in India became more deeply concerned with the well-being of the people of India, who are divided by race, language and religion. Looking back, we may well be proud of what the British have done in India. There have, of course, been failures, but our rule in India will stand comparison with that of any other nation which has been charged with the ruling of a people so different from themselves.

▼ **INTERPRETATION D** Adapted from an article published in a British newspaper in 2017 called '*But what about the railways …?*' *The myth of Britain's gifts to India*, written by Shashi Tharoor, an Indian politician and writer. Tharoor has written many books on India and its history.

> The British ran government, tax collection, and law and order. Indians were excluded from all of these… The death of an Indian at British hands was always an accident, but any crime by an Indian against a British person was always dealt with severely… The construction of the Indian Railways is often pointed out as one way that British rule benefitted India, but the railways were created for Britain's benefit. British investors made huge amounts of money when the railways were built, and they were used mainly to transport Indian resources – coal, iron ore, cotton and so on – to ports for the British to ship home to use in their factories.
>
> British rule exploited India and meant ruin to millions, ending lifestyles that had flourished for many years. In 1600, when the East India Company was established, Britain was producing just 1.8% of the value of all the world's goods and services [known as GDP], while India was generating some 23%. By 1940, after nearly two centuries of British rule, Britain accounted for nearly 10% of world GDP, while India had been reduced to a poor 'third-world' country.
>
> The India the British entered was a thriving society: that was why the East India Company was interested in it in the first place. Far from being backward, pre-colonial India exported high quality manufactured goods much sought after by Britain's fashionable society.

Chapter 11 Assessment: Interpretation analysis

Students will start by looking at the content (Question 1) of the interpretations to find differences when considering opinions of the impact of British control in India. Then the focus will turn to the provenance to explain why those differences exist (Question 2). This will then allow students to write a structured answer explaining how and why the interpretations differ, using both interpretations and their own knowledge (Question 3).

Students are provided with sentence starters, scaffolding activities to help build answers, and questions to ask when evaluating the interpretations.

For the mark scheme, see page 188.

A note about the end-of-chapter assessments

There is an assessment for each Student Book chapter. Each is structured like a GCSE exam-style question, with scaffolding steps to support KS3 students. Each assessment has a total of 20 marks, and is designed to be completed in a typical lesson – each has been written with a time allowance of about 30 minutes.

There is a mark scheme for each assessment. You can choose how to give student outcomes: a mark out of 20; a percentage; a performance indicator (we use a three-stage indicator – 'Developing', 'Secure', 'Extending' – but you could adapt to match any performance indicators used in your school); or a GCSE grade indicator. To convert raw marks to a performance or GCSE grade indicator, use this table:

Raw marks			
0	1–6	7–13	14–20
GCSE grade (9–1) indicators*			
U	1–3	4–6	7–9
Performance indicator			
Ungraded	Developing	Secure	Extending

*Please appreciate that these are approximate grades based on grade boundaries from recent GCSE exam papers. If a student achieves a Grade 7 in one of these assessments, it is not the equivalent of a Grade 7 at GCSE. Instead it is an indicator of the grade the student could expect to get if they continue on their flight path through KS3 and GCSE. Please note:
- the raw-mark boundaries are based on but do not match precisely those for recent GCSE exam papers: this is because our assessments are focused around one exam-style question, likely to be done at the end of a chapter (topic) rather than at the end of the course. Secondly, we provide carefully considered scaffolded steps to allow KS3 students to tackle high level questions and gain confidence through the deliberate practice of building up detailed answers.
- the assessments for Student Book 3 are progressively more demanding in that they use higher-order command words and provide less scaffolded support – if you set one of them for Year 8 students, please take that into account when awarding GCSE grade indicators.

Entering student outcomes into the Kerboodle Markbook

The Kerboodle Markbook records scores and percentages to allow for quick comparison of performance. If you want to use the Markbook to record student outcomes, you will need to enter the appropriate values given in the raw marks row of the table above.

Chapter 11 Assessment: Interpretation analysis

Links to GCSE

By the end of KS3, students should be familiar with the History skill of comparing two or more interpretations or sources. At GCSE, all exam boards specifically ask students to consider historical evidence to make a judgement on the most convincing or reliable account. For example:

AQA:
- How does Interpretation B differ from Interpretation A… ? (4)
- Why might the authors of… have different interpretations… ? (4)
- Which interpretation gives the more convincing opinion about… ? (8)
- How convincing is Interpretation A about… ? (8)

Edexcel:
- Study Interpretations 1 and 2… What is the main difference between the views… ? (4)
- Suggest one reason why Interpretations 1 and 2 give different views about… (4)
- How far do you agree with Interpretation 2 about… ? (20)

OCR A:
- How far do the sources agree with each other?/Which is the more reliable?/How similar are they? (10)

OCR B:
- How far do [interpretations] differ… ? (12)

Eduqas:
- Identify one similarity and one difference… (4)
- Study the interpretations. Do the interpretations support the view that… ? (10)

WJEC:
- Use Sources A, B and C to identify one similarity and one difference in… over time. (4)

Links to KS3 History resources

Student Book

This assessment question links to these lessons:

11.2 *What was India like before the British arrived?*
11.3 *Invasion of India*
11.4 *Indian mutiny… or war of independence?*
11.5 *The jewel in the crown*

Kerboodle

Support for this assessment question on Kerboodle:

RIE 11 Assessment presentation: Interpretation analysis
RIE 11 Assessment worksheet (Core): Interpretation analysis
RIE 11 Assessment worksheet (Foundation): Interpretation analysis

Curriculum and Assessment Planning Guide

Support for this assessment question in this guide:

11 Assessment mark scheme – page 188
11 Assessment sample student answers – pages 189–190

Chapter 11 Assessment: Interpretation analysis

Student name: _____   Date: _____

Mark scheme

Assessment bands	Marks	GCSE grade indicators*	I have...
	0	Ungraded	
Developing	1–6	1–3	☐ identified one difference between the interpretations, but I have not included any supporting knowledge. ☐ written one reason why the interpretations differ, but I have not backed it up with any supporting knowledge. ☐ reached a basic judgement on whether I agree or disagree with Interpretation C, without any relevant supporting knowledge. Key words are not used correctly.
Secure	7–13	4–6	☐ identified one difference between the interpretations, and included some relevant supporting knowledge. ☐ written one reason why the interpretations differ, and I have backed it up with *either* a simple analysis of the interpretations *or* some relevant supporting knowledge. ☐ written a well-supported judgement on how far I agree with Interpretation C, and included some relevant supporting knowledge and comparison with Interpretation D. Some key words are used correctly. NOTE: Marks should only go above 10 if you have included both interpretations in your answer to Question 3.
Extending	14–20	7–9	☐ identified one difference between the interpretations, and included detailed, relevant supporting knowledge. ☐ written one reason why the interpretations differ, and I have backed it up with a detailed analysis of the interpretations *and* with relevant supporting knowledge. ☐ written a well-organised, well-supported judgement on how far I agree with Interpretation C, and included detailed, relevant supporting knowledge and comparison with Interpretation D. All key words are used correctly.

* IMPORTANT: These are approximate indicators devised using publicly available information on the new GCSE grades. They are designed to assist in the process of tracking and monitoring. They cannot and should not be used to replace teachers' professional judgement. Teachers should use their own discretion in applying them, taking into account the cumulative test scores of an individual student (rather than just one assessment point), and should refer to their institution's assessment policy.

Mark: _____

Comment:

Chapter 11 Assessment: Interpretation analysis

Sample student answers

Assessment: Interpretation analysis

STUDENT BOOK PAGES 216–217

> 1. Interpretations **C** and **D** give different views on the impact of British control of India. What is the main difference between the views?
> 2. Suggest one reason why **Interpretations C** and **D** give different views about the impact of British control of the British Empire.
> 3. How far do you agree with **Interpretation C** about the impact of British control of the British Empire? Explain your answer, using both interpretations and your own knowledge of the historical context. (20)

⭐ Sample Developing band answer

1. A main difference is that Interpretation C states that the British were concerned with the well-being of the Indian people. However, in Interpretation D the author says that the Indian people were treated badly by the British.

2. One reason the authors have different views is because the writer of Interpretation C was British but the writer of Interpretation D was Indian.

3. Interpretation C says that the British were concerned with the well-being of the Indian people – I agree a little with this opinion about the impact of British control in India, because the British did build railways in India, which helped the Indian people.

⭐ Sample Secure band answer

1. The main difference is that Interpretation C states that British rule in India helped to develop a country that was 'divided by race, language and religion'. It implies that the British made India a better country than it was before British rule. However, Interpretation D argues that the impact was only negative. Tharoor states that India was more economically developed than Britain beforehand, but that Britain used up India's resources and made the country poor.

2. One reason the authors have different views is when they are writing. Clement Attlee was giving a speech in the House of Commons after India had won independence – he would not want to let British rule seem like a failure to the British people. However, Tharoor was writing in 2017 – he is looking back at the impact of British rule today. Both men have different perspectives because of the time they are writing in.

3. Interpretation C says that although the British made some mistakes, British rule had a positive impact on India. However, Attlee does not give examples of the positive things Britain did. They did build railways and introduced new forms of government, but I disagree with the opinion about their positive impact, as I know that even during times of famine, the British still took valuable resources from the Indian people. Interpretation D offers a different view, saying that the positives brought in by the British benefitted the British only. This is supported by the figures about the income of both countries before and after British rule.

Revolution, Industry and Empire: Britain 1558–1901 **189**

Chapter 11 Assessment: Interpretation analysis

⭐ Sample Extending band answer

1. The main difference between the two views on the impact of British rule in India is the judgement on the lasting impact British rule had. Interpretation C accepts that the British made mistakes but that overall the impact was positive, and that the British united a divided people to create a better country. However, Interpretation D doesn't agree that any of the services and laws put in place by the British did any good for the people of India. The opinion of this interpretation is that the British made India a 'third-world country'.

2. One reason the authors have different views is because of the time they are writing. Attlee was writing at the time of Indian independence, looking back at what Britain had achieved there. He painted a more positive picture of the empire, as this was a time when Britain's empire was in decline, and he wanted to make Britain look good. However, Interpretation D was written at a time when many people felt that the British Empire was something that Britain should not be proud of. Furthermore, Tharoor is an Indian politician, so he can personally see the lasting impact British rule had on his country.

3. Interpretation C says that Britain made some mistakes during its rule of India. I agree with this statement as its response to the famine was inadequate and resulted in the deaths of thousands of people. And although the British brought in a new legal system and government, they often gave the top jobs to British people, not to Indian people. This was unjust. In Interpretation D, the author argues that any of the services – such as the railways – brought to India were created just for British gains. The idea of the British not caring about the well-being of the Indian people directly contradicts what Interpretation C states. An example I know of the British not caring about the Indian people was when the Sepoys were forced to use the animal fat on their guns, and the British did not consider their needs.

To conclude, I agree partly with Interpretation C. The British did make mistakes in India, but they also brought in railways and a legal system, and built hospitals and schools, and under Curzon, developed an irrigation system. However, as Interpretation D states, most improvements were for the benefit of the British, and left the Indian people worse off than they were before British rule.

Chapter 12 From Tudor to Victorian Britain: what changed?

Links to KS3 History National Curriculum

The concepts of 'party politics, extension of the franchise and social reform', outlined in the latest KS3 History National Curriculum Programme of Study, form the basis of several of the sections in Chapter 12. Students are required to gain and deploy a historically grounded understanding of terms such as 'protest', 'reform', 'parliament' and 'politicians', achieved here by learning about the Peterloo Massacre, Swing Riots and Chartists. The chapter provides students with opportunities to select and combine information from sources and text to answer questions, identify links between events, and show how one event led to another.

The chapter demonstrates how pivotal, dramatic and far-reaching the changes that took place in the British Isles between 1745 and 1901 really were. This chapter pulls together topics such as education, health, women in society, Home Rule, Darwinism and social reform. Some sections help students to understand the complexity of people's lives, the process of change and the diversity of British society between 1745 and 1901. Students will be asked to explore historical concepts such as continuity and change, significance and difference, and to offer (and justify) their own opinions about important events in British history.

Skills and processes covered in this chapter

		Lesson/activity in the Student Book
History Skills	Knowledge and understanding	12.1A Over to You: 2
		12.1B Over to You: 3a
		12.2A Over to You: 2a, 2b, 3, 4a, 4b
		12.2B Over to You: 1, 2, 3b, 4, 5
		12.3 Over to You: 1a, 1b; Change: 1
		12.4B Over to You: 1a, 1b, 1c, 1d; Significance: 1
		12.5A Over to You: 1a, 2a, 2b
		12.5B Over to You: 1, 2a
		12.6 Over to You: 1, 4
		12.7 Over to You: 3
		12.8 Over to You: 1, 4
		Have you been learning? Quick Knowledge Quiz: 1, 2, 3, 4, 5, 6, 7, 8, 9, 10
	Interpretations	12.1A Interpretation Analysis: 1, 2
		12.1B Over to You: 3b
		12.2B Interpretation Analysis: 1, 2
		12.8 Over to You: 2, 3a, 3b; Interpretation Analysis: 1
	Sources	12.1A Over to You: 3
		12.2A Over to You: 1a, 1b, 1c, 4a, 4b, 4c
		12.3 Over to You: 4a, 4b
		12.4A Over to You: 1a, 1b; Source Analysis: 2
		12.4B Over to You: 3a, 3b
		12.5B Over to You: 3a, 3b
		12.6 Over to You: 4; Source Analysis: 1
		12.8 Over to You: 2, 3a, 3b
	Significance	12.1B Over to You: 3b
		12.4B Significance: 2
		12.7 Significance: 1

Chapter 12 From Tudor to Victorian Britain: what changed?

		Lesson/activity in the Student Book
	Cause and consequence	12.1B Over to You: 1, 2a, 2b, 3b
		12.2A Over to You: 2c
		12.2B Over to You: 3a, 3c
		12.4A Source Analysis: 1
		12.4B Over to You: 2b
		12.5A Over to You: 2b
		12.5B Over to You: 2b
		12.6 Over to You: 2, 3a, 3b
		12.7 Over to You: 1a, 1b, 2, 4
		12.8 Over to You: 2, 4
		12.9 Change and Continuity: 3
	Diversity/Similarity and difference	12.1A Over to You: 1a
		12.5A Over to You: 1b
	Change and continuity	12.1A Over to You: 1a
		12.2A Change: 1, 2
		12.3 Over to You: 2, 3, 4a, 4b; Change: 2
		12.4A Over to You: 1b, 2
		12.4B Over to You: 2a, 2b, 3b
		12.5B Over to You: 3b; Change and Continuity: 1, 2, 3
		12.7 Over to You: 1b
		12.9 Over to You: 1a, 1b; Change and Continuity: 1, 2, 3
		12 Assessment: Change: 1, 2, 3, 4
Literacy and Numeracy	Literacy	12.2B Over to You: 5
		12.6 Over to You: 4
		Have you been learning? Literacy Focus: 1, 2, 3, 4, 5, 6
	Numeracy	12.1A Over to You: 2

Chapter 12 From Tudor to Victorian Britain: what changed?

Lesson sequence

Lesson title	Student Book pages	Objectives
12.1A 1848: How close was a British revolution?	pp 218–219	• Recall how and why people fought for improved rights. • Judge how successful they were. • Examine events such as the Swing Riots, the Peterloo Massacre and the Kennington Common meeting.
12.1B 1848: How close was a British revolution?	pp 220–221	
12.2A Was this an age of improvement for women?	pp 222–223	• Assess the position of women in the eighteenth and nineteenth centuries. • Evaluate the importance of the Match Girls' Strike of 1888.
12.2B Was this an age of improvement for women?	pp 224–225	
12.3 What were Victorian schools like?	pp 226–227	• Describe what life was like in a Victorian schoolroom. • Explain how and why schools changed in the 1800s.
12.4A A healthier nation?	pp 228–229	• Outline how and why attitudes towards cleanliness changed in the nineteenth century. • Explain how surgeons won the battle against pain and infection. • Assess the significance of important surgeons.
12.4B A healthier nation?	pp 230–231	
12.5A How did people have fun during Victorian times?	pp 232–233	• Identify at least five ways in which people spent their leisure time (or free time) in the 1800s. • Explain why the amount of leisure time increased in this period.
12.5B How did people have fun during Victorian times?	pp 234–235	
12.6 The high street	pp 236–237	• Understand what a typical Victorian high street might have looked like. • Examine where some of our most famous high-street shops began.
12.7 Why are Charles Darwin and a chimpanzee on a £2 coin?	pp 238–239	• Describe Darwin's theory of evolution. • Examine why Darwin's theory caused so much controversy.
12.8 The Great Hunger	pp 240–241	• Outline the causes of the Great Hunger. • Judge whether the British government did enough to help.
12.9 What was Britain like by 1901?	pp 242–243	• Examine the extent to which Britain changed between 1558 and 1901 in key areas such as population, politics and science.
Chapter 12 Have you been learning?	pp 244–245	• Choose the correct answer from the given options for a quick recap. • Explore textual sources and interpretations relating to the St Peter's Field massacre.
Chapter 12 History skill: Change	p 246	• Examine how to respond to questions on change.
Chapter 12 Assessment: Change	p 247	• Structure an answer which responds to a statement about the changes that took places in Britain between 1558 and 1901.

Chapter 12 From Tudor to Victorian Britain: what changed?

Links to the GCSE curriculum

This chapter provides some historical context to the following:

AQA: Health and the People c1000–Present

AQA: Power and the People c1170–Present

Edexcel: Medicine in Britain c1250–Present

Eduqas: Changes in Health and Medicine in Britain c500–Present

Eduqas: Empire, Reform and War: Britain 1890–1918

Eduqas: Changes in Entertainment and Leisure in Britain c500–Present

OCR A: Monarchy and Democracy in Britain c1000–2014

OCR B: The People's Health c1250–Present

WJEC: Radicalism and Protest 1810–1848

WJEC: Changes in Crime and Punishment c1500–Present

WJEC: Changes in Health and Medicine c1340–Present

Exam-style questions covered in this chapter

Exam board	Lesson/activity question location	Command words	History skills/concepts
AQA	12.2A Over to You: 4c	How do you know…	Source analysis
	12.2A Change: 2	In what ways…	Change and continuity
	12.4A Source Analysis: 2	How useful…	Source analysis
	12.4B Significance: 2	Explain the significance…	Significance
	12.5B Change and Continuity: 2, 3	Explain two ways…different Compare… with…	Change and continuity
	12.6 Source Analysis: 1	How useful…	Source analysis
	12.7 Significance: 1	Explain the significance…	Significance
Edexcel	12.1A Interpretation Analysis: 2	Suggest one reason…	Interpretation analysis
	12.2A Over to You: 3	Describe…	Knowledge and understanding
	12.2B Interpretation Analysis: 1, 2	What is the main difference/similarity?	Interpretation analysis
	12.4A Source Analysis: 2	How useful…	Source analysis
	12.6 Source Analysis: 1	How useful…	Source analysis
	12.8 Interpretation Analysis: 1	What is the main difference?	Interpretation analysis
OCR A	12.2A Over to You: 3	Describe…	Knowledge and understanding
	12.2B Over to You: 3c	Explain the part…	Cause and consequence
	12.4A Over to You: 2	Explain how…	Change and continuity
	12.4A Source Analysis: 2	How useful…	Source analysis
	12.4B Over to You: 2a	Explain how…	Change and continuity
	12.6 Source Analysis: 1	How useful…	Source analysis
OCR B	12.4A Source Analysis: 2	How useful…	Source analysis
	12.6 Source Analysis: 1	How useful…	Source analysis
	12.9 Change and Continuity: 3	Write a clear and organised summary…	Change and continuity
Eduqas	12.2A Over to You: 3	Describe…	Knowledge and understanding
	12.3 Change: 2	Outline how…changed…	Change and continuity
WJEC	12.2A Over to You: 3	Describe…	Knowledge and understanding
	12.3 Over to You: 1a, 1b	Complete the sentences…	Knowledge and understanding

A brief history

12.1A/B 1848: How close was a British revolution?

This chapter starts by defining protest and giving students broad causation for why people protest, with a link back to the Peasants' Revolt. All of this will enable students to accumulate more content about protest in Britain. They will be taken through key protests of the period with explicit links made to the industrial nation they studied in previous chapters. After building their understanding of why people protest, they will focus on the consequences of protest, looking at the creation of the Chartist movement. This will be consolidated by evaluation of the successes and failures of protest for electoral reform.

12.2A/B Was this an age of improvement for women?

A man selling his wife makes a sensational opening to the context of women in nineteenth-century Britain. It is an excellent place to start for showing improvements (however small) throughout the century. Students will explore how women gained more financial, legal and political recognition by the end of the century and learn about some key female campaigners. The activities are well placed to get students to look beyond the change in law in order to focus on analysing how much social attitudes changed, and therefore evaluating how much actually changed for women. A case study on the Match Girls' Strike fosters links with the previous lessons on protest – this really is one of the great stories of the century!

12.3 What were Victorian schools like?

The lesson starts with making the distinction clear between the educational experience of boys, girls and different classes. Straight away students will see the problem with the Factory Act 1833 that they learned about in Chapter 7, and how this was addressed with subsequent education acts. Then the key features of a school day are explored, including punishments. This lesson culminates in students outlining how education changed throughout the nineteenth century. To stretch higher ability students get them to explain how changes to education over time differed for different social classes.

Timeline

1811
The Luddites start to protest by smashing new factory machinery that had taken people's jobs.

August 1819
The Peterloo Massacre occurs at St Peter's Fields.

1830s
The Swing Rioters destroy the new farming machines that had taken people's jobs.

1832
The first Reform Act is passed, which gives the vote to middle-class men.

1844
The first co-operative is set up by workers in Rochdale, Lancashire.

1844
The first ragged school for orphans and very poor children is set up.

1845–1849
The 'Great Hunger' famine in Ireland kills over one million people.

1847
A Scottish doctor called James Simpson uses chloroform as an anaesthetic.

10 April 1848
The Chartists meet on Kennington Common with their third petition, which Parliament rejects.

1859
Charles Darwin's *On the Origin of Species* is published, explaining his theory of evolution.

1863
The Football Association is formed.

1865
Elizabeth Garrett Anderson becomes the first woman in Britain to qualify as a doctor.

1870
The government introduces the Elementary Education Act.

1888
Match girls protest for better pay and conditions, with the help of Annie Besant, and win.

1891
School becomes free for everyone.

Chapter 12 From Tudor to Victorian Britain: what changed?

A brief history continued

12.4A/B A healthier nation?

The painting at the start of this lesson gives students everything they need to see the problems with medicine in the eighteenth and nineteenth centuries. The adoption of anaesthetic starts the journey through hospital reform and then Germ Theory. This will be explained by focusing on the role of the individual and how key people such as Pasteur, Lister and Jenner improved health. Students will then be given a chance to show the change and continuity of medicine from the 1700s. A way to take this further would be to link back to medical understanding from the medieval period.

12.5A/B How did people have fun during Victorian times?

How people spend their free time can tell you a lot about a society, and this lesson does just that. It explores how different classes enjoyed their free time while focusing on the new working class in the industrial cities. Music halls are a particularly fun aspect of this period; you could play some of the well-known songs to your students, as they are still entertaining. This leads nicely to the rise of culture (reading, organised sport and day trips). Students will consolidate their understanding by explaining change and continuity with explicit focus on similarities and differences in leisure time.

12.6 The high street

What do you mean they didn't just order it online? This lesson takes the Victorian period context deeper by giving students an insight into how trade changed and how shops evolved to sell more than one particular item. It truly is heartening to see some of the same names on our high streets today, a point that should be highlighted to students. This is a wonderful change and continuity lesson with activities that cement learning. However, one way to take this further is to discuss the popularity of Internet shopping and the impact it is having on the average high street.

12.7 Why are Charles Darwin and a chimpanzee on a £2 coin?

Students will love this lesson on Darwin and his 'new' ideas on evolution. The lesson starts with the period's prevailing viewpoint of the creation story and then charts the rise of Darwin's theories and their acceptance (and, at points, rejection). It would be advisable to speak with your Science department to check how they have covered the content in order to enable you to prevent repetition and deepen the contextual understanding. The addition of Mary Anning and Richard Owen will give students more scope to explain the change and continuity of how people thought about their place in the world.

12.8 The Great Hunger

Many students will be unaware of the Irish famine or even that famine could happen so close to home. This lesson explains the multiple causes of the famine, government reactions to it, and its short-term effect on relations between Ireland and Britain. Students will use sources and interpretations with varying provenance to select two: one that is critical of and one that supports the British government. The suggested class debate would benefit from extra time to research the impact on women and villages, and emigration. The interpretation analysis question will build GCSE preparation for identifying and explaining the differences between interpretations.

12.9 What was Britain like by 1901?

With a curriculum that builds a clear sequence of learning like this, the visual content of this lesson will give students much-needed time to reflect and consolidate their learning. All areas of life, both social and political, that have been studied from 1558 are compared to show change and continuity. Students will then write a clear and organised summary that analyses change from 1558 to 1900. They should consider the extent of change, different social classes, and men and women. This would be a good opportunity to focus on the literacy activities of note-taking and using connectives.

Further reading and links

For teachers:

- *Peterloo* (2018) is a film by Mike Leigh which explores the events of the Peterloo Massacre and links them to the wider context of the franchise and the growing working class. Watching this film will give you more of a narrative to share with the students.

- Read Mary Wollstonecraft's *A Vindication of the Rights of Woman* (1792). Wollstonecraft is often dubbed 'Britain's first feminist'. Exploring her work will help you give deeper explanations of the role of British women in the late 1700s and 1800s. Search 'A Vindication of the Rights of Woman' on the British Library website for context pages from the text.

- Available on YouTube, PBS America have a fantastic four-part documentary called *Queen Victoria's Empire* (2001), which gives more insight into Victoria's personality, the British Empire, technology and the key politicians of the day.

For students:

- Give students access to GCSE and A-Level resources to find out about the Corn Laws and how they affected the Irish famine. This will give more context to the interpretation that lists the things Robert Peel did to try to help the Irish people.
- Students can visit www.timelines.tv to watch a video about the Peterloo Massacre. They should click on 'Timelines' and scroll across to 'Peterloo Massacre' on the 'Rulers and Ruled' timeline.

Beyond the classroom

- 2019 saw the 200th anniversary of Peterloo. Students could research the massacre and how it was remembered 200 years on. This could be a great enrichment task with your Citizenship or Politics department to evaluate the links being made to current affairs.
- Get students to research the work of Alfred Russell Wallace who shared the same evolutionary ideas as Darwin.
- Provide students with extracts from eighteenth- and nineteenth-century literature where the characters go to the sea or promenade towns. How do the descriptions compare? Students could evaluate their historical accuracy.
- Give students time to research the Tolpuddle Martyrs and the protests around their punishment. They should be able to link the group to their lessons on crime and punishment, factory workers and the Luddites.
- Work with your Music department to analyse Irish folk songs that describe the famine and its lasting legacy in Ireland. Something like 'The Fields of Athenry' will allow students to make links to previous lessons on transportation. The students could then create their own folk songs about the famine.

Chapter 12 Answers guidance

Answers guidance

The answers provided here are examples, based on the information provided in the Student Book. There may be other factors which are relevant to each question, and students may draw on as much of their own knowledge as possible to give detailed and precise answers. There are also many ways of answering questions, including exam-style questions (for example, of structuring an essay). However, these exemplar answers should provide a good starting point.

12.1A 1848: How close was a British revolution?

STUDENT BOOK PAGES 218–219

Over to You

1 Similarities: They attacked machinery that threatened jobs, violence/damage to property, were led by an elusive leader. Differences: Luddites smashed up factory machinery (urban), Swing Rioters smashed up farm machinery (rural).

2 There is a link between violence and protest at times when people are hungry/bread is more costly.

3 Student answers should reflect that it was drawn by a supporter of the protesters. The soldiers are shown negatively – as butchers armed with axes. One soldier is shown saying 'Chop 'em down my brave boys…', implying that it is a brave act to kill defenceless protesters.

Interpretation Analysis

1 Answers may include: The massacre was ordered by local people from Manchester (the magistrates) and a small group of soldiers successfully dealt with the protest – and in doing so, did severe damage to the idea of ordinary people getting the vote – so put back the idea of democracy for over 50 years.

2 It might be referred to as a humiliating defeat because nothing came of the protest – in fact, the government tightened up controls. New laws were introduced (known as the Six Acts) that banned meetings of over 50 people, gun laws were tightened, and courts were given more powers to search homes and put people on trial without a jury.

12.1B 1848: How close was a British revolution?

PAGES 220–221

Over To You

1 Answers may include: Chance of a better life – if they could vote in politicians who would change things for them.

2a Lists may include: Only wealthy landowners could vote, women couldn't vote, some places (like Birmingham) had no MPs, but small villages did.

2b Success: More people allowed to vote, some big towns like Manchester and Birmingham given MPs for the first time, some of the old 'rotten boroughs' removed. Failure: You still had to own property to vote, so only one in five men could vote, and no women.

3a Members of a campaign group of ordinary working people who wanted to bring about changes to the voting system; they issued the 'People's Charter' in 1838.

3b Answers may vary but may include:
- Voting laws did not change as a direct result of the Chartist Movement. The 1848 meeting was a washout and the petitions made little impact.
- In the long term, most of their demands were realised. Chartists drew attention to the problems of working-class people and showed that there were national issues that politicians should address. According to the interpretation, it was the 'first nationwide movement of working class protest, and people had become more politically educated'.

12.2A Was this an age of improvement for women?

PAGES 222–223

Over To You

1a He calls her a snake, a curse, a tormentor and a daily devil. Also, he says she cannot make rum, gin or whisky – but drinks them a lot!

1b He says she has a bright and sunny side, can read novels, milk cows, make butter.

1c Answers will vary, but students may say they are shocked with how open he is with his insults – and the fact that he's actually getting rid of her in this way.

2a A suggestion that the members of one sex are less able, intelligent, etc. than the members of the other sex.

2b List can include: Women couldn't vote; once married, the husband owned the wife. An Act of Parliament was necessary to end a marriage, but it could cost £2000 and only two women ever did it. The husband could spend all the money and she could not stop him. If he got into debt, her possessions could be taken to pay off the debts.

2c Students' reasons will vary, but answers may include detail about keeping the men in power, tradition (it was how it had always been).

3 Answers will highlight the role played by two of the women

Chapter 12 Answers guidance

in the question, based on the text on pages 222–223. For example, Caroline Norton began a national campaign to allow her to divorce her husband. Several politicians helped her and their efforts led to the Infant Custody Act of 1839. Along with artist and activist Barbara Bodichon, she was influential in the passing of the Marriage and Divorce Act of 1857.

4a The first British woman to qualify as a doctor and the country's first female mayor and magistrate.

4b A situation in which someone adopts a role the reverse of that which they normally assume in relation to someone else.

4c Students may say that, by showing the man doing what the cartoonist thinks is a woman's job, and the children playing with different toys, the cartoonist is saying that the fact that Anderson is now a doctor has completely changed family life.

Change

1 Students will write down three changes.

2 Answers will outline the difficulties women faced before reform and then outline some of the changes which occurred, in detail. However, students may also point out areas that did not change – they still could not vote in national elections, for example.

12.2B Was this an age of improvement for women?
PAGES 224–225

Over To You

1 A poisonous and explosive chemical used in match-making.

2 Can cause disease. The fumes could rot the teeth and even cause them to drop out. The disease could spread to the jawbone too, and rot it away. Sometimes an infected person's jaw had to be completely removed, and in some cases the poison caused death.

3a Slavery had been banned, so was now illegal, so using the word in connection to white people in Britain was designed to shock.

3b Fear of losing their jobs as they were unskilled and perhaps thought they could be replaced easily.

3c Besant interviewed some of the women in the factory, published her findings in an article called 'White Slavery in London', helped the workers organise a strike, held public meetings and raised money to give to the striking women.

4 Answers will vary but may include:
- Bryant & May factory: Match girl: unhappy with conditions; Politician: happy that the factory is a thriving British business, concerned about the 'trouble' that might be brewing there – or inspiring in other workplaces; Dockworker: inspired by the women; Mr William Bryant: proud of his factory, worried about events.
- Annie Besant: Match girl: sees her as a heroine; Politician: might see her as 'trouble', perhaps a problem, or be inspired by her; Dockworker: a heroine, someone to fight for rights; Mr William Bryant: might see her as 'trouble', perhaps a problem, bad for business.
- results of the strike: Match girl: happy – she has better pay/conditions; Politician: might think that strikes may happen in other places; Dockworker: hopeful that their conditions might change soon too; Mr William Bryant: a defeat for him.

5 Student posters will reflect the poor factory conditions and how conditions could change – and pay.

Interpretation Analysis

1 The strike was an important victory in the history of workers' rights and union history. H = 'regarded as one of the most important events in the history of labour organisation in any country'. I = 'It was a milestone in union history'.

2 H focuses more on what happened during the strike and the role of Besant; I focuses more on the results and the way it inspired other workers (such as the dockers).

12.3 What were Victorian schools like?
PAGES 226–227

Over To You

1a Dame school.

1b 1880.

2 Answers may include: Engineers and scientists were needed to build and design machines, and understand mathematics. Mechanics needed to read instruction manuals, and secretaries and clerks needed to know how to write letters and calculate prices. Factory workers had to be able to read notices.

3 Student answers will vary, but the main differences will be they have greater variety (PE, Geography, Media, Dance etc.) and that boys and girls can do the same subjects. Similarities will also vary, but will probably relate to the fact that some of the lessons are similar (Writing) – and that

Revolution, Industry and Empire: Britain 1558–1901   **199**

Chapter 12 Answers guidance

the subjects are divided into lessons.

4a Answers will vary, but will relate to layout, size, technology, seating.

4b Answers will relate to the punishments (corporal punishment is now banned in schools), lessons are more varied, slates are not used.

Change

1
- 1833 – Factory Act said that children who worked in factories should get two hours of education a day (but this was done very badly, or not at all, in many factories).
- 1844 – Ragged schools first set up for orphans and very poor children.
- 1870 – Elementary Education Act (schools should be built where there aren't any, paid for by local taxes, a school place for every child aged 5–12 etc.).
- 1880 – Education from five to ten was made compulsory.
- 1889 – School leaving age was raised to 12.
- 1891 – School became completely free.

2 Student answers will outline the education system before reform (no government-run schools. Nor were there any laws that said children had to go to school – but there were dame schools, ragged schools etc.) and then outline the key changes that took place in the nineteenth century, based on the information in Question 1.

12.4A A healthier nation?
PAGES 228–229

Over To You

1a Answers will vary but might be similar to this: A patient, in great pain, is being held down by several men while they cut off his left leg with a saw. There is a belt or tourniquet above where they are sawing to try to limit the flow of blood. There are tools laid out for the surgeons to use and they are operating in their own clothes, rather than any specialist clothing. The man is awake indicating that he is not under anaesthetic. (75 words)

1b Answers will vary, but students may focus on the fact that it does not appear to be in a special operating theatre, the men are wearing their own clothes and the patient is not under anaesthetic.

2 Answers will vary but should mention key names and dates and explain the impact associated with the development of anaesthetics from nitrous oxide ('laughing gas') to ether to chloroform.

Source Analysis

1 Anaesthetics were a step forward, but they didn't stop people dying from infections after operations as a result of filthy hospitals/germs etc.

2 Answers will vary, but should relate to the fact that the source is useful because it gives us an insight into medical treatment at this time – the conditions in operating theatres and the things they did and didn't know. For example, they knew that blood flow should be limited (so there is a tourniquet), but knew little of germs (they are operating in their own clothes) or pain relief (the patient is in agony).

12.4B A healthier nation?
PAGES 230–231

Over To You

1a Sepsis: a blood infection or blood poisoning.
1b Pasteurisation: heating of food and drink, for example, milk, to kill germs.
1c Sterilise: to clean an object so that it is free from any germs.
1d Vaccination: using the dead germs of a disease or one similar to build up an immunity (resistance) against the stronger form of the disease.

2a Answers will vary but they should mention: Jenner's successful use of vaccination in preventing smallpox (which led to smallpox vaccination becoming compulsory for babies in 1853); Pasteur's Germ Theory about germs causing disease (and that germs could be killed by heat); Lister's work on antiseptics and his successful operations/lower death rate that were a result of his work; and Florence Nightingale, who campaigned to improve hospital hygiene, and helped to raise standards of nursing by setting up a professional nurse training school in 1860.

2b Answers will vary. Students may choose Pasteur over Lister – because Lister's work was a result of Pasteur's theory. Or they might choose Jenner relating to their experiences of vaccination – or Nightingale based on the improvements clearly made since Source A (page 228) was painted. Some students might talk about the combination of all to the gradual improvement of heath.

3a Source A will mention the patient in great pain, no anaesthetic, no specialised operating theatre, doctors in own clothes, patient awake. Source E will mention patient asleep, doctors in specialist clothing, operating theatre.

3b Students should write, for example, that operations have become more hygienic (special clothes worn), anaesthetics used, operating theatres used, patient in no pain.

Chapter 12 Answers guidance

Significance

1 A substance that kills germs.
2 Answers should outline the dangers of infection before antiseptics, then briefly write about Pasteur's Germ Theory, Lister's work on antiseptics and then the impact of Lister's work in his own hospital and the fact that, by the 1880s, doctors and surgeons all over the country were trying antiseptic sprays and other cleaner ways to work. They should include that hospitals waged a war against germs: walls were scrubbed clean, floors were swept, equipment was sterilised, surgeons started to wear rubber gloves, surgical gowns and face masks during operations.

12.5A How did people have fun during Victorian times?
PAGES 232–233

Over To You

1a
- Music hall: venue that puts on a wide variety of entertainment acts; cheaper to visit than a theatre
- Melodrama: musical play with very dramatic plot and exaggerated emotions.

1b Richer people would go to large, elegant, expensive concert halls or theatres to watch classical music concerts, operas and plays. For poorer people, there were music halls, melodramas and going to the pub.

2a Answers will vary but should be similar to: spare time after work has finished and all other jobs relating to family have been completed.

2b A series of new laws and improvements to workers' rights meant people worked shorter hours than ever before and found themselves at home earlier in the evenings, and off work on Saturday afternoons.

12.5B How did people have fun during Victorian times?
PAGES 234–235

Over To You

1 There was a variety of entertainment for both. The rich went to concerts, operas and plays. There were also health resorts, ski resorts and the Grand Tour. Poorer people went to local pubs or music halls. They might also take short holidays at the seaside.

2a Activities that involve hunting for animals, wounding or killing them, or betting on fighting animals.

2b Answers may say they began to die out because people viewed them as cruel; also the RSPCA was set up in 1824.

3a Student descriptions will vary but will focus on the crowded beach; they may also mention pier, Punch and Judy show, ice-cream seller, seafront hotels, 'bathing booths', railway station, which brought visitors right up to the sea front.

3b Answers will vary, but they might mention people wearing fewer clothes, more sports being played, no bathing booths, more pollution.

Change and Continuity

1 Answers will vary but will probably contain activities such as 'socialising', playing online games, engaging in social media, playing sports etc.

2 Answers will vary but students may mention that less time is spent in music halls, concerts, the pub, for example. They may say that the Grand Tour is not really done any more, and trips to the seaside are not as popular. They may also mention the rise of other forms of entertainment – TV, online gaming, cinema etc. Blood sports not common.

3 Answers will vary but students may mention that holidays to the seaside are still popular (but not as popular as they were because of foreign travel). Reading, cycling and organised sports are still popular.

12.6 The high street
PAGES 236–237

Over To You

1 Answers might include: WH Smith (London, 1848), Boots (Nottingham, 1849), Sainsbury's (London, 1869) and Marks and Spencer (Leeds, 1884).

2 Workers saved up to buy a stock of food and opened a shop. They sold their goods at fair prices and shared the profits among their customers. Their co-operation with each other gave its name to their first shop – The Co-operative.

3a Local councils checked the quality of food – so food quality improved.

3b
- Shop owners: wider variety of food that could be kept for longer.
- Customers: wider variety of food.

4 Students' information panels will vary, but should include a basic description of the scene (an image of Eastgate Street in Chester in the late 1800s – a great example of what a Victorian city high street would have looked like) as well as detail in the scene and what it says about Victorian Britain.

Source Analysis

1 Answers will vary, but better answers will reflect on the fact that this image shows detail of one particular city (Chester) at one particular time (late 1800s), and shows what a town centre might have looked

Revolution, Industry and Empire: Britain 1558–1901 201

Chapter 12 Answers guidance

like and the developments of the era (trams, shops, street lights etc.), but it does not show the whole picture because students know (using contextual knowledge) that town and city centres were also places of overcrowding and industry, which isn't reflected here.

12.7 Why are Charles Darwin and a chimpanzee on a £2 coin?
PAGES 238–239

Over To You

1a Answers may say that so many people believed in the biblical explanation of life on Earth that any other explanation went against their belief system.
1b Answers will vary but may include: There are different origin theories around the world, and many people believe in the one relating to their own religion which has been established for a long time.
2 Answers may vary but should focus on Darwin's significant achievement in scientific theory.
3 A famous fossil hunter.
4 Many people thought that God created the universe, and also human beings, around the same time. Mary Anning and Richard Owen's discovery of prehistoric animals and fossils from animals might have led some people to wonder about the creation story told in the Bible and whether the world was a lot older than previously thought.

Significance

1 Student answers should briefly describe Darwin's theory and how it changed the way people thought about the birth of human existence at the time – and how this theory has continued and is still taught in schools today as accepted science (or similar).

12.8 The Great Hunger
PAGES 240–241

Over To You

1 A time of famine in Ireland between 1845 and 1849.
2 Answers will include: A million people died (Interpretation A), a million people emigrated (Interpretation B), peasants were evicted from their homes by English landowners (Interpretation E).
3a Answers will vary, but Sources and Interpretations A, B, D (partly), E and G are critical – E, for example, says 'The British Government was slow to give help. Worse still, it gave no protection to peasant farmers.'
3b Answers will vary, but Sources and Interpretations C and D support – D, for example, says that the 'British prime minister, Robert Peel, ordered Indian corn to be bought and handed out to the starving Irish.'
4 Class debates will vary in the opinions expressed.

Interpretation Analysis

1 B criticises the government and blames it completely, indicating that it did nothing to help and made matters worse – 'Its effects would not have been a tenth as bad if the British Government of the time had made the slightest effort to relieve the starvation.' D contradicts this and says that the government did try to help – 'The British prime minister, Robert Peel, ordered Indian corn to be bought and handed out to the starving Irish.'

12.9 What was Britain like by 1901?
PAGES 242–243

Over To You

1a Answers will vary, but be based on the differences between life in Tudor times and life in late Victorian Britain. For example, students might say that the way people travelled was very different – much faster in fact – and then explain the changes to travel. In Tudor times, richer men and women travelled by horse and carriage, while the poor walked, but by 1901 travel was much faster. The train was a common mode of transport. London to Edinburgh took nine hours by train. The roads were better too and the motor car had been invented.
1b Student answers will vary.

Change and Continuity

1 Student answers will vary, but most will probably come down on the side of the second point – the things that changed a lot would be transport, communication, population, empire etc. – but women still didn't have the vote and society was still very divided.
2 Student answers will vary.
3 Student answers will summarise the changes that took place in this period, covering the main themes. Students could also conclude with their thoughts on what changed the most/least.

Chapter 12 Have you been learning?

Answers guidance

Chapter 12 Have you been learning?

Quick Knowledge Quiz

PAGE 244

1. **a** Luddites
2. **c** Education should be free for all
3. **b** Elizabeth Garrett Anderson
4. **b** the Bryant & May factory
5. **b** dame school
6. **c** chloroform
7. **b** Louis Pasteur
8. **c** music hall
9. **b** The Co-op
10. **c** Charles Darwin

Literacy Focus

PAGE 245

Reading for meaning

1. Interpretation A: Samuel Bamford (helped arrange the meeting at St Peter's Field)
Source B: William Hulton (ordered the soldiers to go into the crowds)
Interpretation C: Lieutenant Jolliffe (one of the soldiers)
2. Interpretation A: The soldiers on their horses cut their way through the crowd of people who were trying to stop them.
Source B: The people tried to cut off the soldiers on their horses who had made their way into an open crowd.
Interpretation C: The crowd turned on the soldiers who tried to move them without cutting them.
3. Source B and Interpretation C agree with each other as they both suggest the crowd turned on the soldiers.
4. B and C: The cavalry started cutting everyone instantly/A: They went into open space
B and C: The people tried to break and move away/A: The people cramped in around the soldiers
B and C: The soldiers cut and harmed people/A: The people were not hurt
5. Interpretation A is an account from someone who organised the meeting whereas Interpretation C and Source B are linked to the soldiers.
6. No. They are both trying to justify their actions which means we have to be cautious about trusting them.

Chapter 12 Assessment: Change

Assessment summary

The assessments in this textbook have been carefully designed and tested with History teachers to support student progression throughout the course. This specific assessment is written to support Year 8 or Year 9 students in tackling questions relating to change:

> ⭐ How far do you agree that science and medicine saw the largest change between 1558 and 1901 in Britain? Give reasons for your answer (20)

Students will be expected to explain changes in science and medicine over the time period, and then identify and explain other areas of change (Question 1). Then they must make a judgement on the biggest change (Question 2). Using this judgement, students will directly answer the exam question (Question 3) and respond to the given statement. Finally, students will provide details to explain their response and write a conclusion (Question 4).

To support students with this question we have provided sentence starters and key areas of focus.

For the mark scheme, see page 206.

A note about the end-of-chapter assessments

There is an assessment for each Student Book chapter. Each is structured like a GCSE exam-style question, with scaffolding steps to support KS3 students. Each assessment has a total of 20 marks, and is designed to be completed in a typical lesson – each has been written with a time allowance of about 30 minutes.

There is a mark scheme for each assessment. You can choose how to give student outcomes: a mark out of 20; a percentage; a performance indicator (we use a three-stage indicator – 'Developing', 'Secure', 'Extending' – but you could adapt to match any performance indicators used in your school); or a GCSE grade indicator. To convert raw marks to a performance or GCSE grade indicator, use this table:

Raw marks				
0	1–6	7–13	14–20
GCSE grade (9–1) indicators*				
U	1–3	4–6	7–9
Performance indicator				
Ungraded	Developing	Secure	Extending

* Please appreciate that these are approximate grades based on grade boundaries from recent GCSE exam papers. If a student achieves a Grade 7 in one of these assessments, it is not the equivalent of a Grade 7 at GCSE. Instead it is an indicator of the grade the student could expect to get if they continue on their flight path through KS3 and GCSE. Please note:
  - the raw-mark boundaries are based on but do not match precisely those for recent GCSE exam papers: this is because our assessments are focused around one exam-style question, likely to be done at the end of a chapter (topic) rather than at the end of the course. Secondly, we provide carefully considered scaffolded steps to allow KS3 students to tackle high level questions and gain confidence through the deliberate practice of building up detailed answers.
  - the assessments for Student Book 3 are progressively more demanding in that they use higher-order command words and provide less scaffolded support – if you set one of them for Year 8 students, please take that into account when awarding GCSE grade indicators.

Entering student outcomes into the Kerboodle Markbook

The Kerboodle Markbook records scores and percentages to allow for quick comparison of performance. If you want to use the Markbook to record student outcomes, you will need to enter the appropriate values given in the raw marks row of the table above.

Chapter 12 Assessment: Change

Links to GCSE

By the end of KS3, students should be familiar with the History skill of change and continuity. At GCSE, all exam boards expect students to analyse change within and over long time periods. For example:

AQA:
- Compare... with... In what ways were they similar? Explain your answer with reference to both periods. (8)
- In what ways...? Explain your answer. (8)

Edexcel:
- 'The main change... was...' How far do you agree? Explain your answer. (16)
- Explain one way in which... was different from/similar to... (4)

OCR A:
- Explain why... (10)

OCR B:
- How far do you agree that...? Give reasons for your answer. (18)

Eduqas:
- Outline how... changed from... to... In your answer you should provide a written narrative discussing the... across three historical eras. (16) (SPaG 4)

Links to KS3 History resources

Student Book
This assessment question links to these lessons:

1.1 *What was Britain like in 1558?*
12.1A/B *1848: How close was a British revolution?*
12.2A/B *Was this an age of improvement for women?*
12.3 *What were Victorian schools like?*
12.4A/B *A healthier nation?*
12.5A/B *How did people have fun during Victorian times?*
12.6 *The high street*
12.9 *What was Britain like by 1901?*

Kerboodle
Support for this assessment question on Kerboodle:

RIE 12 *Assessment presentation: Change*
RIE 12 *Assessment worksheet (Core): Change*
RIE 12 *Assessment worksheet (Foundation): Change*

Curriculum and Assessment Planning Guide
Support for this assessment question in this guide:

12 *Assessment mark scheme* – page 206
12 *Assessment sample student answers* – pages 207–208

Chapter 12 Assessment: Change

Student name: _____   Date: _____

Mark scheme

Assessment bands	Marks	GCSE grade indicators*	I have...
	0	Ungraded	
Developing	1–6	1–3	☐ given a basic explanation of one or two areas of change in Britain between 1558 and 1901. ☐ written an answer that shows limited knowledge and understanding relating to the changes.
Secure	7–13	4–6	☐ written a detailed explanation of at least two areas of change in Britain between 1558 and 1901, suggesting that one change is larger than the others. I have reached a judgement that answers the question. ☐ written an answer that shows a range of accurate knowledge and understanding that relates to the question.
Extending	14–20	7–9	☐ written a well-organised answer with a well-developed explanation of three areas of change in Britain between 1558 and 1901, leading to a judgement that is backed up by reasons, and answers the question. ☐ included a wide range of accurate and detailed knowledge and understanding that is relevant to the question.

* IMPORTANT: These are approximate indicators devised using publicly available information on the new GCSE grades. They are designed to assist in the process of tracking and monitoring. They cannot and should not be used to replace teachers' professional judgement. Teachers should use their own discretion in applying them, taking into account the cumulative test scores of an individual student (rather than just one assessment point), and should refer to their institution's assessment policy.

Mark: _____

Comment:

Chapter 12 Assessment: Change

Sample student answers

Assessment: Change

STUDENT BOOK PAGE 247

> How far do you agree that science and medicine saw the largest change between 1558 and 1901 in Britain? Give reasons for your answer. (20)

☆ Sample Developing band answer

Science and medicine changed from 1558 to 1901 in many ways. Many people before the nineteenth century were still dying from terrible hospital conditions. However, after the discovery of germs and how they can kill people in surgery, things improved and fewer people died. Another area of change was society – life also changed for normal people during this time, as women got more rights.

☆ Sample Secure band answer

In the Tudor period, in the 1550s, science and medicine had improved with more knowledge of the human body and how it worked. Life expectancy was still low, and going into hospital was dangerous as they were dirty. However, by the end of the Victorian period, there was an understanding of how germs caused disease and that they were causing people to die in large numbers. This was called Germ Theory, and it showed how germs could be killed by heat. This resulted in operations becoming much safer and led to Joseph Lister discovering the role of antiseptic, which further reduced deaths. Therefore, the key changes in science and medicine were that surgery became safer because we had cleaner hospitals.

There were other changes that were important too, such as education. Most children in the Tudor period did not attend school because education was not compulsory. Education then was for the rich and mostly for boys. By the end of the Victorian period, school became compulsory for all children between 5 and 12 years of age. This was a big change, since in the early 1800s poorer children were working in factories or in mines, and education was something that only the very rich could afford. But by the late 1800s the government introduced education acts which said that school was compulsory and free. This changed education as all children were then able to have a chance to improve their knowledge and their lives.

In conclusion, I agree that science and medicine experienced the largest change between 1558 and 1901. The numbers of deaths from surgery fell dramatically, and I think this change is more important than changes to education.

Chapter 12 Assessment: Change

⭐ Sample Extending band answer

In the Tudor period, life expectancy was still low and going into hospital was very dangerous due to a lack of cleanliness. However, by the Victorian period, Louis Pasteur had published the Germ Theory (1860), which had a great impact on the safety of surgery. This was a change from the Tudor period because back then, instruments were used on several patients before being cleaned. More medical changes occurred when Joseph Lister discovered that carbolic acid could be used as an antiseptic in 1865, which further reduced deaths. This showed that hospitals should be sterile and fit for recovery, not just for rest. So science and medicine changed, as there were fewer deaths and the approach to surgery and patient care changed too.

There were other areas of change during this period. The most important change was in society. In the Tudor period, the monarchy and the ruling class were the most powerful and made all the laws. The poor had no say over matters about how the country was run. By the end of the Victorian period, society had changed – those at the bottom, the working class, now had more of a say. Two in three men got the vote. This was a big change since the working class had protested throughout the late 1700s and 1800s to gain more representation. The Chartist movement had sent three petitions to Parliament to try to get the vote for all men, and to demand wages for MPs in order to allow the working class to work in politics. This was a great change, as it impacted on how laws were passed and forced the government to recognise the needs of all people in society, not just the rich. This also resulted in workers gaining better conditions and pay.

Another area of change was the way people spent their free time. In the early Tudor period entertainment was still largely divided by class, with the rich enjoying hunting and the poor engaged in blood sports. But by the end of the Victorian period, people had started to go on holidays to the seaside. This was down to bigger changes in society, like weekends off and better pay for the working class, along with improved transport around the country. The new music halls were popular with both rich and poor too.

In conclusion, changes to society had the biggest impact in the period, as they ensured that most people in society had a say and created a more equal society. Although science and medicine had seen big advancements, there were still no antibiotics. Also, this area had been changing consistently across the period whereas the rights of the working class changed rapidly towards the end, affecting the whole of society rather than just one area, like science and medicine. Changes in society led to the changes in entertainment, because without more rights for the working class, they wouldn't have had time off for holidays. Furthermore, entertainment did not see a total change, as the rich still hunted and went to expensive concerts.